I've travelled the world twice over,
Met the famous: saints and sinners,
Poets and artists, kings and queens,
Old stars and hopeful beginners,
I've been where no-one's been before,
Learned secrets from writers and cooks
All with one library ticket
To the wonderful world of books.

© Janice James.

The wisdom of the ages
Is there for you and me,
The wisdom of the ages,
In your local library.

There's large print books
And talking books,
For those who cannot see,
The wisdom of the ages,
It's fantastic, and it's free.

Written by Sam Wood, aged 92

THE MAN WHO LISTENS TO HORSES

This is the life story of a man whose unique methods reveal the depth of communication that is possible between man and horse. His powers may seem like magic, but Monty Roberts' amazing 'horse sense' is based on a lifetime of experience. He started riding at the age of two and has never looked back. He has always worked with horses, schooling them, studying their behaviour in the wild, listening to them, caring for them and learning their language. According to Monty, anyone can learn the language of the horse and anyone can learn Monty's 'join up' methods. In this book he tells you how.

MONTY ROBERTS

THE MAN WHO LISTENS TO HORSES

Complete and Unabridged

CHARNWOOD
Leicester

First published in Great Britain in 1996 by
Hutchinson
London

First Charnwood Edition
published 1997
by arrangement with
Random House UK Limited
London

Hutchinson thanks Pat Roberts for her drawing
'Equus, the Flight Animal' which illustrates this book

British Library CIP Data

Roberts, Monty
The man who listens to horses.
—Large print ed.—
Charnwood library series
1. Roberts, Monty 2. Horse trainers—United
States—Biography 3. Horses—Training
4. Large type books
I. Title
636.1'088'092

ISBN 0–7089–8963–2

Published by
F. A. Thorpe (Publishing) Ltd.
Anstey, Leicestershire
Set by Words & Graphics Ltd.
Anstey, Leicestershire
Printed and bound in Great Britain by
T. J. International Ltd., Padstow, Cornwall

This book is printed on acid-free paper

THIS book tells the story of how I learned to listen to horses and to communicate with them across the divide which our separate species naturally defines for us.

It only occurred to me to write down my discoveries after a particular turn of events one December evening in 1988, when I was 53 years old.

I received a telephone call from a friend and neighbour of mine, John Bowles. His Southern accent was unmistakable.

'Monty?'

'Yes.'

'Guess what, the Queen of England wants to meet you.'

He went on to describe how Her Majesty the Queen of England wanted to investigate my work with horses and perhaps see for herself what I claimed to be able to do in terms of communicating with them.

Now, John Bowles is a man not above playing a practical joke or two, so naturally this is what I thought I was dealing with. I asked him how come he, plain John Bowles, was carrying messages for Her Majesty?

He answered that an English friend of his, a certain Sir John Miller, was a former Equerry to the Queen — that's to say, her horse manager — and she'd instructed him to find me. Her

Majesty had read articles printed in *The Blood Horse* and *Florida Horse* magazines, which explained the demonstrations I'd been doing, she had been intrigued.

John Bowles said it was the easiest task he'd ever had, to find someone who lived 5 miles away and whom he'd known for 15 years.

Not long afterwards, Sir John Miller came to meet me at my farm in California, to see what I could do.

After I'd given him a demonstration, he became very excited at what he'd seen; as we went back into the house for lunch and during the meal, he started telling me particular dates during the following year — Her Majesty's itinerary. She would be at Balmoral for such and such a time, and so on. I began to cotton on that he was about to fit me into this schedule somewhere along the line.

Sure enough, he advised me that Her Majesty would be inviting me to come to England in April of 1989 and spend a week at Windsor Castle as her guest. He asked in his upper-class British voice, 'I wonder if a demonstration such as I've just seen could be accomplished for Her Majesty in the mews?'

What the hell was a 'mews'? I didn't know, but I assured him we could make it work somehow.

He ended by telling me that if the Queen was convinced that my work was worthwhile, she would arrange for me to go on a tour of several British towns and cities. Most importantly, she would want Newmarket and Gleneagles in

4

Scotland to be part of that itinerary.

Two weeks later, I received a formal letter of invitation from Buckingham Palace. Now I knew it was going to happen for real — I was on my way to meet the Queen of England!

For various reasons which will become clear during the course of this book, for most of my life I've had to keep my work secret.

From a young age I have been physically beaten, reviled and accused of trickery when I have chosen to show people what I could do, and what I've learned. And yet I would take the opposite view: that what I have achieved is the result of long hours of observing horses in the wild, but that it is essentially a simple thing and based on common sense. There *is* something magical about it, sure, but it's the magic of an undiscovered tongue — a primitive, precise and easy-to-read language. Once it's learned, it allows a new understanding between man and horse. But there's nothing weird about it and it isn't exclusive to me — just recently I had my farrier achieving similar results in a few minutes.

So, it would constitute the greatest possible reward to me if I could prove to Her Majesty's satisfaction that my work was credible and important, and thereby bring my methods to the broadest possible audience.

I landed at Heathrow airport on 5 April 1989 to be met by Sir John Miller. We drove directly to Windsor Castle, a distance of only ten or fifteen miles.

Parked at Windsor Castle were some vehicles

that looked more like Sherman tanks than passenger cars. Sir John told me that the Queen was having lunch with the Russian President Mikhail Gorbachev and his wife Raisa, and they'd shipped in their own cars for the occasion.

The interior of Windsor Castle was a revelation. Behind these doorways and in these corridors which I was now walking through, great affairs of state had been conducted for hundreds of years. This family — the royal family — had been leading owners of racehorses for hundreds more years than my country had even existed.

Let's just say that as a country boy from California who'd worked long and hard in the field of horsemanship, I knew I was going about as far up in the world as it was possible to go.

Sir John took me down to a meadow in front of Windsor Castle, where he showed me 15 horses of all colours, shapes and sizes. In a separate paddock there was a thoroughbred filly — making a total of 16 horses.

None of them had been ridden. All were green and raw, but they had been halter-broken. These were to be the horses I would communicate with during my week-long series of demonstrations here.

Then Sir John took me to the stable area to one side of the castle itself; so this is what was meant by a 'mews'.

Next we went to see the indoor riding school. It had the appearance of a chapel building, with gothic-style windows and a high, vaulted ceiling. At one end of the building was a balcony with a glass and wood front to it. This was the soundproof viewing stand from where the Royal Family would be watching.

In the centre of the riding school was a 50-foot wire-mesh round pen which Sir John and I had arranged to be delivered and set up by the Lodden Equipment Company.

It was an attractive set-up, but I'd never demonstrated my techniques in a wire-mesh pen before and I wasn't sure how the horses would react. They would be able to see through to the outside of the wire, which meant they weren't going to focus so much on what I was doing.

However, there was no other option. I would have to trust that it would work as a sufficient barrier and not distract them too much.

Sir John told me that the Queen had invited up to 200 people to watch me during the coming week. She herself would only be spending an hour with me on the Monday morning — her prior commitments wouldn't allow for more time than that — but she would probably watch the days' events on a video recorder in the evenings.

After our tour, Sir John and I walked back to Windsor Castle. Mikhail Gorbachev and his wife Raisa were about to leave, and we walked into the large-scale security operation necessary to get them away from the lunch table.

It was an eerie feeling watching the Russian guards mingling with British security officers, with men walking around the ramparts of the castle carrying machine-guns.

Suddenly, after an upset between them, one of the senior British officers came down towards Sir John and shouted, 'By God, we stopped them in the Crimea and we'll stop them at Windsor Castle!' That guy sure knew how to hold a grudge.

Soon afterwards Gorbachev and Raisa came out and drove right past us. Several cars preceded them and several more followed. It was turning out to be quite an experience for me in all kinds of ways.

At 9 o'clock on the following morning we were back at Windsor Castle. Today, Sunday, I was going to introduce the horses to the round pen. I've found through long experience that my demonstrations work more effectively if the horse isn't overly distracted by its surroundings. If you can imagine a raw horse taken out of the field, perhaps never before having been handled by mankind, it's a large step to lead it into a 50-foot round pen, observed by hundreds of people. The horse's powers of concentration are certain to be affected. It doesn't make the demonstration of my techniques impossible; it simply adds 10 per cent to the time factor, since there's the odd pause now and again while the horse checks out the enemy on the other side of the wire.

Anyway, when I arrived at the stable I immediately sensed a cold, separated feeling from the grooms — mostly girls — who were working there. I could tell that the head groom, in particular, was thinking I was treading on his toes.

8

I'd asked a few times for some assistance in shepherding these horses into the round pen, so that they could become acclimatised to it. I wanted to catch them one by one and lead them through and — their being to a greater or lesser extent wild — I would have appreciated some help.

So I was pacing back and forth trying to muster someone to come and join me when I saw a lady dressed in beautiful riding clothes coming out through the riding hall.

I watched her walk straight up to Sir John and start talking to him. The transformation that came over him was remarkable. Suddenly he was a different person. His stance changed, and so did the tone of his voice.

He was talking to the Queen.

For some days I had been wondering what would be the proper term to use, should I meet her. I considered 'Your Royal Highness' or 'Your Majesty', but I wasn't certain of the difference between the two. I wondered if I should bow, or whether a handshake was the order of the day. However, it had never been officially announced that I would meet her in person at all.

Now she was coming towards me and I hadn't prepared or researched properly into the required code of conduct. Far away from home, the guest of a foreign nation, I wanted to do the right thing.

In the event she offered me her hand, which made it easy for me. I shook it and said, 'Your Majesty,' and let it go at that.

9

It didn't seem to cause any raised eyebrows, unlike what would happen later on . . .

She was quick to put me at my ease, saying, 'Come, Mr Roberts, and show me this lions' cage in the centre of the riding hall. I want you to tell me about it.'

Together we walked into the riding hall and looked at the wire-mesh round pen. She said, 'It appears to be the sort of thing you need a whip and a chair to enter with.' I agreed with her, although the similarity hadn't occurred to me before.

Then I gave her a summary of what I intended to do the following morning. I was gratified at her curiosity in my work, and pleased that she wanted to know as much as possible beforehand.

Then she was gone.

I felt like I'd made a good start. The relationship between us was relatively informal, and I had the impression of a straightforward woman who was making happen what she wanted to happen.

At midday on the Sunday my wife Pat, my son Marty, and my rider, Sean McCarthy, arrived and came directly to Windsor Castle.

I've been married to Pat since I was 21. Sean McCarthy was primary rider for me in the round pen for nine years, and in that time he's probably gotten on over 1,400 horses as the first rider in their lives. It was nice to have reinforcements arrive — people who were on my side.

Sean and I went over our equipment in the round pen, then I took him out to show him

10

the horses in the field.

He was surprised at the diverse range of animals. There were two or three that would have been mostly thoroughbred and the one filly who was a registered thoroughbred standing in the separate paddock. There were two very large Shire Piebalds that would go on to be drum-horses in the ceremonial division of the royal stables. There were a few warm-blood crosses, a couple of other large horses, and then a few smaller types going right down to the Fell and Haflinger ponies.

Nevertheless, I was reasonably confident that none of them would kill me.

Our preparation done, we went to spend the evening at Sir John's home, Shotover House, near Oxford, which has been in his family for over a century.

Together with Major Dick Hearn — who was Her Majesty's racehorse trainer for many years — and his wife Sheila, we enjoyed a good dinner that night which went a long way to steadying my nerves for the following day.

The next morning, at 9 o'clock, we were due to meet the Queen, Prince Philip and Queen Elizabeth, the Queen Mother at the riding hall.

When they turned up, it was to create a different atmosphere from before. Suddenly, this was an official event. The woman in riding clothes whom I had talked to the previous day was now the Queen of England attending an engagement. She and her party were surrounded by security personnel and subject to rules of protocol.

Sir John Miller introduced us as though we hadn't spoken the day before. The glassed-in viewing gallery was indicated as the position from which the royal party would view the demonstration, as though we hadn't been talking about this for the last two days.

The event began to take on a life of its own.

I have to admit, I was nervous. As a rule I am a relaxed person; it is a necessary precondition to the work I do. It was disconcerting to feel my pulse rate shoot up and my concentration become less steady.

The royal family, accompanied by Pat and our son Marty, adjourned to the viewing gallery and took their seats, ready for the demonstration to begin.

I was charged first of all with 'breaking in' the young thoroughbred filly, which happened to be owned by the Queen Mother herself, who would obviously be watching intently.

As I entered the round pen, it occurred to me that if I couldn't relax, I'd be unable to communicate with the horse as I normally do. The filly would not then be receptive. It wasn't impossible that this would be the most embarrassing day of my life. As I closed the gate behind me, I pictured myself humiliated and a sense of terror swept over me.

Then the filly was brought in by her handler and released. She was adolescent, skittish and wide-eyed with fear.

I recognised a creature more scared than I was and needing my assistance. She depended on me for some comfort in the situation in which we both found ourselves. The instant I saw this, the presence of this raw young animal settled my nervous system and I started to work with her.

In just a minute or two, I could feel things begin to come right. She began to give me the signals I was looking for. Suddenly, we could proceed with the demonstration.

I'm not going to go into the details of my communication with horses at this point because I'll be doing so later on. The purpose of this book is to carry my understanding of the horse's language as it came to me, in the hope that the reader's comprehension will be as well-founded in fact and in observation as my own.

Suffice to say that this young, untouched filly behaved exactly as I predicted. Without putting any kind of rope or harness on her, she was following me around the ring within seven minutes of our starting work together. If I turned and walked in a circle, she did too, her nose just a foot or two from my shoulder. Where I went, she followed. In her predicament, she trusted me. I was her comfort.

The royal family watched from their seats on the viewing deck.

Within 15 minutes this highly-strung young thoroughbred, who'd hardly been handled at all in her whole life, stood steady as a rock while I fixed her first saddle on her. I still hadn't attached any type of restraint to her head.

After just 25 minutes, she had quietly accepted the bridle and snaffle bit, and Sean was on her back riding around the ring. It was as if she had been looking forward to doing this all her life.

Finally Sean dismounted and she was led away.

As I left the round pen, I saw the Queen, Prince Philip and the Queen Mother rise from their seats to come down and join me. Pat and Marty followed. In addition the security people stirred and moved with them.

The Queen was the first to emerge from the door connecting to the viewing gallery. With a warm smile on her face, she put out her hand to shake mine and said, 'That was beautiful.' She said she was amazed by what had happened and how the filly had responded, and she advised me to be proud of the work I was doing.

Suddenly I realised just how long I'd been waiting to hear someone say such positive things. My round pen at home had been constructed using solid walls and without a viewing area, expressly to prevent people seeing what I was doing and disbelieving me. This was the mother of all turn-arounds.

Shortly afterwards, Prince Philip came through. He shook hands and asked me if I could maybe work with the young men who were 'breaking in' some of his Fell ponies that week.

I was delighted by the response to my demonstration from the Queen and Prince Philip, but I confess I was waiting especially for the reaction from the filly's owner, the Queen Mother.

In a few minutes she too appeared through the door, and I was bowled over by the warmest appreciation I could have hoped for. Tears stood in her eyes as she very quietly and firmly said to me, 'That was one of the most wonderful things I've ever seen in my life.' She was visibly moved by what she'd seen her filly do, and by witnessing what is possible in terms of the communication between man and horse.

Seeing her emotional reaction, I was caught up in the moment and I forgot who she was and where we were. It felt the right thing to do to put my arms out and give her a gentle hug.

The security guards stiffened with surprise and stepped forward. Realising no one was supposed to touch the royal family in this intimate way, I immediately dropped my arms and stepped back a full stride.

However, she didn't seem in the least offended. Still talking in a very soft voice, she told me she hoped I would continue my work and bring about a different, more humane relationship between man and horse. I think back on her reaction as being the one which would satisfy me for the rest of my life.

The account of my visit to Windsor Castle doesn't end there, but for the moment that's where I want to leave it.

There's more to tell: that very Monday afternoon there was an attempt made to undermine what I'd achieved, but again I've left that story until its rightful place in the book.

It was Her Majesty's suggestion that I give an account of my experiences and methods in communication with horses, and it is largely due to her influence that I started out on the long and difficult task of remembering what happened to me in my life, and how I came to love horses so much that I was led to try to reach out across the divide that separates our species from theirs.

I WAS born in the middle of the Great Depression, on 14 May 1935, in the little town of Salinas, California.

The region was the setting for many of Steinbeck's classic novels and he might have drawn his characterisations from my ancestors, who were typical of the immigrants and natives who came to settle in the Edenic land of California.

The first thing I would have seen when I was carried outside the house would have been 2,300 acres of prime land situated in what's called the Salad Bowl of America — fertile soil blessed with a temperate climate.

However, this wasn't exactly a rural setting. It was situated on the edge of town and was in fact a built-up area — but with a difference. Every building had to do with horses, from box stalls to a show-ring with raked seating, to enclosures and breeding barns. It was a horse facility.

And on this facility, my parents worked.

Before I'd reached my first birthday, I joined my mother in the saddle, sitting in front of her. It wasn't just for a moment or two as a diversion, as might happen to other infants; I was up there for many hours at a time as she gave riding lessons. The ears of a horse flicking back and forth, the neck in front of me, the mane bouncing as the horse's stride carried us along — all this was as familiar to me as the sight and sound of a human being.

By the time I was just two years old I was spending most of the day on a horse, having graduated to a mount of my own. It was certainly a unique position to be in: there are few people who could say they were born and raised on the Salinas Rodeo Competition Grounds.

These Grounds came to exist because of a certain Mr Sherwood who, when he died, left the city of Salinas 2,300 acres in his will. He stipulated that these acres would have to be used solely for horse-related activities.

The estate and the city of Salinas called on my father to manage the land. He agreed, and shortly thereafter construction began on more than 800 box stalls and a competition arena including a 20,000-seat spectator grandstand. The facility still exists today.

In addition to being manager of the facility, my father was also running his own riding-school on the Competition Grounds. Every day my mother would make the rounds of the local schools in a large station wagon, picking up students and bringing them to the Grounds for their lessons, then returning them to class. The grammar and high schools in Salinas had physical education classes which included horseback riding, and the students were enrolled in my father's riding academy.

Also, he was training and boarding horses for private clients, and he leased the facilities to various horse trainers so that they could conduct their businesses on the Competition Grounds, as stipulated by Mr Sherwood in his will. So my parents were there as managers of Mr Sherwood's gift to Salinas, as well as on our own account, running a business.

The first horse I was given was called Ginger. He was 17 years old, a reined cow horse from the Uhl Ranch who in his time had been fairly good in Western competition. Now, in his retirement, he was required to be a baby-sitter for me. He had the perfect temperament: he was well-disciplined, steady, and he was assigned as my teacher.

He'd done all this cowboy stuff for years and he knew it backwards. He couldn't help it if this kid on his back thought he could do better. Ginger was patient with the three-year-old bouncing on his withers and flapping his arms and legs in every direction. It wasn't a noble or a peaceful retirement for him but I think he had a lot of fun, too.

Of course, in my eyes he could do no wrong. He was my buddy.

It didn't take my father long to notice that my riding abilities were better than average. I could walk, trot and canter a horse. I could do flying lead changes and perform figure-of-eight manoeuvres without a great deal of trouble. It seemed like an ordinary level of skill to me, but I can remember people saying, 'That boy's just three years old.'

My father planned to use my abilities to his advantage. I was not yet old enough for kindergarten when I was told that I must start

21

to practise harder and to spend more time riding than I already did. He seized on me rather than on my brother Larry because Larry was younger — and also had been born with a condition that in his early years made him somewhat more frail than me. Larry needed looking after; I could be pushed to the limit.

I was entered in horse shows regularly, and competed almost every weekend.

I still have some shaky old movie footage of Larry and me entering the junior stock-horse class when I was four years old. The grainy, flickering film shows us running our horses round, spinning them, stopping them and racing them back and forth like miniature versions of the cowboys who'd taught us — all in the eerie silence of the films made in those days.

When I look at myself and Ginger and see the way I hauled his mouth around and mistreated him — only out of ignorance — it makes me very sad, and I hope he understood that I was only a small child and didn't know what I was doing.

It was the Salinas junior stock-horse class and most of the kids were older than me, but I had Ginger on my side and he knew better than anyone how to go about scoring high marks in these events; he'd been doing it for years against stiffer competition than this. I'm sure he decided all by himself that it would be nice to take this trophy home — so he did. I won the class.

The publicity given to my family because of this unlikely competition win of mine on Ginger had an intoxicating effect on my parents. There was a sudden increase in their business. Mr and Mrs Roberts were plainly the best teachers, because they had a boy of only four years old who won a trophy.

It confirmed my father's belief that I was to be the child who would make the Roberts name famous in the world of show horses.

I should take a moment here to describe my father, because he was an important figure in my life. That's not to say that other members of my family are less important. It's simply that my family is not the subject of this book.

My wife and children, our 47 foster-children, my brother Larry and my mother — none of them features overmuch in the following pages because they'd require a book all to themselves.

The subject here is my relationship with horses — my working life. Nonetheless, to give this account is a deeply personal and emotional experience for me.

Aside from the rest of my family, I take special licence to describe my father in more detail since everything I have achieved has come to me because of the early and concentrated exposure to horses that he gave me. At the same time, if my professional life can be described as having a direction, it is facing away from him. The vigour with which I have pursued that direction is a consequence of my outright rebellion against him and his methods.

My father was a tall man of a slim, muscular build, with chiselled features under light brown hair. He was as neat and orderly as circumstances allowed. If he met a fraternal friend in the town, I'd say he could be a friendly, inviting man.

However, from the outset he turned a cold and critical eye on me. He was unforgiving and scrutinised everything I did, more often than not holding it up to ridicule.

His methods of dealing with horses were what I would describe as conventional — but that is to say, cruel.

The standard way of breaking in horses in those days was a method that is popular even today. A television show made in 1989 to celebrate 20 years of space travel claimed that while outer space is the great frontier of our era, the 'Wild West' was the previous great frontier. As the programme pointed out, some things haven't changed since those times. One of their featured examples was the way we break in horses.

My father had a special corral built, with six solid posts fixed at equal distances around its perimeter. In this way he could break half a dozen horses at the same time.

First he fitted on their head-collars. This might have involved running them through a crush to gain close enough access. Next, he attached strong ropes to their head-collars and tied them one to each of the posts, wrapping the rope about six feet off the ground and tying off the end on the rails.

So, he would have six animals tied 30 feet apart around the edge of the corral. The horses were already terrified.

Next, my father stood in the middle of the

corral with a heavy tarpaulin or weighted sack attached to the end of a rope. He threw the sack over the horses' backs and around their legs, moving from one to the other.

When the sack dropped on their haunches and around their rear legs, the horses panicked. Their eyes rolled and they kicked, reared and pulled back against their restraints as though their lives depended on it — because in their eyes, it did. Who could tell them that this wasn't the end of everything? Fear is in their nature, and they were driven wild with it and plunged back and forth and sideways on the ends of the ropes, fighting for their lives. Their necks and heads swelled up and frequently they injured themselves. It was — and remains — a desperately cruel sight.

This process is called 'sacking out'. It continued for maybe four days, its purpose being to break the horses' willpower and thwart their capacity for resistance.

The next stage was to tie a leg up, usually the near hind leg first of all. A rope would be caught under their rear pastern and pulled tight to a collar placed around their necks.

With the horse disabled in this way, a second period of 'sacking out' further reduced their ability to offer resistance. They struggled valiantly, heaving their weight pitifully on three legs and groaning in pain at the pressure on their head-collars.

Each leg in turn was tied up — and 'sacking out' was now taking a shorter and shorter time as the spirit was being driven out of them.

Then, with the hind leg again tied off, a

saddle was fixed on. The horses renewed their resistance, fighting the girth. More 'sacking out' wore them down. Some fought for many hours; others gave up more quickly and descended into confusion, waiting for more pain.

By now 8 – 10 days had passed. The horses had blood tracks on their pasterns from where the ropes had worn through the skin; in places the hair had been burned off from the friction. Frequently there was bruising and more serious injuries to their legs. Their relationship with their human masters was now defined — they were working out of fear, not out of willingness. To destroy the willingness in a horse is a plainly daft, unforgivable thing — it's among the dominant characteristics of the horse, and if it's nurtured it can grow into the most solid and rewarding aspect of their working lives. Of the horses I've held dear in my life, I've enjoyed most their willingness to try for me, over and over again.

At this stage the six horses were untied one by one and a hackamore fitted; this is a rawhide noseband without a bit.

They were long-lined for a further week.

When my father came to ride on them for the first time, their rear legs would be tied up again to prevent them from bucking. He got on and off, kicked them in the belly, tried to raise some fight in them any way he could. If they moved, they were whipped.

When he was convinced they were 'broken', he'd untie them and ride them in the round pen. Those who weren't yet able to be ridden spent part of the day with their legs tied up.

The whole process took a minimum of three weeks for the six horses.

Now, let me make a straightforward, heartfelt claim: if you gave me those same six horses today, I would have them ready to ride away without having used any tethering, and without having inflicted a moment's pain or discomfort. I won't have a whip anywhere near a horse. I will use only my voice to a certain extent, but mostly just my body language. In this way, you'd have a willing animal who'd try hard for you for the rest of his working life. To accomplish this for all six horses, it would take me just three *hours*, not three weeks.

★ ★ ★

My father was standing next to a stranger, beckoning me over to him. 'Monty, this is Mr Don Page.'

Don Page loomed above me, holding out his hand for me to shake. 'Pleased to meet you, Monty.'

'How d'you do, sir.'

It was 1940, and I was five years old; my brother Larry and I were in competition here at the Pickwick Riding Stables in Burbank, California. This area was also the home to many Hollywood movie studios such as MGM, Paramount and Warner Brothers.

My father continued, 'Mr Page works at one of the motion picture studios, Monty.'

They were both looking at me expectantly,

27

and I waited to hear what was coming. Mr Page dropped to his haunches so he was near the same level as me and explained, 'You know, horse stories are real popular at the moment. You seen any?'

'I've seen some with horses in them.' It was true; theatre marquees up and down the country were showing various films about a horse and a boy or a girl.

Don Page asked, 'Did you know that the author of *My Friend Flicka*, Mary O'Hara, is a screenwriter at MGM?'

I didn't know; I was only five years old, after all.

Don Page went on, 'It's like, everyone's hungry for stories with kids and horses and nice things like that, so they can forget all the trouble we're in, what with the Depression, and the war over there in Europe, and so on. And we plain haven't got enough kids who can ride for us.'

I squinted across at him and began to think I knew what he was after. Sure enough, an invitation arrived which I was ready to grasp with both hands.

'Back at the studio we're having real difficulty finding young riders. And your dad tells me you can ride pretty well. How d'you feel about coming along to show us what you can do?'

Mr Page suggested we should stay over for a day and come to a nearby location where the studio's stunt team kept their horses and worked out their stunts. My father agreed; and we were all set for an 'audition'.

At the appointed time we turned up at this studio facility and were greeted by a whole line of people who were waiting to watch me and judge what I was capable of. I don't know who they were, but I imagine they might have been stunt directors and casting directors. I just had a bunch of 'hellos' and handshaking to go through first.

They had a steady, predictable horse ready for me, which presumably was used to this type of fun and games. He was a bay gelding and led the low-status life of a studio mount in those days when the film industry wasn't so concerned about the safety of animals.

One of their number called out, 'OK, Monty, just canter past from left to right.'

This I did.

'And now back the other way, if possible.'

I successfully completed this difficult manoeuvre.

'Now, can you pull up to a dead stop, and jump off?' He asked this with more of a questioning tone.

It was all right with me. I'd been doing this sort of thing for a couple of years by now.

There was some whispering then, between my father and the line of studio observers. The guy who'd been doing all the calling-out came over to where I was standing my horse, waiting for the next instruction. He looked at me and asked in a serious tone, 'You see the sandpit over there?'

I found what he was pointing at.

'If you're comfortable about it, could you just ride over the sandpit and sort of . . . fall off?

While the horse is moving?'

I cantered the studio's gelding over the sandpit and took a dive off the right-hand side. A sporadic outbreak of applause was led no doubt by my father, who'd seen some of the brand-new vehicles parked at the entrance to the facility.

I stood up and brushed the sand off my clothes; someone had caught the gelding and was bringing him back.

Now they were in the swing of things and had me doing all sorts of tricks. 'Can you fall off the rear end?' 'Could you just canter him past us and be invisible, hanging off the other side?'

Like most kids, my brother and I had been watching motion pictures on Saturday mornings. After the picture was over, Larry and I would go home and try to copy the stunts. We even had a trick-riding saddle that our father had found for us in an old saddlery store, with the specialist grips built into it.

I left that studio facility pretty beaten up, but I'd got myself into the movie business and over the following years I was to appear in many films.

Once I was doubling for Roddy McDowell. The crew were setting up the massive film camera they had in those days, pointing the wide-angle lens into the corral. We all gathered round to hear what was going to happen.

The director gave me his instructions. 'OK, Monty — so you rope the horse here in the paddock. The pretty little girl is watching you from over there, sitting on the fence. Got that?'

'OK.'

'The horse yanks you off your feet, but you cling on to the end of the rope as though your life depends on it.'

'All right.'

He frowned — obviously quite worried. 'Now don't forget to let the horse drag you around the paddock for quite a while, because we have to get coverage of that.'

'No, I'll hang on to the rope until you tell me to stop.'

That cheered him up. 'Great! And we'll cut the sequence back-to-back with Roddy McDowell bringing the girl here and then taking off with her afterwards.'

'Got it.'

'So if you go along to wardrobe now, they'll fit you out in the same clothes as Roddy's wearing.'

It was a simple requirement, although my father was strolling back and forth behind the camera, shaking his head and telling the producers how dangerous this was going to be and suggesting the price should reflect the level of risk his son was being subjected to.

I roped the horse and dug my heels in, so as to make it seem like I was pulled over by the horse. I bit the dust, literally, and was dragged along the ground as planned.

Then there was this shredding sound; what no one could have foreseen was that the pants given me by the costume department were of a thin, crêpe-like material and, with this rough treatment, the backside was ripped out of them.

I got to my feet mortified with embarrassment. I stood there without my pants, and no one could help me out of that predicament quickly enough.

What was worse . . . they had no replacement pants. They had been brought along specifically to match the pair that Roddy McDowell was wearing for the rest of the sequence, and they didn't have any others.

There was some consternation among the crew and quite a bit of running about. Then they all agreed they needed some more shots of me being dragged, so I was to carry on, but wearing my own jeans instead. They'd just have to do what they could with the continuity problem.

When we went to see the finished movie, there was a section where Roddy McDowell was wearing off-white pants one moment, and then the next moment he was wearing a pair of jeans while he roped a fairly wild-looking horse, and afterwards he was back in his off-white pants again, without a single costume change. So we all knew you can't believe everything you see at the movies.

There were many child artists I doubled for. I was Elizabeth Taylor in *National Velvet*. I was Micky Rooney, Charlton Heston and Tab Hunter, and many more. It was a good career for a boy just starting grade school.

My father made all the decisions in dealing with the studios. He did the negotiations and signed the contracts. He was not legally obliged to consult me or inform me how much I'd earned. At the time, there were no laws governing the use of minors in film production. There was no provision for schooling, no minimum wage, and safety rules did not exist back then.

Nowadays, a six-year-old who performs in films would have an agent, an attorney and a trust fund. His or her parents would have to deal with their child by certain ethical standards.

As my filming schedule increased, my father often congratulated me on how well I was doing financially. He told me he was investing the money on my behalf, so that it would be waiting for me when I reached an age when I'd be sensible enough to use it wisely. If I asked for some of it to buy a new saddle or suchlike, he would shake his head and sternly emphasise to me, 'Monty, I'm telling you, I'll keep the money for you.'

I have to admit, he stuck to his word; I never saw a penny of it.

* * *

I didn't know if there were more horses or people, or which was making the most noise. The crush threatened to carry me away, and I had to hang on to the sight of my father so as not to get lost. There was a lot of squealing and calling going on, the auctioneer hammering away in his high-octane sales patter, and horses of every description were hurried into the ring to be put through their paces. For a seven-year-old kid, the excitement of the sale was intense.

We squeezed into a spot more or less ringside

and watched the first few horses without my father taking any interest. Then a skittish chestnut filly which the auctioneer's programme had written down as eight years old came into the ring. She was playing up and pushing her nose in the air, bothered by the halter rope and walking into the back of the man who was leading her, as though she were only a two-year-old. She was undoubtedly a horse with problems, and no one else was interested. However, she was exactly what my father was waiting for. He raised his hand, and bought her for peanuts.

My father signed the ticket and then took hold of my shoulder. 'Monty, time to go to work. Follow me,' he said.

I thought, 'Here we go again.'

My father scooted around the back of the sale ring to the stalls, to find the chestnut filly he'd just bought. I ran along behind.

When he had the filly, we hurried to a spot where we were out of sight of the sale ring. On the way, my father had picked up lunge ropes, a saddle and bridle and a whip.

When we were a safe distance away, he fixed on the saddle and bridle and attached the lunge ropes. He ran the filly around in a circle, turning her in both directions for about ten minutes. Then he reined her in and took the lunge ropes off.

'Overfed and under-used,' he said, making a snap judgement as to what was causing the animal's unsociable behaviour. 'Ride her hard for about an hour, then bring her down to a walk and cool her off. Have her take backward

34

steps every quarter of an hour. Clean her up, and we'll put her back in the ring in three hours' time. We'll do the usual show.'

Left with my instructions, I watched him hurry back to the sale ring to conclude his business there. It was just me and the chestnut filly for the next three hours.

My affinity with problem horses — or, as I call them, remedial horses — dates from these early, rather dubious experiences with my father at the sales ring.

I was given the horses whose difficulties he thought came from maltreatment by youthful riders. He felt that I was the best person to deal with a 'child-spoiled horse', because when I got them right the transition to the regular rider would be easier.

I took this chestnut filly and did as I was told. But every time I did this, I was also trying to figure out for myself what was causing her behavioural problems.

Close to three hours later, my father returned. 'Let's see,' he said.

He watched as I rode the chestnut filly steadily in circles at a walk, a trot and a canter. Then I slipped off, ducked my head and walked underneath her belly. I repeated this several times.

'OK,' said my father. 'Let's go.'

Back in the sales ring, buyers looked on as I rode what appeared to be a well-broken, gentle animal into the arena and put her through some impressive manoeuvres. I dismounted and walked underneath the horse's belly and then back again. I could sense the buyers pressing around the ring; they were impressed no end.

I heard the voice of the auctioneer quicken and rise a notch in tone as the figure rose to twice, then three times what my father had paid earlier in the day. Looking back on it, I assume the auctioneer must have been aware of what my father was doing. There was nothing illegal about it, of course, but clearly this wasn't a technique whereby the problems of any particular horse were comprehensively solved, only quickly masked over. However, the sheer range of horses I rode made it an experience hard to equal. It meant I was able to develop the ability to read and understand problem horses quickly and accurately.

During the years when I was doing this type of thing for my father, I tried to learn what was troubling the horse through observing their actions and reactions. I developed an inner ear. I believed the horses were telling me something and, most importantly, I learned hardly ever to believe the people connected with the horse. It's not that they were lying, but simply that they weren't listening.

Over the years this came to be the foundation stone of my thinking, so much so that it's become like a saying, repeating itself over and over as my experience in the field of horsemanship proved it to be true, time and again: '*A good trainer can hear a horse speak to him. A great trainer can hear him whisper.*'

★ ★ ★

The hard California sun was hammering the dry earth as my father and I moved across the corral he used to break horses in. His every movement was followed by a deep black shadow, like a presence from which he couldn't escape. He came over and leaned against one of the six upright posts — almost as tall and thin as he was — which were used for tethering the young horses.

He was coiling a rope to leave it neatly hung on the post, ready for the next poor animal which would dance on the end of it like a fish stuck on a line.

He suggested, 'Maybe it's time you learned how to break a horse.'

I was seven years old. There's no chance that I'm wrong about the year, because events that would change everything were shortly to happen. I didn't know it then, but this was to be our last summer living at the Competition Grounds for some time.

When he made his suggestion, I didn't answer. I didn't want to play any part in 'sacking out'. I had witnessed the tying-up and the beatings, and I'd seen the injuries they caused. Even the posts standing around the perimeter of this corral were like grim sentries guarding the reputation of this terrible procedure.

He added, 'There's nothin' much you can't manage, despite your being only a kid.'

We strolled over to a nearby corral where my father squinted into the sun and pointed at two young horses. 'There. Those two.'

I watched them for a while, and they seemed

of a gentle enough disposition. Then we climbed the rail and walked closer. The two young horses stirred and moved away quietly, but they were receptive to our voices. They had obviously been handled before.

'We'll have you do the pair of them together, OK?'

No, I wanted to reply, I wasn't ready to go through with sacking out and tying-up a horse; I never wanted to do that if I could possibly help it, not in my entire life.

Given my silence, my father continued, 'I'll let you know when I've got the time to take you through it and instruct you.'

I asked, 'Can I have a few days?'

He didn't sense my reluctance. To him, it would have been incomprehensible to want to 'break' a horse in any other way. 'A few days for what?' he asked.

'You know, maybe get to know them a bit, first.'

'To get to *know* them?' he asked, mystified.

'Maybe.'

'Well, OK, but don't go messing it up. And don't go trying any fancy business. A horse is a dangerous machine, and you'd be wise to remember that. You hurt them first — or they'll hurt you.'

I took the horses to a round pen way out back and simply got to know them. I wasn't in any danger, because there were other people around who were working their horses and they were keeping an eye on me.

I merely walked around the pen following

38

them and trying to cajole them into allowing me to move closer to them. I didn't really know what I was doing, but on the third day I was surprised to find that one of the horses was following me around. Wherever I went, so did this gelding. To my astonishment, I could stand on my tiptoes and push a saddle on his back. There seemed to be no rhyme or reason to it — but it happened.

I was wildly excited by what I'd accomplished and ran immediately to the house to tell my father. I asked him to come and watch.

He reminded me that he'd told me not to go messing around as he followed me out of the house and over to the round pen, a distance of some 200 yards. I couldn't judge his mood. Maybe it was reluctance to waste his time coming over here for nothing? Perhaps he'd sensed my disobedience already, and was angry about it.

When we arrived, he didn't say anything. He didn't ask me about what he was going to see, or what on earth I was going on about. He simply took up position on the viewing stand just above the fence and waited.

I was confident as I brought the gelding into the round pen. The horse and I wandered here and there together, like an odd sort of dance with neither partner knowing what the moves were, but eventually I was standing next to him.

Then, moving quietly and calmly, I reached up as high as I could and slid a saddle on his back. It was a magical experience.

At this point I looked up at my father, who

was staring at me with his mouth open. I was uncertain how to read that look, but I was hoping it was astonishment and maybe pride at my accomplishing this after only three days.

Slowly, he stood up, still fixing me with this look which could have meant any number of things. The first words he uttered were, 'What the hell am I raising?' As he jumped off the viewing platform, I saw there was a four-foot stall-chain in his hand. He came bursting into the pen and grabbed me by one arm.

He repeated, 'What am I raising?' I think he truly believed there was something evil in what I'd done.

Then he raised the stall-chain and brought it down hard, again and again, on my thighs and buttocks. I felt my nerves whip tight from head to toe with the shock of it and the blood drained from my skull, making me feel faint. The impact of the solid iron chain hitting my body seemed to make it certain that something would break. I can still remember the grip of his left hand on my upper arm, inescapable, as he used his right hand to wield the chain. The beating seemed to continue for several minutes while I writhed in his grasp.

I was left in a pitiful, grieving state. He was giving me the same treatment which he used to whip horses into submission, and I felt the same anger and the same sense of failure and — I can report now — I've suffered a lifelong sense of resentment. It was a lesson in how *not* to win respect and allegiance; instead it only enforced a reluctant obedience and instilled fear.

With this blur of pain and disappointment, I learnt a second lesson. I would never show my father any part of my work in starting and developing young horses, I promised myself that.

As it turned out, I wouldn't take him into my confidence again — not for 44 years. In 1986, just before he died at the age of 78, I would invite him to take up position on the viewing deck of a round pen once again.

★ ★ ★

Later on that year, in September of 1942, a stranger appeared unannounced at the gates of the Salinas Rodeo and Competition Grounds.

He was a stocky man, shorter than my father, with the athletic conformation of a rugby player — a low centre of gravity. He was dressed in a jacket and tie and carried a briefcase — not a normal sight. My father and mother greeted him and they stood in a knot, talking amongst themselves.

From where my brother and I were watching, we saw my father raise his hand and point in different directions. When they started to move off, we followed at a discreet distance, poking our noses around the corners of barns to see where they were going next.

It wasn't long before we realised that this stranger was visiting areas of the Competition Grounds which weren't a normal part of anyone's agenda. At the ages of six and seven, Larry and I had a clear pattern of where people

41

went and why; and as we trailed around after them, we knew something odd was going on.

From time to time we saw him writing down measurements he'd made by striding up and down the lengths of the barns. He examined the perimeter fencing, and we saw more pointing and taking notes.

A month afterwards, a letter arrived. My father read it aloud as we all listened: ' . . . it has been confirmed that the Competition Grounds, owned by the city of Salinas, are to be requisitioned and used by the US Government as a Japanese-American concentration camp.'

We were stunned. What was a concentration camp? Pearl Harbor had brought America wholeheartedly into the war the previous year, but I had no idea what this meant.

My father and mother explained it to us by turns. We were at war with Japan, so Japanese immigrants and their families were considered enemies of the state and were to be interned for the duration of the war.

But these people were our friends and neighbours; some of them had been living around here for as long as we could remember. We were confused.

Our parents could do no more than press on and explain to us that everything was going to be different while the war continued. The Japanese-Americans who lived in our area would be brought here, to the Competition Grounds.

Uncomprehending, we asked, 'Where will they all live?'

'The government plan to house them in the box stalls.'

'In the box stalls? What about the horses?'

My father was silent, looking again at the letter. Then he read out, 'Other buildings will be constructed to provide communal facilities.'

I'm certain that Mr Sherwood could never have predicted such a turn of events when he gifted the land to the city of Salinas.

Of course, moments later it occurred to Larry and me that this wasn't only going to affect our Japanese-American neighbours, it would also affect us. We had a line of questions for our parents.

My father folded the letter and explained the situation, that we were being asked to choose the lesser of two evils. We would have to reduce our riding-school and horse-training activities almost to zero if we wanted to stay living at the Competition Grounds. Otherwise, we might choose to leave.

This was a traumatic experience not just for me and my younger brother Larry, but for my mother and father as well. If we chose to stay in our house, we'd be living under cramped conditions behind barbed-wire fences, as though we were prisoners also. Whether we stayed or left, we'd have to sell most of our horses.

To add to the confusion, it was difficult for Larry and me to understand why we were at war. We'd been attending elementary school and had many Japanese classmates. Some of them were friends of ours who lived nearby and whose parents operated successful farms.

43

Now they were to be imprisoned all around us, on what we had come to think of as our home, although technically it was owned by the city of Salinas.

I remember the arguments going back and forth — and the atmosphere in the house suddenly blackened with this news. In reality, there was no option.

We decided to leave.

As far as I was concerned, my life had come to an end. I couldn't sleep, and cried through most nights. Many of my concerns were selfish, as those of a small child tend to be. I already believed I was to be a champion rider, with a future in showing horses. Now, all our horses and their equipment were to be sold.

Kicking our heels by the front gates, Larry and I watched resentfully as an endless line of vehicles came and went, putting this plan into effect without delay. Some brought materials for the conversion of the box stalls into the most basic of living quarters for the Japanese and the erection of makeshift facilities for communal use. Other trucks removed our equipment and our horses.

Many of them were sent to the notorious Crow's Landing for slaughter. Truck-load after truck-load of animals were taken away and killed. Larry and I, more upset than we'd ever known was possible, watched as they rolled out of the Competition Grounds in clouds of dust, never to be seen again.

To help us understand this decision, we were told that horsemeat was required for the war

44

effort. All over the world, US soldiers not so very much older than ourselves were living in desperate conditions. The outcome of the fight against tyranny depended on keeping these young soldiers fit and as well-fed as possible. The horsemeat we were providing would go towards saving their lives and winning the war.

In truth, of course, there was nowhere else for the horses to go. No one could afford to buy them. Gas was rationed, and no one could pay even for the transport.

Ginger was among those who were taken and killed.

* * *

We moved to a small house in the centre of the city of Salinas. It had concrete kerbs in the front, and it was the only house I've ever lived in which had a number on the door: 347 Church Street.

It was a 1920s clapboard house with three bedrooms and an elevated floor; there was a lot of porch to go through before you were inside. There was a yard out the back with a large magnolia tree growing there; I was to prove allergic to its blooms. It was a city lot, with neighbours in every direction.

This was different from anything I'd known, and I didn't like it one bit. My mother tried to console me. She picked up our large world globe, brought it to my room and asked me to find Japan. After some delay, I found the right place.

45

Then she asked me to find America. 'There.'

'Now, Monty, look at those two places. Japan is a collection of tiny islands. The United States is a massive country, isn't it? So, when you compare Japan with America, you can understand why, in just a few months, the war will be over and we can return to the Competition Grounds.'

It helped, but there was plenty of evidence to the contrary and I began to doubt my mother. If the war was going to be over soon, why were people putting stickers in their car windows asking, 'Is this journey really necessary?'

Also, my father was asked to become a policeman. He was 34 years old and therefore not eligible for service in the armed forces at that time, but the shortage of young men and the fact that he had once been a forest ranger made him ideal material to be an officer in the Salinas police department.

When the news of his appointment came through, it seemed to me the change in our lives was going to be more or less permanent. We would never go back to the Competition Grounds.

However, one thing happened which was to prevent my life from straying too far from the course which I had so firmly fixed for it. My father managed to rent a smallholding on the edge of town. It was only a barn surrounded by a few acres, and was nothing compared with what we were used to, but it would allow us to keep 10 – 15 horses in training.

We went at that place with a hose and cleaned it out thoroughly. We hammered up partitions, mended gates and scrubbed concrete floors until they glistened. We walked over the ground inch by inch to clear any nails and the remnants of any fencing wire which might damage the horses' feet. We fixed up the water supply and put the gates back on their hinges, and made up a bin for the feed. We went hammer and tongs at it to make the place fit for equine habitation, including storage for hay and straw.

The smell of horses was in my nostrils again, and that meant happiness.

Although my father was a cruel and frightening man, he gave me back what I wanted most in the world: a future with horses.

More specifically, my future lay with a small brown gelding called Brownie, who was one of the first arrivals at the Villa Street facility.

Brownie was a 15-hands-high gelding, his mother a mustang mare and his sire a thoroughbred — one of the government remount stallions. This was a project whereby the US Cavalry took thoroughbred stallions and set them loose to run with the mustangs on the open range. The ranchers would receive a payment if they could shoot a mustang stallion in order that the thoroughbred stallions would take over the females and breed a class of horse which would be suitable for the Cavalry. The US Cavalry had the first call to come back and capture the young males for themselves, while the ranchers could keep the fillies as a further payment for their co-operation in this initiative.

As his name implied, Brownie was a medium brown all over, except for about eight inches of softer, doeskin colour on his muzzle and a very small white dot between his eyes, which gave him a concentrated, pointed look. He had well-shaped feet with flint-hard sidewalls — a legacy of his mustang heritage.

The minute Brownie arrived and I knew he was to be mine, I wanted to bond with him closely.

'OK,' said my father, 'let's break him.'

My heart sank. How could I be this animal's best friend when his tentative trust in human beings was about to be abused? But I was too frightened of my father to do anything to stop it.

I watched him prepare for the sacking-out procedure. As Brownie waited in his stall, my father rooted among some old slatted boxes used for the commercial transport of vegetables which were lying in a pile awaiting burning. He found what he was looking for — a cut of heavy, crêpe-like paper which would have been used to line the bottom of the crate and protect the vegetables. He twisted one end and tied it to the end of a rope.

Brownie was taken out and tied to a single post which had been driven deep enough into the ground to withstand the punishment. He stood patiently while my father walked around behind him, coiling the rope with the paper tied to the end of it.

My father lobbed the paper and Brownie jumped sideways as if his life depended on it — which to his way of thinking it did. His head snapped around, brought up short by the rope. This was just the beginning.

As I watched Brownie's eyes widen and roll in fear as he waited for what would happen next, I felt dread and sympathy in equal amounts. I cursed inwardly and wanted more than anything to untie the rope. I tried to think of how I might make it up to him, but I didn't know of a way.

The sacking out continued, and I became more and more determined to find one. I was left wretched and disgusted, but there was nothing I could do. It wasn't just my father's method — this was the way it was done — and it still remains an acceptable practice in the eyes of many people around the world.

Time would tell of the impact of this experience on Brownie. For his entire life, he was phobic about paper. Anything that sounded like it would send him into a panic, and he'd be dangerous to himself and others. He would bolt madly, and no one could tell him that it was only paper, that it was nothing to be afraid of. I could never be angry with him for this blind spot in his nature and accepted it as our fault, our crime against him.

★ ★ ★

When my father became a policeman, our car became a police car.

The war had made vehicles of any description difficult to come by. When he joined up,

49

my father was told he would earn a higher salary if he offered to equip his family car for police work.

Consequently, a lot of policemen's private cars were being taken and fitted with red emergency lights, sirens and radios. Special spotlights and lighting systems were installed to adapt the car for driving in blackout conditions. The West Coast was vulnerable to enemy attack, and blackouts were common.

Our family car was an unusual one. I recall my father coming home one day — this was when we were still living at the Competition Grounds — and saying we needed a larger vehicle to cope with picking up the riding students. He said the Mullers, who owned a mortuary in Salinas, had just the car for us.

It wasn't exactly a hearse, but it was the limousine in which the immediate family travelled in the funeral procession. A huge 1932 Cadillac sedan with enormous running boards, it was fitted with every option under the sun — the kind of car that Al Capone would drive. It had acres of space inside, and would accommodate many more riding students than any new car which we might have been able to buy for the same price. Like many automobiles of its day, it didn't have a traditional trunk or boot; rather it had a large metal box, like a foot-locker, which bolted onto the back of the car.

It didn't take long for the riding students to reduce it from its former immaculate condition to something resembling a stable on wheels.

When we moved into town in 1942, we took the car with us and it was subsequently fitted up as a police car. I can remember riding with my father when he got calls over the radio, or when he saw someone violating the traffic code. The red light would come on, the siren would sound and we'd race off and 'apprehend the suspect'. He carried his badge with him at all times, and there was always a citation pad and a pair of handcuffs in the glove-box. Also, there was usually a hand-gun.

Late in the evening of one spring day in 1943, we were driving home. It had been a long day of riding our horses and attending to their keep in the Villa Street facility on the outskirts of town. Now it was getting dark.

Just as we arrived at the city limits, a call came over the radio saying there was an armed robbery in progress at the Golden Dragon saloon bar on Soledad Street in Chinatown.

My father picked up the hand microphone and responded, 'I'm just a block and a half from the Golden Dragon and I'll answer that call.' The radio dispatcher asked, 'Are you armed?' My father replied, 'Yes.'

A bolt of fear ran through me. In all the times I'd been with him in the car when he answered police calls, he'd never had to defend himself with a gun.

The Cadillac's speedometer leapt to 60 miles an hour. He flipped the switches for the siren and the flashing light. The car listed wildly from side to side as it covered the distance to Chinatown at breakneck speed. The headlights picked up people leaping out of our way.

He barked at me, 'Get down on the floor!'

My knees turned to jelly as I realised the seriousness of the situation. I quickly slid from the seat and into the footwell underneath the dash, and waited.

I was about to witness an incident that changed me for ever, and which I was subsequently to push to the darkest corner of my mind. But in that dark corner, it remains as crystal-clear as if it had happened yesterday.

When I sat down to write an account of my life, I wondered whether or not I ought to include this incident, and I listened to advice from some members of my family who recommended it should be omitted.

However, it is probably the single most important influence on me. In particular, the way in which I deal with horses was strictly reinforced by what I saw on that day in 1943, although not a single horse features in it.

It could be said that I was born in 1943 at the age of eight. Before that day I was a different person entirely.

In recounting this story, I must stress that I'm not attempting to vilify my father. He was brought up in the tough and sometimes cruel world of the American pioneer, and his upbringing and experience caused him to be the type of person he was. The single generation which divided us might have been 100 years long, in terms of what happened in those few decades at the turn of the century in America. During his upbringing, he would have faced up to the natural law of 'kill or be killed' almost daily.

He mellowed as the years went by. When my own wife and children came to know him, he wasn't the cold and rigid man that I had known as a youngster; he'd had the fight drawn out of him.

I'm also at pains to point out the difficulty my father had with the issue of race. Half Cherokee Indian, he had suffered racial abuse as he was growing up. Yet he was angry that the Second World War had brought black people to our otherwise white community. The military installation of Fort Ord was a 20-minute drive away, and many black servicemen were stationed there. It's perhaps true that those who are victims of racial prejudice are the first to inflict it on others when circumstances give them the chance.

This is not to excuse what happened, but it is my attempt to gain the most understanding view of my father's actions. Often I learnt from him what I *didn't* want to be, rather than what I might want to be.

As the car sped towards the scene of the crime, my father gave a second order: 'Get me the gun and the handcuffs.'

I reached up and sprang the latch on the glove-box. I quickly removed the handcuffs, but I could not feel the gun. Frantically, my fingers swept through the maps, pens and other debris in the glove-box, but it wasn't there. He was cursing at me to hurry.

When he knew for certain that the pistol

wasn't there, he said, 'Damn, I was sure I brought it with me.' He'd already grabbed the handcuffs and shoved them into his pocket.

Just then the Cadillac slid to a halt a few doors down from the Golden Dragon. He leapt from the car almost before it stopped moving, shouting to me just before he slammed the door, 'Stay in the car, *on the floor.*'

I lay there, curled under the dash, as the red, yellow and green lights of the Golden Dragon filled the car with an eerie blinking light. It was cramped and the smell of horse, dirt, sweat and damp wool was pretty bad. I wrestled with the urge to sit up, partly to escape the smell but mainly to see what was happening.

As I unfolded my legs and crept on to the seat, my eyes were now level with the bottom of the passenger window. I had a direct view of the entrance to the bar some twenty yards away.

The street was lined with people, some of them talking to him and pointing towards the saloon. They were agitated and whispering amongst themselves. I could see my father about to go inside.

Even though I was stiff with panic, I found my hand reaching over to the handle and easing the door open.

I crept forward. Everyone was focused on what was going on just inside the doorway, so no one saw the eight-year-old boy crawling along, making his way closer to the object of their attention. I crabbed sideways to gain a spot near the door.

It seemed like everything had gone silent,

because all I could hear was the thumping of my heart as I peered into the bar.

Inside, no more than five feet away, I saw my father with his back to me. The bar's patrons were scattered to the furthest corners of the room, huddled together. A tall, heavy-set black man was the only person moving.

He swerved to point a knife that looked the size of a sword in the direction of the bartender and shouted, 'Put the money on the bar!' The frightened bartender pulled bills from the register, scattering coins to the floor in his haste.

The robber had spread his coat on the bar and there were already watches, rings, bracelets and wallets collected on it — evidently he had been cleaning out the patrons up to now. When he had the money from the takings, he'd be ready to fold it all up in his coat and make a getaway.

At this point my father lifted his badge high in the air so that everyone could clearly determine his authority, and he shouted, 'Police! Stand where you are. Put down the knife and place your hands on the bar.'

For one second, everything was frozen in time.

Then, instead of obeying my father, the black man turned to face him, his knife pointing directly in front of him.

At this point I silently begged my father to give way.

He didn't. Instead he stepped forward, walking towards the knife. Serious injury or even death

55

awaited him; he didn't have a weapon with which to defend himself. It was a brave act, but terror overtook me; in those few seconds I feared I was to be without a father.

All this raced through my mind as I watched him approach the man, saying, 'Don't do this to yourself; put the knife on the bar, turn around and put your hands in the air, give it up.'

When they were inches from each other, virtually eyeball to eyeball, and just when I thought the black man would give way after all, he made his attack. He closed the gap between them with a quick thrust of his knife hand, aiming for my father's ribs.

My father's hand snaked out and grabbed the man's fist exactly where it closed on the knife handle.

With a quick folding action he locked the robber's elbow backwards and sent the knife spinning to the floor. The thrust on his twisted arm caused the black man to fall back and his head cracked on the edge of the bar. Bouncing off the wooden counter, he continued to fall to the floor and hit his head again on the brass foot rail.

He lay motionless, in a heap. It was all over.

I experienced a rush of emotion. My father was alive and, without the use of a weapon, had brought down an armed robber.

He had turned from being a defenceless, unarmed policeman to being a hero.

I watched then as my father stood over the black man's unconscious form. I saw him gather his body to its highest point. He paused for a moment, then he dropped the whole 220 pounds of his weight, driving it through his knee and directly on to the robber's chest, surely breaking his ribs.

Now I didn't know what to feel. My father had crushed a man when he was down. He might have committed a murder.

My father put the cuffs on him. The people in the bar and observing from outside were now aware that the tables had turned in no uncertain manner. They were no longer the frightened victims; now they were on the winning side.

My father walked over and picked up the knife by the tip of the blade, handing it to the bartender to carry for him. He grabbed the chain connecting the handcuffs and hauled on it, dragging the black man who was limp as a sack of feed.

As he turned towards the doorway, the realisation hit me that I wasn't where I was meant to be and I turned and ran back to the car. Just as I was sliding into the driver's seat and closing the door behind me, I saw him emerge from the bar, surrounded by onlookers. He gave the torso an extra lift and then released the chain, dropping the back of the man's head on the sidewalk.

My father went round and opened the passenger side of the car, taking the knife from the barman and placing it carefully on the seat beside where I was sitting.

Then he went to the rear of the Cadillac and opened that big, trunk-like box. From there he took some empty grain sacks and laid them over the rear floorspace so that blood wouldn't stain the interior.

He opened the doors wide, heaved the black man on to the grain sacks, and then got in the car himself. Because the knife was occupying the passenger seat, I was huddling close to him to avoid touching it. He told me to pick it up by the blade and put it in the glove-box. It's some indication of the size of a 1932 Cadillac's glove-box that it fitted inside.

As we set off, I could hear sounds coming from the man's throat, but my father was unconcerned. He told me the man was faking his injuries, adding, 'He'll be just fine.'

By now, other patrol cars had joined us on our way to the police station. Positioned in front and behind us, their sirens joined ours in a wailing sound that fitted my inner feelings exactly.

My father was talking on the radio and explaining how the robber had attempted to cut him with the knife. The story of the arrest was told with bravado.

Turning behind me, I watched anxiously to see if the man was still breathing. He was . . . just.

I prayed we'd arrive at the police station quickly. At the station, he'd be safe.

When we arrived, my father opened the car door and dragged the man on to the sidewalk. For good measure, as if he was testing him for any resistance at all, he drew the black man's shoulders up a few feet and dropped him with a crack on to the cement.

The other officers coming out of the station and getting out of their cars laughed and hooted.

My father picked up the chain again, lifted the man's head and torso off the sidewalk and backed up the set of concrete stairs fronting the police station.

He would take a couple of steps, hoist the man, take a couple more steps and repeat the process.

No one made an attempt to find a stretcher, and no one helped him. This was his trophy. He'd bagged it, and now he was going to bring it home to display in front of his brother-officers.

They hollered and laughed behind him, side-stepping the trail of blood.

Inside the station, at the top of the stairs, was the sergeant's desk. Dragging the black man the last few feet, my father dropped him on the concrete floor opposite the desk. 'I've pulled a driving licence from his pocket. Here's his name; book him, send someone to get his prints.'

A booking sheet was fed into the typewriter and the keys began their staccato beat, filling in the blanks from the information on the licence.

People lit cigarettes. There was laughter as the story of the man's arrest was retold, with more violence and drama added to what had already occurred.

I begged my father to do something about the dying man. He looked down and shouted, 'You get back in the car and shut up. The man is just faking it! There's nothing at all wrong with him.'

At this point the black man regained consciousness and struggled to his feet. No one raced to stop him as he staggered like a wounded animal, heading for the door.

My father told me again, 'Get in the car, Monty,' and turned to follow him.

He hadn't got far; he stumbled at the top of the steps and dived headlong, striking his head against a tree that was growing there. Once again he was motionless.

At this point I was crying uncontrollably. My father again yelled, 'Get in the car!'

I ran for my life back to the Cadillac and buried my face in the upholstery, sobbing. Then I heard the sound of the car door opening and slamming shut, and the scrape of the key in the ignition. We were on our way home.

Four days after the robbery, I asked my father what had happened to the man he'd arrested in the Golden Dragon Saloon. He replied, 'Oh, he died.'

He must have felt my shock, because then he quickly invented a story. 'He didn't die of his injuries; he died of pneumonia. That boy refused to pull the blankets over him at night, and he caught pneumonia and died.'

I believed him. From then on, throughout my boyhood, I was careful to pull the blankets up to my chin, making sure my chest was covered.

Years later, I found out that the black man had lain with his ribs broken, his lungs pierced and his skull cracked, until he died.

Later, in psychology courses, I'd learn how kidnappers and child molesters will kill small

60

animals in front of their victims in order to traumatise them and instill in them such a sense of fear that they are unable to fight back.

In this sense, I understand now that I became a victim of my father's aggression. But I didn't see it that way back then; all I knew was how much I feared him. From that point forward, well into adulthood, I had to control my life and direct it away from his involvement.

There is a postscript to this incident.

Two months later, my father asked me to come with him one evening. 'We're going to the fights,' he said, 'and you're going to meet a very special man there.'

We drove to the National Guard Armory, passing crowds of people as we pulled up outside.

We passed into some small rooms at the back of the exhibition hall, entering a particular room where a very large black man was seated on a table.

My pulse shot up. He was the first of his race I'd seen since the time of the robbery.

My father drew me closer and said, 'Come on, Monty. Meet Joe Lewis, he's the heavyweight champion of the world.'

Joe Lewis greeted my father, 'Hi, Marvin.'

'Hi,' said my father; and then he added, 'Meet my son, Monty.'

I refused to go closer. The champion boxer said, 'Come on, I won't hurt you.'

I shook his hand, but couldn't look him in the eye. Hoping to get past my shyness, Joe Lewis pointed at his shoulder and said, 'Hey, little man, hit me, I dare you.'

I couldn't play that game with him. In the end he took my hand and folded it into a fist and tapped it against his shoulder, mocking that it hurt him a bit. 'Now,' he said, 'you can say you knocked out the world champ.'

A photographer was setting up nearby and he called out that he was ready.

My father put his arm around Joe Lewis so that the picture could be taken.

★ ★ ★

There's a breed of horse which was known originally as 'Copper Bottom' and then a touch later on as 'Steel Dust'. These curious names for what was, back in the 1930s, a small, specialist breed came about because they were the names of the two principal sires.

They were stout, easy keepers with well developed feet and calm, trainable minds. Typically quite small, their conformation might be described as the muscular 'bulldog' type, with exceptionally well-rounded hindquarters and deep hearts.

They were bred for ranch work because their terrific acceleration made them ideal for roping cattle and cutting a cow out of a herd.

During the week they'd be worked on the ranch, then at weekends they'd be taken to rodeos and entered in the roping events and steer wrestling.

When done with those, they'd be given a few minutes' rest and then they'd trade their Western

62

rigs for the jockey's 'postage stamp' and be raced on the bush tracks that surrounded the rodeo arenas.

In shorter races, typically less than a quarter of a mile, there was nothing that could beat them. They just blasted out of the starting gate like a bullet out of a gun. In fact many of them never drew a breath until after they'd passed the finish line, were slowing up and they realized they needed a change of air in their lungs.

They're the horse equivalent of drag-racers and, because of the distance involved — a quarter of a mile — the breed became known as the quarter horse.

My father was attracted to this new type of competitive event, sprint-horse racing, and I loved the excitement.

Of course the smallest boys were up in the saddle to achieve the minimum weight on the back of the animal, and I rode at that time for a fee of $5 to ride and $10 to win.

Little towns up and down California — Salinas, King City, Fresno, Victorville, Stockton — held these 'short horse' or 'quarter horse' meets which were run for a jackpot. Each owner put up a little money and the winner took everything.

There were larger amounts of money, though, changing hands with the betting that went on among the spectators and owners. The gambling was unregulated, without sanction by any association. This of course made it fiercer and faster and more contentious — a heady atmosphere which is meat and drink to the mind of any serious gambler.

There was no licensing of the riders, nor much concern for their safety, and I rode a lot of races without a protective helmet.

Mr Frank Vessels was one of the principal owners of this type of horse, and his trainer was a man called Farrell Jones.

One day, I was watching him down at Frank Vessels' track; I say 'track', but this was no more than a strip of land set down between stacks of hay. Mr Vessels had a bunch of horses so he needed the hay, but he took the opportunity of piling it alongside this rough track for spectators to sit on.

That day, Farrell Jones had a young quarter horse wheeling about behind the starting gate, eyeing the contraption like it was akin to the jaws of a crocodile and shying at the track like it was laid down especially to spook him, with these square blocks of hay ready to fall in and catch his flanks, and the ground ready to open up beneath his feet, and the sky looking pretty dangerous too.

Accompanying this young animal was an older stablemate who knew what this rough-and-ready racing game was all about, and who could tell the old war stories about the times she'd overhauled the leader in the last breath of a race that only ever lasted a number of seconds.

'Right, then,' said Farrell, 'let's load him into the gates.'

In training quarter horses to bolt from the starting gate, it was common practice at that time to shut the novice horse inside and then put the whip on him to drive him into a frenzy so he'd be pretty anxious to escape once the gate was flipped open. The thinking was that each time thereafter he found himself in a starting gate, the thought process would be repeated and so the fear, the instinct to run, would guarantee a better performance. It wasn't that uncommon to apply electric shocks to the horse, to achieve the same effect.

I watched as Farrell Jones now took his young animal and walked him *through* the starting gate. He didn't close the door in front, nor the one behind; he simply led the horse in the back, through, and out the front again, while the older stablemate was held in close proximity.

Then he went around again. And again.

This continued until the few of us watching began to get *dizzy*; and I might guess the horse himself was on the edge of being bored stiff with the darned circle he was taking over and over.

Then Farrell Jones led him into the stall and shut the front gate, offering a mouthful of feed in a bucket to make him feel at home. His stablemate was nearby, easily visible through the slatted sides.

We all hung around wondering whether this was going to be a training session for getting this novice to jump into an effective start in a quarter-horse race, or was it his new stable?

Once he'd grown comfortable with being inside with the gates shut, they were opened and he wasn't led out — oh no, that would be too much altogether. He was allowed to take his time. It was his decision whether he wanted to leave, ever. When he did so, it seemed like an exciting moment.

What Farrell Jones was doing was taking every ounce of pressure out of the training procedure.

Next of all, I began to see an additional reason for having the stablemate on hand. With the gates closed and the novice horse inside, the stablemate was walked alongside and down the track a way. The gate was opened and without any encouragement the novice of course stepped daintily out of the stall and strolled up the track to catch up with his girlfriend.

A while later, the pace horse was set going at a faster walk, and she was allowed to reach a little further down the track. It might even have been necessary for the novice to shrug into a gentle trot to catch her up.

Not many hours after that, Farrell Jones had his novice horse entering the stalls without the slightest fuss, waiting with his nose pressed against the front gate in a state of great anticipation, thinking only of going forwards, ready to fly out of the gate of his own free will and canter down to the pace horse, who was always held back a touch to allow the novice to overtake and 'win' the race.

He was having fun.

I was incredibly impressed by what I witnessed Farrell Jones doing, and I wanted to know all about it. I asked him how he'd arrived at his method.

He sucked some more on the wad of tobacco he had parked down the side of his back teeth, and explained, 'You know, I've watched a whole lot of these races and I've watched them pretty carefully — as you do when there's maybe a sum of money riding into your pocket if you make the right choices. And I saw an interesting thing. It ain't the horses who're all jazzed up who're starting the quickest. Those ones are so busy banging about from side to side and running on the spot and thinking about what evildoer is behind them, that they've less time to notice whether the gate's flying open. No, it's the animals who are the most relaxed — they're the ones making the flying starts.'

Farrell Jones proved to me that this cruelty — whipping the horses in the stall to make them afraid and want to escape — was not only unnecessary, it was also having a contrary effect: it was making them slower off the mark; it was counter-productive.

Learning from this example, it became part of my way of thinking that a man should never say to a horse, 'You *must*.' Instead, he should invite a horse to perform because, 'I would like you to.'

Taking that a step further — to ask a horse to perform isn't as clever as causing him to *want* to.

Horses want to run, it's natural to them, and if they're trained right we can harness their willingness to do just that, to race to their utmost potential — and they can enjoy running as much as we enjoy watching them do it. As it was to turn out, I would work for most of my life in the thoroughbred racing industry,

67

and to this day I am fervent in my belief that whips should be banned; there's no need for them if training procedures take advantage of a well-bred horse's overpowering desire to run. Certainly, I want no whips anywhere near my establishment — not for any reason.

I probably rode in about 200 sprint races when I was 8 – 12 years of age, most of them quarter-horse races. I didn't have any serious accidents, although I fell off a time or two.

Frank Vessels was to start the Quarter Racing Association in 1945 and he built a dedicated race-track, something very different from how he started, when it was simply that path through stacks of hay.

Soon he was to elevate sprint racing beyond its origins in ranching and turn it into the same class of event as thoroughbred racing.

The American Quarter Horse Association would be started in 1946, with a team of inspectors touring the United States taking those horses with the right conformation on to their register.

It would be 1949 before I rode my last race in King City, California. It was just a ranching town, but there were two owners there who became very important to quarter-horse racing: Gyle Norris and the McKensie brothers. The McKensie brothers owned a top-class mare named Lady Lee whom I was lucky enough to ride a couple of times. They also owned a quarter horse called Dee Dee, who was 1946 champion older male of the breed.

By 1949 I would be unable to keep my

weight down below the 130-pound mark any longer, unlike Tucker Slender who was a tall, thin man, three or four years older than me and a much better jockey. He later went on to become the head starter at many of the major tracks in southern California, and he's still the head starter at Santa Anita and Del Mar.

Farrell Jones was to become the leading thoroughbred trainer in the United States several times over. His methods and his original thinking have stood me in good stead since I learned that first lesson from him. His son, Gary Jones, is currently one of the top trainers in this country.

So, from hanging on to the neck of a particular type of horse as it blasted down those rough tracks, we all started the quarter-horse racing industry, a university for me at the starting stall.

* * *

When I was nine years old, my Uncle Ray told me a story from way back, a story from our Cherokee ancestry.

My grandfather was born in Wales, in the United Kingdom, in 1870. My love of horses might have come from him, because he farmed with them and also used them for fox-hunting and pleasure riding. He was called Earl Roberts, and he emigrated to the United States aged 17 years.

He was quickly lured to the West by the promise of steady work, building roads over the

Sierra Nevada mountains. The Spanish name, Sierra Nevada, means 'snow-covered mountains' which is an unassuming description for the massive natural barrier which forms the border between California and Nevada. It is second in size only to the Rocky Mountains.

When Earl, my grandfather, travelled west to build these roads through the Sierra, crews could only work six months out of the year. The rest of the time, the passes were closed. I can only try to imagine the amount of work involved in cutting through the Sierra Nevada using only man and beast.

Earl was hired to supply horses to pull the equipment on these road projects, as well as to provide saddle horses for the foremen as they directed the efforts of the crews.

The labourers were immigrants like my grandfather, but there were also Indians of the Cherokee nation, who were brought to Nevada from their reservation in the mid-west by the United States government.

Among them was the woman who was to become my grandmother, a young Cherokee girl in her late teens. She was called Sweeney, taken from the name of the agent who transported her family to Nevada. They lifted his surname from the paperwork and gave it to her as a forename.

Among her few possessions were papers qualifying her as a full-blooded Cherokee, entitled to specific native-born rights.

Earl petitioned her family for her hand in marriage and she bore him nine children in quick succession — five of whom survived, including my father and my Uncle Ray.

When Ray, her youngest child, was 11 years old, Sweeney decided that her marriage contract with Earl had been fulfilled. One day when the family got up in the morning, she'd gone.

Months passed while they searched for her. Ultimately, they discovered that she had walked from Tulare back to the Cherokee Indian Reservation, a distance of 600 miles.

Shortly thereafter, 11-year-old Ray developed pneumonia. Earl decided to take the boy back to Sweeney on the reservation, where Ray was adopted into the Cherokee tribe and raised to adulthood. He had the benefit of learning the Indian way as well as the white man's way.

My Uncle Ray told me that when Cherokees wanted to capture wild horses on the great plains of the mid-west of America, they faced the problem of how to get close enough to rope them. They overcame this obstacle in a remarkable fashion.

Instead of driving them into the neck of a valley or building other traps of that sort — which would be difficult given the landscape — they used a much quicker method.

First of all, they followed the herd of horses. They weren't driving them hard, but simply walking after them, pressing them away.

This would continue for a day or two.

Then, when the time was right, the Cherokees would turn and walk in the opposite direction.

Invariably, the horses would turn round and follow them. There was a yo-yo effect.

The Cherokees would simply lead the wild herd into corrals between 2 – 5 acres in size.

Apparently the Cherokees used similar tactics to get close to the beasts they hunted to eat. They used this same yo-yo effect to hunt deer, antelope and buffalo. To be effective with the bow and arrow, the Cherokee Indian needed to be within 40 – 50 feet of his target. They'd press the animals away from them for a while, then turn around and head back the other way. The animals would turn and follow them.

After this oscillatory movement had been repeated a few times, they found themselves near enough to make an easy kill.

Later on, I would come to understand the reasons behind this curious tendency of horses to turn back and seek intimacy with their pursuers, when I was to have the opportunity to observe them in the wild for myself. I would give the phenomenon a name, 'Advance and Retreat'. It would form the basis of my technique in working with horses.

But for the nine-year-old boy that I was at the time Uncle Ray told me the story, it was a mystery. I believed it to be true, but didn't know why. The years of the Second World War had been filled with death — and I guess war always brings that to everyone in one way or another, either metaphorical or not.

In the small world of a boy aged 8 – 11 years at that time, the death of my dreams looked certain for a while when we first moved away from the Competition Grounds.

I'd seen my Japanese-American classmates rounded up and interned at a prison camp located at my former home. I'd witnessed the death of the black man at the hands of my father, which caused me to lose respect for him and to seek my own path in life.

At the same time as I was trying hard to dissociate my life from his, he was giving me what I wanted more than anything else — a life with horses.

Now, with the war over, it was a mad scramble by everyone to return to normality. For my father, this meant gearing up to return to our business at the Competition Grounds and entering me in as many equine competitions as could be found starting up again around the country.

This was exactly what I wanted to do, but it was frantic. The return to the Grounds was like a circus, a festival.

The Japanese had gone, but the camp was in a horrible state. We had to drag magnets around for weeks because the workmen who had dismantled the living quarters of the internees had left the nails and the roofing tacks on the ground, where of course they were a threat to the horses' feet.

We had to put the stables back in order. We put the feed-stalls back in, repaired floors and mended roofs. My mother's entire family turned up to volunteer their help.

The Cadillac had the back sawn off it to turn it into a pick-up, and it went back and forth to the dump, carting away the rubbish.

73

I recall the day when the new saddles arrived — 20 or 30 of them, all dumped in the yard at the same time, and I was there — tearing at the packages to get them out and fitted up with the proper parts ready for the start of lessons the following day.

With the cost of this equipment, not to mention the horses themselves, there were heavy overheads involved in going back into business. We had family conferences, held around the table back in our old house.

It was decided that my father would remain in the police force, because he'd risen to the rank of lieutenant and his salary could help to fund our debts.

My father told us that if we were to succeed, we'd have to do it on our own without much hired help. We could afford only one man, the same Wendell Gillott who'd worked for us before and now had returned from Hawaii. He was a good man — without the highest IQ in the world, but crazy and fun and hard-working.

My brother Larry and I were told that our schooling would have to be cut back to the bare bones, so that we could fit in the necessary work to help Wendell out.

So we were back home, but we had to hit the ground already running.

Wendell arrived at 4.30 in the morning and immediately started in on feeding all 60 horses we were now stabling.

I rolled out of bed some time before 5 o'clock and struggled into the same working clothes which had lain in a heap on the floor where

74

I dropped them the night before. I was in a hurry — I had 22 stalls to muck out before breakfast. My brother Larry would be up and about in a while, also. He had 10 stalls to complete — fewer than me because he was younger and not as strong due to his early illness as a child.

I'd barely call a greeting to Wendell before starting work, cleaning each of the 22 stalls right to the bottom and raking it, rolling the bedding back (no cheating), adding the necessary straw — and then on to the next one.

As I went, I counted: the aim was to take no more than 3½ minutes for every stall; so, all 22 stalls were done in just under an hour and a half. It was like a race; when I threw the pitchfork back against the wall I would raise both hands in the air like the calf-ropers in the rodeos do to stop the clock when the calf is stretched flat on the ground with feet bound.

Breakfast was from 6.30 – 7 a.m. As Larry and I ate, we listened to our father while he issued instructions as to which horses we should ride and what we should do with them.

After breakfast, Wendell cleaned out the remaining 30-odd stalls while Larry and I were out riding. From 7 – 9 in the morning, I rode perhaps six horses with a variety of training programmes and tasks to be accomplished.

After that, we trotted back to the house and showered and changed, ready for the start of school at 9.30.

At 1.30 we returned to the Competition Grounds and were straight back in the saddle training 5 – 6 horses apiece, so by mid-afternoon I'd have had four hours of riding behind me.

Then all of us — my father, mother, brother Larry and I — gave riding lessons. The classes ranged in number from 6 – 12 people. Their ability went from complete beginners and upwards. Some were scared stiff of horses, others were above it all, some were attentive. We pressed on, doing the best we could.

At 5.30 p.m. my mother toured the neighbourhood, delivering the children back home.

Larry, Wendell and I would finish up by putting the horses away, cleaning the tack and feeding.

My mother was preparing the dinner by 6.30 and I was her helper, which started me being interested in cooking. Then, after dinner, there was always a period of time for school work.

Even though I was only in school for about 10 per cent of the normal time, my father insisted I kept up the best possible grades. By anyone's standards, he was a hard task-master.

A child's capabilities are elastic at that age and he stretched mine to the limit, but perhaps as much credit should go to Miss Parsons for tutoring me and making it so that I wanted to take the school tests at all. Her kindness and understanding would allow me to achieve straight A grades at school, despite my prolonged absences from the classroom.

I guess I had the carrot in front of me and the whip behind, like in all the best cartoons.

With the war over by now, there was a surplus of military hardware for sale.

Among all the local ranchers there was this new fashion to zip around in nearly-new military Jeeps or armoured cars, which they could buy for very little money. I'd guess there was some spare weaponry banging around, also.

My father joined in this craze for military surplus, but in a different way from anyone else. It sounds extraordinary to say it now, but he leased an ex-US Cavalry railroad car. There it stood, large as life, our own railroad transport. The payment to secure it for a number of years was minimal. Designed to take officers' horses around the country on the rail network, it had shipping stalls for 15 horses built into it.

My father's idea was that even though competitions were fewer than pre-war and less publicised, in the railroad car we'd get there, however far away they were.

Also, with the war over, the competitions would increase and he wanted to be able to take full advantage of the return to normal life.

That railroad car was to criss-cross America to further my father's and my ambitions. He employed builders to take out six of the stalls in the railroad car and in their place construct a bunk-room, a feed-room with a bin for the grain and a large container for water. In addition there was a minimal kitchen area — a hotplate and a spot for making coffee.

For the next ten years or so, this railroad car

would become a home away from home for me during long spells of the summer months.

My father and I would consult the advertised schedules for horse shows up and down the country. We'd select those shows we thought the best and which we were capable of getting to. Then we'd take our itinerary to Southern Pacific and make our bookings. They would give us a series of pick-up times and sidings numbers. So we would be car 21 in siding number 56, for example, and on the dot of our pick-up time a switch-engine would pull us from the siding on to the main track. The train would then back up to us and hitch up, then off we'd go.

My father stayed behind to attend to his duties as a policeman and as a trainer/manager of horses. Travelling in the railroad car would be my own favourite, Brownie, plus anything up to eight other horses, a groom, myself and Miss Marguerite Parsons.

Marguerite Parsons was a figure of central importance in my life. She had been our nanny since I was two or three years old, and now she became my teacher as well. Neat, clean and as steady as a rock, she read me stories and made learning fun. Above all, she was instructive.

She understood me better than my parents did and sympathised with my problems. She not only taught me how to communicate with people but also encouraged me to relax, and to understand that if I was to pursue a career as a horseman with such single-minded dedication and from such a young age, I would have to pace myself in order not to burn out.

She was only about 20 years old, but it seemed to me that she was always right in what she said and did. She wasn't to leave us until 1949.

In the bunk-room in the railroad car, Miss Parsons slept on the other side of a curtain strung along a pole. When we all retired for the night, I remember hearing this noise from the other side of that curtain — I could never figure out what it was. It was like a whispering sound, but this wasn't any noise I'd heard a horse make before, so it wasn't one of them; it had to be Miss Parsons. What could it be?

Quite a few years later, I would come to know that it was the sound of a woman's underclothing, but meanwhile it merely added to Miss Parsons' mysterious qualities.

One of the first occasions when we used the railroad car, we were heading for a show in Pomona, in southern California.

I was very excited at the preparation involved. The saddles and bridles were all cleaned and sorted and put into a box arrangement we had fitted to one wall of the railroad car. This was because they would need to be transported carefully from the car to the showground; the idea was that we could simply lift out the boxes and stack them in the van so the equipment wouldn't be damaged or dirtied on the way.

In addition Miss Parsons was busy sorting out the homework she wanted to take with us, so I could keep up with my schooling.

Wendell was the groom on this trip and we all loaded the horses and equipment, ready to hitch a ride with the Southern Pacific engine which was due to pick us up.

'Ramp up, ramp up!' exclaimed Miss Parsons as soon as we were inside. She was worried about mice, which were in plentiful supply in all the railway sidings, because that's where the grain was spilled during transport, giving them a healthy food supply. Miss Parsons hated mice and maintained a keen vigil and a comprehensive extermination programme inside the railroad car.

On the dot of the appointed time, the switch engine pulled us on to the main track and a gentle bump and the clink of the hitch told us we were now just one of many wagons hitched to the engine we could hear steaming away at the head of the train.

Southern Pacific took us down through San Luis Obispo, Santa Barbara, Ventura, towards the Los Angeles basin. Peering out through the heavy wire mesh guarding the windows, it was an amazing sight to cut through the mountains, dipping in and out of what must have been as many as fourteen tunnels.

Running alongside the sea was a different experience — one of tranquil beauty, and the slow rhythm of the wheels rolling over the tracks settled all of us into a routine as we made our way south.

Wendell attended to the horses and the equipment. He had a shoe to fix on to Brownie's off-fore, and busied himself with double-checking the equipment.

Miss Parsons was a perfectionist. She had lists of rules and regulations posted around the car, which we were asked to read every day. She prepared my homework and wrote out tests for me to do at the little desk she set up there, usually waiting until one of the long stops we had to put up with at various places, so that neither of us would become too seasick with reading and writing while in motion. Then a woozy sleepiness would creep over us, and it was all you could do to stay awake sometimes. Usually I found myself doing homework at night, when the train was stopped, and then Miss Parsons would check it the following day as well as preparing more.

When she wasn't running around the place chasing the mice, Miss Parsons also had her crusade to keep on top of the dust. To her continual frustration, it seemed like she no sooner wiped a surface than it grew a layer of the stuff right in front of her eyes — just to spite her.

After the tunnels and the slow trail alongside the sea, we reached Los Angeles. This was an eye-opening experience. I'd never seen so many people squeezed into one place before. The number of cars and buildings all scooped up together, side by side, amounted to an alien land for me and I was in awe that so many people lived there.

Finally, we arrived at our destination in Pomona. This was an upscale show, fiercely competitive, and I was facing it with real trepidation. Some of the shows I went to, I could be reasonably confident from the outset that I'd win, but here it was different.

It was also unique in that the owner of the facility — Mr Kellogg of Kellogg's cereals — had paid to have a spur line put down to connect him to the main Southern Pacific network. So we didn't have to park in a siding and transport ourselves and our horses and equipment to the showground — not a bit of it; we simply chugged down this little spur line, dropped the ramp and there we were, in prime position with the main arena dead in front of us, like we'd ordered it that way on a whim.

The other contestants stopped in their tracks and looked on in amazement at this kid just turning up next to the arena with his own train, so he didn't have to be stabled a mile away like the rest of them. It was a good psychological tactic — I'd already won pole position.

The moment the ramp dropped, this whole scene greeted my eyes — a 2,000-seat stadium, the competitors walking back and forth superbly equipped and mounted on expensive horses. I knew this was a serious event, and I'd have to give Brownie all the help I could possibly muster to cut a path anywhere near the top.

Brownie, too, sensed the importance of the occasion. A current of excitement coursed through him and he was as charged up as I was. Because of his breeding — part aristocrat and part mustang — his nerves were always highly tuned, and he knew this was something special.

As I led Brownie out and then went back to help Wendell with the other horses, a line of children began to watch and so we had a small audience. They continued to observe impassively as I warmed Brownie up, putting him through his paces in the same way as any athlete would want to do, to warm up the ligaments and tendons, to push his blood around his body a bit faster and charge up his batteries after the long journey with inadequate exercise.

As they watched, I had the sense that Brownie and I were the 'other team' — that we'd been noted as the opposition.

While I was doing this, something snagged my eye — a horse in a ring some distance away coming to a dead stop from a gallop, a cloud of dust under his belly from where the hind feet were tucked underneath, taking the strain of the sliding halt. I was impressed — elated, yet depressed at the same time because I thought: there's the winner of my junior class, surely.

As I rode over I saw — with no small measure of relief — that this was an adult, so we wouldn't be in the same class; he would be riding in the open division. Drawing closer, I recognised Clyde Kennedy riding Rango, the southern California champion reined cow horse. Now I knew why I'd been impressed, even from that distance away. I was determined to meet him.

Having warmed Brownie up, I put him back in the railroad car until the junior stock-horse class began. In the present company, and somewhat daunted by the professional atmosphere, I was doubting if we would do very well. Somehow, the railroad car and the fact that our home base was right there on the showground would make any failure on our part more visible. I felt real trepidation.

When it was time for my class, Wendell brought Brownie across to me. Watching him stride over, the single white dot between his eyes like a third eye as he carried himself along in his usual, steady fashion, I suddenly knew I had the best horse. When I was in the saddle and with my hand on his neck, I sensed his low pulse rate and his capable attitude and adopted it myself to calm my nerves. I had doubted him, but now I didn't any more. We felt like professionals. We were here, we were doing our thing. We went into the ring.

Figures-of-eight were Brownie's Achilles heel, but he hit the flying lead changes on this occasion unusually well. Somehow it was working — and I knew Clyde Kennedy was watching me. I'd found a new hero, and I wanted to impress him.

When it came to doing the stops, Brownie accomplished the first two reasonably quickly, but without any reaction from the crowd. The third stop I can remember to this day because I asked Brownie, 'Whoah!' when we were galloping dead in the centre of the ring, and he slid to a quivering, perfect halt in 30 feet and we stood in this cloud of dust while the crowd roared; the applause went up like the winning goal at a football game and I knew then, before we even did the backing-up and the offsets, that we'd done OK.

At the out gate, Clyde Kennedy was there to congratulate Brownie on his performance and to ask me if I had a trainer. I told him no, but that I'd seen him on Rango earlier and I'd take any lessons I could from him. Clyde came over to the railroad car and looked around inside, intrigued by the whole arrangement.

That night, Clyde Kennedy came with Miss Parsons and myself to the railroad workers' cafeteria a short way back up the track, where we had arranged to eat. As we sat down to our meal, I learned about the rivalry between Jimmy Williams, the local favourite here in Pomona, and Clyde. Over the next day or two this rivalry would be settled.

Clyde also continued to ask questions about the railroad car. Miss Parsons was proud to tell him how strictly we were tied to a low budget. There was no candy or soft drinks for young Monty Roberts, no sir; if he was lucky, he'd get to open the box of scrap leather and mend some of his equipment, that's if he ever had a spare moment in between collecting used Coca-Cola bottles so he could get the deposits back.

Clyde shook his head in amusement.

That night I couldn't sleep. As I lay in the railroad car I could hear kids whispering and running around outside, looking for Brownie who had become a bit of a hero by now. Certainly, at the end of the next day he was receiving a stream of visitors, most of them kids asking, 'Can I give Brownie a carrot?' or 'Can I stroke his nose?' There were a whole line of rosettes pinned to the outside of the railroad car, as well as spurs and belt buckles and other prizes. He took this celebrity in his stride, as though he thought it was his due. It wasn't like he was an arrogant horse; he was simply a steady character who remained unworried by most experiences, just so long as they didn't involve paper.

On the last day of the show, the rivalry between Jimmy Williams and Clyde Kennedy was settled, when in front of 2,000 people they fought for the top spot in the open division.

Jimmy was good — his horse Red Hawk could spin on a dollar piece and cut a steer out of the herd moving as quickly and as agile as if he were a dog, not a horse, while his stops could be seen for miles around, the dust like Cherokee smoke signals. It helped that the crowd was rooting for him, too.

Clyde Kennedy, though, was superb riding Rango. He really only had me, Miss Parsons and Wendell to cheer him on, but Rango executed the figures-of-eight with real style, effortlessly flying from one lead to the other like he was ambidextrous and didn't care which foot he led with. His pirouettes were a blur — all the while holding his head and neck straight, and not allowing his front feet to tangle as he spun in both directions. His stops I'd already seen, so I wasn't surprised when he won the division, but it was thrilling. Our applause made up for the rest of the crowd, who were disappointed not to see Jimmy Williams win.

With the show over, Wendell, Miss Parsons and I loaded ourselves and our horses back into the railroad car, ready to be hauled back to the main line.

Next stop: Tucson, Arizona, over eight hours away.

My whole life was in front of me; it seemed to be as straight and as uncomplicated as the railway track itself.

Very recently, I had occasion to revisit that showground in Pomona. A 60-year-old veteran of the show ring, the rodeo and the race-track, I stood in the middle of this wild, grassy area and said to my wife Pat, 'Hang on, I've been here before.'

'What d'you mean?'

'Follow me and I'll show you.' I cut a path through the undergrowth and we went a short distance up the valley.

'I bet you,' I said to Pat, 'there's a disused single-track railway line up here.'

She looked at me as if I was mad, but followed anyway.

A little way off, I found the track. Kicking at the ground, I exclaimed, 'Here it is!'

We both stood looking down at the length of iron I'd uncovered. 'See? A railway line. I came down here when I was a kid.'

We walked down the track until we came to where the showground had been. I pointed out to Pat where the spectators' grandstand had been dismantled but the main ring itself was still discernible, the railings grassed over and choked with weeds and visible only as an oval shape.

Suddenly, that day half a century ago sprang clear as daylight to my memory, and I relived the triumph and excitement. The reality of the place, the showground itself, was slowly being eroded; the event lived only in the minds of the people who'd taken part. It wouldn't be many years before all trace of it would be gone.

We stood there, the pair of us, married for 40 years and with grown-up children and lives that hadn't gone in a straight line at all, and we felt good having achieved our maturity, and we were proud of our memories.

★ ★ ★

My brother Larry and I were used to picking up the Coca-Cola bottles at horse competitions and bringing them back in the railroad car to earn the deposits. Now I thought I saw an occasion when the bottles were going to come to us — and how!

In 1947, in Salinas, the first post-war rodeo was to be held at the Competition Grounds. It was going to be an enormous event — perhaps the second or third largest horse-related activity in the country — which would take place over four days.

It would be held in the outdoor grandstand which allowed for 25,000 spectators. The grandstand was a huge structure with a concrete wall at the back and at each end. The wooden seats started at the back wall and sloped forward and down to the ground about 30 metres ahead, creating an enormous triangular space underneath the seats where the public wasn't permitted to go. There were very large steel doors set into the back wall which were kept locked.

A short while before the rodeo, I went to Doc Leach with a proposal.

Doc Leach — a short, bespectacled man with a sophisticated sense of humour — was our dentist, but he was also at this time president of the association which was elected every now and again to oversee the Competition Grounds and decide on what should happen there.

A blue-ribbon member of the community, he was also in a general sense very helpful to us Roberts brothers. Often he'd offer us a dollar to take care of his horses, and then give us two dollars when he saw we'd done a good job. It had become a bit of a joke to see how far we could take this quest for excellence with him.

In this case, I had a more elaborate idea to put to Doc Leach. In his capacity as president of the association which ran the Competition Grounds, I asked him, 'Doc, who goes in and cleans up under the seats when the rodeo's over?'

He hadn't thought about it. He said, 'We have a clean-up crew, but none of us talked about the space under the seats.'

Trying to hold my voice steady, I offered our services. 'We'll do it: Larry and me. We'll clean it up just for the coins and stuff we might find.'

He wasn't sure. 'It'll take you too long a time, surely?'

'I promise my brother and I will clear it out and have it neatly raked for you, no papers nor broken glass or anything.'

He looked sceptical and wondered vaguely why we might volunteer for so much work just

89

for the odd coin or two, but he agreed. 'If you want to, then go ahead, that'll be fine.'

Doc Leach wasn't to know I was after the deposits on the Coca-Cola bottles that would fall down the gaps in the seats. He wouldn't have known about the deposit system anyway, because prior to the Second World War there hadn't been one — and anyway, he certainly wouldn't have got as far as having Coca-Cola in his kitchen yet; that'd be far too newfangled a thing for him to have about the place.

The day after the rodeo, however, I was to receive a warning that perhaps we weren't going to do as well as we thought.

We hadn't opened up the doors to see what our haul was, but I'd asked my father to put me in touch with a representative of the Coca-Cola Bottling Company because I was reckoning we'd need wooden crates stacked up by the doors and a whole queue of trucks to come and take them away. I had in mind a very busy scene, with Larry and I in charge.

A Mr Carlson was the representative from Coca-Cola, and he warned us that people were catching on to the idea of the deposit and he doubted there'd be many bottles underneath the seats at all. He said most people would have taken along a bag to put their used bottles in, so as to take them away and get back the deposits for themselves, and he predicted we might be about to do a lot of work for very little money.

When my brother and I first opened the doors, we were greeted by an amazing sight. The entire area was ankle-deep in rubbish. Sunlight filtered through the slatted seats, throwing wide stripes of light and shadow across the ground.

We stepped forward into the sea of paper, anxious to find the first bottle. When we did so, we held it up to a shaft of light to see if it was broken. It wasn't. In fact, we couldn't find a broken one at all to begin with. We were safe.

It took my brother and me two-and-a-half months to complete the job of cleaning up underneath those seats!

Most of the work had to be done at night so as not to interfere with the heavy schedule my father had us on. We fixed up auxiliary lighting so that we could see what we were doing.

We turned in over 80,000 unbroken Coca-Cola bottles and, just as I had imagined, there was a convoy of trucks to take them away. There was one unbroken bottle for every ticket sold over the four days.

This was sufficient to earn us $800 each — a small fortune at that time.

There were only about a thousand broken bottles under the seats, which is a tribute to the glass Coca-Cola used in those days, because the highest seats were about five storeys high.

Doc Leach wrote an article about it in the local paper. He quite cheerfully admitted his mistake, and accused us of being entrepreneurs taking an old guy like him for a ride. The Rodeo Association had missed out on making quite a profit. He admired the ingenuity with which the agreement with the Roberts boys had been worked out in advance of the rodeo, and he stood by his word. I think he had a laugh about it.

He wasn't about to repeat the same mistake, though. In subsequent years, the clean-up crew had it as part of their contract to clean up under the seats.

Coincidentally, Mr Carlson, the Coca-Cola representative, subsequently came to be an owner of horses himself, and I was to do some training for him. I would also appear in commercials for Coca-Cola.

I don't have to think about it for long to relive the same sense of achievement as I felt all those years ago, earning such a large amount of money from an unsuspecting Doc Leach when Larry and I were just 10 and 11 years old.

★ ★ ★

In 1947, Doc Leach had found it difficult to get hold of wild horses for the Salinas Rodeo Wild Horse Race which was an important part of the show.

Normally, it would have been easy. He'd have called around the usual people and said in effect, 'Come on, folks, I need a hundred and fifty mustangs to be delivered to Salinas by July the first' — and it would happen.

However, with horsemeat being used in the war, the numbers of mustangs had dwindled significantly. By 1947 the herds in northern California, Nevada and southern Oregon had diminished by as much as two-thirds, and they were now located almost exclusively in Nevada.

In 1947, Doc Leach's phone calls fell on deaf ears. 'What mustangs?' the ranchers asked. 'You come up here and see if you can get them yourself.' So the Salinas Rodeo Association had to scrape together what they could find for 1947, and it was a fairly tame Wild Horse Race. It was more like a trickle of horses who were all too old for the job or not capable of putting on the necessary athletic display of resistance for all those rodeo fans.

In 1948, I saw an opportunity to provide Doc Leach with a service which would salvage the reputation of the Wild Horse Race — and at the same time save the lives of around a hundred or more horses. I knew that in previous years, the mustangs were sent to Crow's Landing to be slaughtered for dog food once the rodeo was over and they were no longer needed. If I could somehow make them worth more than that . . .

I was fresh from our success with the Coca-Cola bottles, and this is what I proposed to Doc Leach.

'What about if my brother and I go to Nevada and get the mustangs?'

Doc Leach's eyebrows popped up above his glasses. 'How you going to do that, walk?'

'No, we've made a lot of friends from our trips to horse shows there. I know we can ask for help from the Campbell ranch. We can take our own horses with Tony Vargas driving the truck because he has a licence, sir, and maybe we can do the whole job for you.'

Watching him consider this, I added, 'I know

we can do it, Larry and me.'

'Good for you.'

'We'd ride on up to the ranges with some of the day hands from the Campbell ranch, and I bet we could promise to secure one hundred and fifty head.'

'Head of what, chickens or horses?'

'Strong and healthy mustangs, Doctor Leach.'

Like I've said, he had a sophisticated sense of humour, but I didn't like the way he wasn't taking us too seriously. After all, we were the ones who'd had the last laugh with the Coca-Cola bottles.

'Then we'd hire transport from Irvin Bray to run the mustangs back here to Salinas,' I went on, 'and Larry and I could care for them at the Competition Grounds until the rodeo's held. They'll be ready on the spot, with the pair of us on hand to see they're all right.'

Doc Leach shifted his pipe from one corner of his mouth to the other and blinked a couple of times. I could see him thinking about it.

Finally he asked, 'What's in it for you two boys?'

'Larry and I were thinking, sir, that after the rodeo we could break in the mustangs and maybe have an auction sale afterwards, so they'd be worth more than Crow's bait.'

This was the euphemism used for animals taken to the slaughterhouse at Crow's Landing — 'Crow's bait'.

I explained to Doc Leach that I thought he wouldn't have to send any animals for slaughter this year. 'There'd definitely be more than a few

94

that would go through the sale ring ridden by my brother or myself and maybe provide someone with a useful mount, sir.'

He was still thinking about it and I went on, 'And perhaps show a profit for the Rodeo Association at the end of the day, more than the slaughter value anyway.' Doc Leach was a touch wary of the Roberts boys since losing out on our deal concerning the Coca-Cola bottles, and for a while he hunted around for any aspects of this arrangement which he might not have immediately seen.

When he couldn't find any, he agreed. 'OK. There's no harm in it. We'll see what you can do, anyway. It can't be any worse than last year.'

We thanked him and assured him we'd earn his trust for this plan of action. He nodded and offered to call up Irvin Bray and contract him to provide us with transport for the return journey.

Finally, we agreed that the net proceeds of any sales we managed to secure were to be divided equally between the Association on the one hand and my brother and myself together forming the other party.

So at the ages of 12 and 13, Larry and I were on our way to Nevada to gather 150 head of mustangs. It would prove to be the most important opportunity of my life: to study horses in their natural groups, in the wild.

For the next three years I'd be going over the Sierra Nevada to the high desert beyond, to live alongside wild herds for several weeks at a time. This is the land they call Federal

Land, just north of Battle Mountain, because it's owned by the Bureau of Land Management. It is a vast, empty tract.

From this experience I'd begin to learn a language, a silent language which I have subsequently termed 'Equus'. I'd learn the basic theories which were to allow me to define accurately and convincingly the principles of my life's work.

So come June 1948, Dick Gillott, Tony Vargas, my brother and I put our horses and our equipment in the van and headed off, weaving back and forth around the foothills before climbing the Sierra Nevada, driving along roads cut by our forefathers into the stern, harsh landscape.

Beyond Battle Mountain lay the high desert — our destination the Campbell ranch.

The air was thinner — that's what I noticed first as the door of the truck swung open. Climbing down from the cab, I knew already that this landscape would be like nothing I'd encountered before. The horizons lay against a sky that over-reached us further than I'd ever seen, and there was the sense of being on a different planet. The soil was silky and cool to the touch in the early morning, yet burned your skin at midday; it was like a lunar landscape covered in rough grasses and brush and cut by deep barrancas (a ravine or small canyon) overgrown with stunted trees.

The high desert . . . somewhere in this vast natural wilderness were the horses we were looking for.

The Campbell ranch had some Indian day-hands working for them, who were detailed to help us. I was half expecting them to recommend the same trick as had been explained to me by my Uncle Ray four years before. As I related earlier, Ray had told me that his Cherokee ancestors — before they tried to drive the mustangs towards the trap — pushed them in the opposite direction for a day or so. The horses' tendency would be to press back against the control inflicted on them.

However, this was not the case. The Indian day-hands explained to us the way in which we would trap the mustang horses.

Some 50 miles distant from the homestead, they'd built a corral approximately a quarter of a mile long. They'd searched for a heavily travelled canyon or barranca and set it at the bottom end. From above it looked the shape of a keyhole, with two sides angled into a narrow gap and a circular area beyond. The posts and fencing were obscured with sage and brushwood to make it near invisible.

It was a two-day ride for us to reach this makeshift structure, and when we got there the day-hands walked us around and explained how the mustangs should be driven into the wedge at the bottom and funnelled through the narrowest part into the circular arena, where they would slow up, forced to turn. They'd be accustomed to going through this barranca and they wouldn't have seen a vehicle or a building or even a fence-post to scare them off.

Riders would come down the wings and

close the gate across the narrowest part of the 'keyhole'.

First things first, though — where were the horses?

They weren't to be seen by any casual scanning of the earth's surface — a large part of which seemed to lie spread in front of us, a fissured plateau baking in the sun.

The Indians pointed here and there — the whereabouts of the wild-horse herds could not be guessed accurately, and they were happy to allow Larry and me to head off and start bringing them back for ourselves. They had work to do, but they'd ride out and help us over the last bit when they saw we'd got close enough.

I had two saddle-horses and two pack-horses for this undertaking. Brownie was my number one saddle-horse, naturally, but in addition I had Sergeant and Burgundy as well as a second packhorse, Oriel. The going was rough and the barrancas in particular made for precarious riding, so I'd be leading Brownie a lot of the time; his being more precious to me meant that I wanted to save him from too much wear and tear if I could.

Larry and I prepared ourselves thoroughly and strapped our supplies on the pack-horses. We were ready to go, and I was anticipating the adventure of a lifetime.

I had a feeling of prescience as Brownie took his first steps into this cracked and thirsty land; after all, this is where he came from, his mother was a mustang and I couldn't help feeling that something was about to be shown to me. He was always a steady and good-mannered horse — apart from his fraught relationship with paper — but the conviction with which he carried me into his home territory hinted that he knew something I didn't . . . and that I'd soon be shown.

Larry and I broke camp at dawn and hurried to stamp out the remains of the fire and bury it, kicking at the loose earth, enjoying the burst of activity if only to warm ourselves in the thin, chill air. We wore yesterday's clothes, and as we mounted our horses and started to peel the oranges that our mother insisted we eat every day, the sun rose like a golden disc, watery at first but then burning with increasing strength as the morning wore on.

Things began to go wrong — as I would see it — as soon as we saw the first herd of wild horses, numbering some 50 head.

Brownie was the first to catch their scent as we were traversing a barranca which had the usual large stones littering its slopes, around which the stunted trees struggled to suck enough water and take advantage of the shelter. You could ride down the same paths scoured out by flash flooding on the sides and along the bottoms of these canyons, but nevertheless they made for dangerous riding. Brownie's heels dragged behind him as he tried to load more weight on to his hocks to take the strain of the descent. When he stopped dead, concentrating on something that I couldn't see or hear, I knew from his lack of agitation — and the fact that he was keen to move on in the same direction as his ears were pointing — that he'd smelt a herd of his brothers and sisters, the mustangs of northern Nevada.

However, when we caught up with them — and they were already moving away, fully aware of our presence — then the difference between what Larry wanted to do and what I wanted to do became painfully clear.

Larry, not unreasonably, wanted to press on and simply drive the horses back towards the ranch. Because we had to cover 50 – 60 miles of ground on the return journey, we would have to go relatively fast to stick to our schedule.

I wanted to stop in our tracks and observe the horses. There was something compelling about seeing them as a family, the alpha male or breeding stallion circling and lifting his tail, stepping out with a high, proud action and whinnying at our presence. It made me want to melt into the background and see what could be seen, without their being subject to our interference.

It was almost as if I wanted to be a horse myself, so thoroughly had I taken their side; these horses weren't only Brownie's brothers and sisters, they were mine also, perhaps as much as Larry was. I wanted to understand them — and I was more than ever certain that I didn't know as much as I thought I did.

As a result of this unspoken conflict of interest between Larry and myself, of course there was an unspoken compromise to the situation. He hurried me along, and I slowed him down. We neither of us got what we wanted; we were only kids after all, out there doing what we said we were going to do, so this anxiety on my part to slow down and do something different went largely unvoiced.

Meanwhile, as the herd moved ahead of us at a distance of up to a mile away, I observed only what I already knew: that the squeals of discontented mares serve notice of their anger. There's the normal whinny of the horse who is attempting to attract the attention of other horses; anyone who has been involved in the feeding process in a stable knows the nicker of a horse who is calling to you at feeding time.

As we pressed them ahead of us, we heard the foals call out to be identified and to identify, as would the young of any species.

All these signals are obvious to anyone who's had anything to do with a horse. A pair of forward ears showed their interest in something anterior or in front. Forward ears with the head high denoted interest in something ahead or in front of them at a distance. Forward ears with the head held low indicated interest in something up close, near the ground.

The head held in normal position with a 'split ear', one forward and one back, showed interest in something in front, but also at the same time a concern for anything that might exist to the rear — ourselves. The ears directed us to what was attracting the attention of the herd. If their ears were hanging relaxed and they were standing maybe resting one hind leg, Larry and I could assume that we were unobserved; these horses had no concern for their safety at that moment.

If a horse pinned his ears back on his neck, then he was angry. We watched one of them moving in such a manner so as to position his rear legs to take action against another animal or person, and we saw that he was angry, aggressive and dangerous.

Once or twice we saw the stallion pin his ears back on his neck and stick his nose straight out in front of him as far as he could reach; he had his head lowered to just below the wither height, so that from the shoulder forward the neck and head looked like an arrow with the nose being the point; his eyes were steely, and he was moving forward in a stalking mode. From observing this stance, we could judge he possessed very active testicles. It's the movement of the full-grown adult male virtually exclusively. Only as the male reaches potential for supremacy within the family group are you likely to see this particular display.

As Larry and I circled this first group, and scooped them up and turned them this way and that to point them back towards the trap set for them in the barranca, I learned that a horse's field of vision is nearly 360 degrees, with only a slim cut of land right behind him which he can't see, and an even slimmer cut right in front. Trailing the herd and watching the alpha male keep his defensive tactics in position as we manoeuvred them, we grew to appreciate how complete was their visual coverage of any given area.

Watching the stallion chivvy the mares in his defensive role, we could confirm that when he switched his tail — other than when clearing insects off his body — he wasn't content. He was unhappy. This we knew already — if you're a trainer who puts too much pressure on a horse with spurs or whip, you are often going to make a switch-tail horse — and in horseshow competition in the western USA you'll lose significant points if your horse switches its tail in the course of its performance.

Perhaps the most important piece of knowledge that I had confirmed to me — engraved as it were more indelibly — during that first trip to Nevada, was that there are two types of animal — the *fight* animal and the *flight* animal. It bears repeating, that the horse is a flight animal. If I knew that before, only now could I understand just how true it was, with the mile or so that nearly always separated Larry and me from the horses.

It sounds obvious, but it is critical to remember that given the slightest excuse a horse will say, 'I don't want to be near you. I am going away. I want to be away from you. I feel there is danger if I stay. I am in flight!'

The flight animal only wants to do two things — reproduce and survive. And fear is the tool that allows him to survive. This has to be respected in any dealings with a horse, otherwise he is misunderstood.

Man, however, is a fight animal. His preoccupation is with the chase, and having dominion over others in order to eat them or use them for his own ends.

So the horse is at the far end of the flight animal spectrum, while mankind is way off the edge of the opposite, the fight animal spectrum.

In order to gain a horse's trust and willing co-operation, it is necessary for both parties to be allowed to meet in the middle. However, it is the responsibility of the man, *totally* of the man (I'm speaking generically, to include women) to achieve this, and to get to the other side of this hurdle. He can only ever do it by earning the trust of the horse and never abusing its status as a flight animal.

If I learned anything on that first trip, it was that I needed a much longer time if I was to get what I was looking for — a true understanding of how horses behave in the wild.

I was already a skip into it, knowing what I wanted. The frustration was that it couldn't happen under these conditions.

The truth was, when we got back to the trap in the barranca we merely jammed a bunch of horses into the circular pen and brought up the hired transport on the dirt roads and carted them off. There was no selection of suitable animals, no grading by age or sex. We loaded in lactating mares and older animals along with the more suitable younger adolescent colts.

In short, we were inexperienced.

However, I knew what I wanted to do the next time round.

★ ★ ★

Dick, Tony, Larry and I arrived back at the Competition Grounds in our convoy of trucks with a haul of 150 mustangs banging and kicking in the back.

We dropped the backs of the trailers and they scooted off the ramps and ran into their new home — a corral with fences around it and a whole lot of barns and other buildings in view, including the arena where, unknown to them, they'd be racing in just a month's time in front of thousands of people. They snorted and blew and ran round the perimeter of the corral, astonished at their new circumstances. It was a far cry from Nevada.

I rushed into the house and was proud to relate to my parents what we'd done — and I was especially anxious to tell what I had planned for the following year. 'You know, Ma, I'm going to take longer next year, and then I can see what they get up to for real. They're not even going to know I'm there.'

My mother was receptive and listened intently. 'What d'you think you'll find out?'

'I don't know, but something. The way they communicate, like, as a family. That's what I hope.'

'Well, I hope you do, too.'

My father was not pleased at all. 'You'll find out it's cold at nights and hot in the day, is about all. You'll find out those mustangs don't want to have much to do with you or your fancy notions.'

It was his opinion that horses understood one thing only, and that was fear. If you didn't hurt

105

them first, they would hurt you.

Certainly, in the case of these 150 mustangs, we — that is to say mankind — were going to hurt them quite badly. They were to be entered for the Salinas Wild Horse Race.

I don't know how many people were there to watch this part of the rodeo, but it was one of the most popular events so the grandstand was pretty much full up with people, ready to shout and holler and stamp their feet.

Larry and I were in among the crush of people pressed right up against the fence. Now we would see what would happen to our horses.

Waiting in the middle of the arena were a number of teams of three men each, all of them kitted out in the full cowboy regalia. They were as likely to get hurt as the horses were, and you could tell they were nervous by the way they couldn't stand still. The teams milled about some distance apart from one another, waiting to have their wild horse delivered to them, each team with a Western saddle parked ready on the ground nearby.

The minute the Rodeo Committee men rode into the ring on their saddle-horses, each one literally dragging a wild mustang on the end of a 15-foot lead rope connected to the horn of his saddle, the crowd started up their hollering and cheering. There were more riders running behind the mustangs to push them forward as well.

Our mustangs were bucking, running and diving and pulling on the ends of their ropes. The crowd was jeering and whooping, their

106

adrenalin shooting sky-high, seeing these wild horses dragged in.

The Committee men then handed the lead rope of each mustang to the first member of each team, called 'the anchor', who is the biggest and heaviest of the three men.

The anchors dug in their heels and set about trying to keep these 900-pound wild animals as much as possible in one place.

The second man in the team is called 'the mugger' — and it's probably the most dangerous part of the job. Now the muggers were travelling down the lead ropes, hand over hand, turning this way and that to follow the line as the mustangs fought and plunged like the wild animals they were. As fast as they could, the muggers had to grasp the horses around their necks, effectively trying to put them into a head lock and pinching their top lips to cause them enough pain so that they wouldn't think about anything else such as a man trying to put a saddle on them.

My heart was in my mouth as the battle began. Some of the men were thrown off the ropes before they reached the horses; others had better luck and were already hanging in there, trying to wrestle with these animals like they were in a bar-room brawl.

Now the third members of the teams — 'the riders' — were darting in, carrying saddles on their arms, to try to throw them on and buckle the girths.

The noise and the confusion can be imagined. My nerves were screwed to the highest pitch, just watching. Several men were limping off, too injured to continue, while other men ran forward to take their places. One man was dragged out unconscious from under the feet of a horse and had to be carried off.

By now some of the riders had managed to buckle the girths and were jumping up and aiming to stay on long enough to be handed the lead rope, which is their only method of guidance.

It was a scene of utter confusion, with horses bolting in all directions, some with riders on board and some without. The riders who had managed to get mounted were attempting to race each other once around a half-mile track, and were having to use whatever methods of hazing they could. They were shouting and spurring their horses and pulling at the rope to try to turn them the right way.

I lived the excitement of it as would any 13-year-old reared to the culture of rodeo, but at the same time I recoiled against the mad cruelty. There were some crashing falls, and I felt the impact of each and every one of them as though it was happening to me. One horse, I learned later, had broken its jaw. An excited voice exclaimed behind me each time there was a horse writhing on the ground — 'Crow's bait, Crow's bait!' I knew what he was saying: the casualties were taken to Crow's Landing, the canning facility.

By the time there were some riders up in the saddle and racing around the track, the roar of the crowd doubled in volume and the horses

108

were running for their lives, their heads held low and ears pinned back to their necks. They raced once around the half-mile track and the winner threw his hand in the air and continued sailing around until his horse had slowed enough for him to leap from its back and take his applause standing to face the audience, his expression one of the utmost excitement and triumph.

The Wild Horse Race causes several deaths among horses every year, and I believe it should be abolished.

★ ★ ★

Therefore, it was somewhat less than 150 head which were left to us at the Competition Grounds. We turned them out in the Green Corrals, where they were no doubt glad to relax after the trauma.

They weren't allowed to rest for too long. In October they'd be sold at auction, so it was the task of my brother and me to 'break' as many of them as possible in just 60 days — during August and September. If we hadn't done this, they'd have been sent to Crow's Landing anyway, injured or not. The economics of our arrangement with Doc Leach meant we were attempting to make them worth more to him alive than dead. My brother and I agreed that I would take roughly two-thirds of them, to his third.

My first concern was to hide my new ways of thinking from my father.

I wanted to continue experimenting with the

communication skills that interested me so much. I wanted to start to refine a technique that used the horse's respect and co-operation, rather than a method that demanded their servitude with such cruel penalties attached.

I believed it was important to concentrate on this not only because of the deadline facing us, but because I felt in my bones that I'd cottoned onto something new which would change the way human beings related to horses.

I was able to obscure from my father that I was developing a methodology different from his because a pair of barns ran down either side of where I was working, so it was closed off from his view.

Although my technique was to improve dramatically after the following year's expedition to Nevada, nevertheless even at this stage I had come to think of my process as entirely different from that of 'breaking' horses. That word, 'breaking', has connotations of violence and domination, and damage done to the object concerned.

I changed the nomenclature. From that day on, I called my method 'starting' horses. My aim was to head in the opposite direction from the 'sacking out' procedure. If sacking out was designed to cause fear in the horse, then I wanted the opposite. I wanted to create trust.

If sacking out involved ropes and tying horses' heads and legs, then I wanted no part in any rope or tying procedure. A significant moment came when I realised I could long line (or 'lunge') a horse without attaching ropes to his head.

Sacking out involved physical punishment; so I wouldn't have a whip within sight of a horse and would never raise hand nor foot against him.

In short, instead of telling young horses 'You must', I wanted to ask them a question, 'Will you?'

I'm not going to detail where these thoughts took me in terms of my starting technique, because I'll be doing so a little later on; it was after I had arrived at a startling new development that I knew, then and there, was going to change my life and hopefully the lives of many horses.

For now it's enough to say that I knew horses could be started in a way that engaged their trust and co-operation, and right from the very beginning I never doubted that it could be done. My technique was haphazard and unrefined, but I got there.

After the starting process, I recruited four or five of my top students to ride for me and so brought on about 80 out of my 100 mustangs to a good standard. The students were willing volunteers, and together we learnt a great deal from each and every horse. I felt I'd really achieved something.

On the day of the sale, I rode my 80 horses through the ring and my brother rode his 30 mustangs. Altogether, the sale took in just under $6,000.

Doc Leach was happy with the results; not only had he got back his investment in the herd of about $5,000, but he'd made a small profit. This was a big plus for him, because normally he'd have to wear a substantial loss on the whole operation.

My brother and I were less happy, financially speaking. Our share of the profit amounted to a $250-payout each, for two months' work. Even in those days, that was not a wage to boast to your friends about. It was more like a nod and a thank you.

No doubt Doc Leach thought he'd got his own back this time. I'd like to tell him that from what I had started to learn in those few months, I was the winner.

★ ★ ★

'Larry, would you mind dropping out of the picture, this year?'

I watched him think about it. He was my younger brother and we did a lot of things together, so he might just want to decide against my doing anything on my own.

However, I was happy asking him to withdraw from gathering the mustangs this year because I was sure he didn't want to go.

He squinted up at me. 'OK.'

The next person I had to talk to was Doc Leach. He was often around the Competition Grounds because he was a member of the committee which oversaw the operations there, so it was no trouble to run into him.

'Doc?'

'What can I do for you, son?'

112

'I have an idea how to improve the Wild Horse Race this year.'

'Let's hear about it, then. You didn't do so badly for us last time.'

'How about we reduce the number of mustangs we haul back here?'

'And that's to improve the race, is it?'

'Well,' I explained, 'I noticed that you didn't use all the hundred-and-fifty head. You picked out the best two-thirds of them.'

'That's right, we did.'

'And the others just stood by and watched.'

'So what're you saying?'

'I'm saying, what if we choose the best two-thirds of them up there in Nevada instead of down here in Salinas; then we'd only be transporting a hundred head instead of one-fifty, and we could lower the overheads.'

Doc Leach looked down at me. 'Who's going to judge the best one hundred head — you?'

'That's right, sir. Then we can avoid bringing the lactating mares and the older animals in the first place.'

Doc Leach smiled and said, 'You've got a point, I have to admit.'

I recommended to Doc Leach that we gather 500 head and pick off the best 100 adolescent colts and fillies (if they weren't pregnant). 'Adolescent' in terms of a mustang would equate to an animal 3 – 5 years old, as their nutrition and environment delays their maturity.

Then we would transport only 100 head, reducing our transport charges by one-third.

So I was heading off to Nevada again, but

113

this time without Larry and also three weeks ahead of my helpers and the trucks. I was 14 years old and had a driver's licence, but I was not qualified to drive a truck loaded with horses, so I used the services of the haulage company to transport myself, Brownie, Sergeant and Oriel up to the Campbell ranch.

I was going to be up there, just me and my horses, for three weeks. I'd have the time to move slowly and observe the mustangs without interfering with them in any way.

The Campbell ranch had prior information as to where the family groups were likely to be. There'd be a group here and a group there — maybe 10 miles apart. I intended to bring each family group towards the trap in the barranca one by one, very slowly, observing them as I went.

Once again, I was glad to have Brownie as one of my saddle-horses for this all-important experience. I patted his neck as we rode out over the high desert ground. Oriel and Sergeant walked along behind, and in addition I had a dog, three pairs of binoculars, a hand-gun and a rifle. 'This time, Brownie, we'll see what'll happen, won't we?'

When we reached the first horizon I twisted around in my saddle and watched the outbuildings belonging to the Campbell ranch disappear from sight as we tucked down the opposite side of the slope. We were on our own.

It was great to be riding across this open ground again, with its rocky barrancas where cottonwood and aspen trees grew. I knew I must be extra vigilant for rattlesnakes and for the invisible crevices which were maybe six feet across, treacherous for horses.

As before, it was hot during the day and cold at night. Occasionally, rainstorms would lash down for an hour. Big, billowy, high-desert clouds would give rise to electrical storms.

I was living on a diet mostly of jerky — a cured meat — and pancake mix and salami, as well as oranges.

To find the first family group of horses, I was having to look closely for where they'd be getting their nutrition. They'd eat the sage and the chamis if they were desperate, but they preferred the grama, brome and rye grasses.

When I caught up with my first group, my aim was to integrate with the herd as closely as I could. Either they'd accept me as no threat — which meant I'd have to stay over a mile distant — or I'd have to get closer without their knowing I was there.

They caught my scent from a mile away and began to move off. They were little more than dots on the plateau, and already they were going away.

I left Oriel, my bay pack-horse, because he was proving rather clumsy and often stumbled over stones, the noise of which carried over vast distances — not that he cared. I was beginning to wonder about this Oriel character. His ears were always at half-mast, neither forwards or backwards. Either he was a deep thinker or a little dumb, or maybe both.

Having lightly hobbled him and leaving

Sergeant as well to keep him company, I continued on foot, leading Brownie.

The wild herd saw us pressing closer, and it was an achievement to get within a quarter of a mile of them. We used the barrancas as cover and stayed down-wind, moving quietly.

Given the time to move slowly and think about what was happening, I was surprised by how hypersensitive the herd was to our presence. If Brownie just scuffed a rock, I could see their ears flick in our direction.

Now I was within a quarter of a mile of the herd, and I couldn't get any closer. I'd run out of cover and even though I was downwind of them, they wouldn't allow us any more ground.

This was OK for a while. Brownie and I settled down by a cottonwood tree and I counted them up, trying to log their markings so that I could learn to distinguish one from another.

My binoculars became incredibly important. Nowadays I see young people strapping the virtual reality helmets on to their heads, entranced by the world they enter. This reminds me of the feeling I had when I looked through my binoculars at this herd of wild horses. Suddenly they were close enough to touch. I could observe their every movement in detail. I was there, among them.

I noticed in particular a dun mare with a dark stripe along her back and zebra stripes above her knees. Older than most of the others, with a heavier belly that hinted at many more pregnancies, she seemed to give a lot of commands in the group. It was she who ordered her group to move off. She started and the others followed; she stopped, and so did the others. It seemed she was the wisest, and they knew it.

What I was observing, in fact, was the dominant mare. No one had told me that wild horses were controlled by a dominant mare before, and I suspect a lot of people today still think that it's the stallion who runs the show. That isn't true. The breeding or dominant stallion, sometimes called the alpha male or lead male, will skirt the herd and defend it from marauders. His motivation is to prevent anyone or anything from stealing his harem.

But it was the dun mare who was in charge of the day-to-day running of this group. There was no mistaking it.

And then I saw an extraordinary sequence of events. A light bay colt was behaving badly. He was about 20 months old, I guessed, with a vast amount of feathering around his fetlocks and down the backs of his legs and a mane running down well below his neck line. Right in the middle of the group, he took a run at a filly and gave her a kick. The filly squealed and hobbled off and this colt looked pleased with himself. He was only about 550 pounds in weight, but very aware of the fact that he was the owner of a pair of testicles.

As I watched, he committed another crime. A little foal approached him, snapping his mouth in a suckling action to indicate he was no threat but subservient, only a little foal. That didn't cut any ice with this colt; he launched himself

117

at his younger cousin and took a bite out of his backside. He really was a terrorist — if he wasn't kicking, he was biting. Immediately after the attack, he pretended nothing had happened; he went neutral. It was as though he was trying to avoid having the blame pinned on him.

Each time he behaved badly, the dun mare — the matriarch — weaved a little closer to him. I became certain that she was watching to see if there was going to be any more of this behaviour. Even though she showed no sign of interest, she'd left her station and was getting closer to him all the time.

She witnessed about four such episodes before she made her move. Now she was within 20 yards, but this sugar-coloured colt couldn't help himself; he launched at a grown mare, grabbed the nap of her neck and bit down hard.

The dun mare didn't hesitate. In an instant she went from neutral to full-on anger; she pinned her ears back and ran at him, knocking him down. As he struggled to his feet, she whirled and knocked him down again.

While this chastisement was going on, the other members of the herd didn't turn a hair. It was as if they didn't know it was happening.

The dun mare ended by driving the colt out of the herd. She drove him out 300 yards and left him there, alone.

I thought, what in the hell am I seeing? I was amazed. The dun mare took up position on the edge of the herd to keep him in exile. She kept her eye on his eye, she faced up to him. She was freezing him out.

He was terrified to be left alone. For a flight animal, it's to be under a sentence of death; the predators will get you if you're separated from the group. He walked back and forth, his head close to the ground, executing this strange, uncomfortable gait several times. It looked like a sign of obedience, similar to a bow made by a human being.

Then the light bay colt made his way around to the other side of the herd and attempted to come back in that way, but the dun mare had followed his circle. Again she drove him out, running at him until he was about 300 yards away before returning to maintain her vigil on the edge of the herd. She kept her body square on to him, and she never once took her eye off his.

He stood there, and I noticed there was a lot of licking and chewing going on, although he hadn't eaten anything. I remembered the foal and how it had snapped its mouth, which is an obvious signal of humility and as though it was saying, 'I'm not a threat to you.' Was this the more adult version? Was this colt saying the same thing to his matriarch?

By this time, some hours had passed and it was rapidly getting dark. I thought, Where's the moon? Am I going to see how this ends up?

I scooped up Brownie's reins and rode back to where Sergeant and Oriel were waiting. My intention was to take up a position for the night from where I could continue to observe what was happening with this confrontation between the dun mare and the adolescent colt.

When I got back, Oriel was standing with his nose in a bush. Then he lifted his head sharply, his whole body tense with surprise. A cloud of bees surrounded his head.

This was an emergency. Oriel took a few paces backwards and then tried a couple more sideways. He tried it with his head held low and then jerked it up again.

No luck.

Then he shook himself like a dog coming out of the water, but afterwards he was astonished to realise the bees were still there. This was a puzzle all right, and he'd nearly run out of tricks. There was only one thing for it: tossing his head up and down like a Texan 'nodding donkey'. His thinking obviously was, that if he did this for long enough the bees would get bored and leave.

Brownie, Sergeant and I kept our distance until the bees had gone. Oriel didn't seem unduly perturbed by the experience. It was one of life's many mysteries.

The sun sank surprisingly fast down the western slope of the sky, as though itself desiring rest from a hard day's work. I made camp and hurried to settle Brownie, Sergeant and Oriel with their feed.

Looking at the silhouettes of Brownie and Oriel as they stood nose to tail, no doubt conferring on the day's experiences, I wondered again about Brownie. Where used he to live? Who was his dominant mare? How did he relate to the family group?

The moonlight gave a different tint to the

landscape and, since it was reflected from such a vast sky, it seemed to me that there was quite a lot of light available. I picked up my binoculars and found I could see clearly for quite a distance. In fact, unknown to me I was aided in my night-time observations by the fact that I was (and remain) totally colour-blind. This is a rare condition, quite separate from the more ordinary condition of confusing colours or being unable to separate them normally. When I was young, no one believed that I could only see in black and white, but I've subsequently learned that I see in a very different way from normally-sighted people. Professor Oliver Sacks, in his study of 'The Case of the Colour-blind Painter', describes how his subject had a car accident which caused him to lose all perception of colour: 'People's figures might be visible and recognizable half a mile off . . . his vision had become much sharper, "that of an eagle".' Particularly at night, it seems, the artist could see far better than a normal person, suddenly finding himself able to identify a number-plate from four blocks away. In fact, this artist was so distressed by his loss of colour that he took to being nocturnal.

Focusing and swinging the twin circles of the eyepiece here and there, I caught sight of my herd. I wanted to find out what was happening.

To my astonishment, the dun mare was now grooming the light bay colt. She was giving him little scrapes on his neck and hindquarters with her teeth, and generally fussing over him. She'd

121

let him back in; and now she was keeping him close by and giving him a lot of attention. She worked away at the root of his tail, hips and withers.

So . . . after his purgatory, came heaven. As I watched, she groomed the hell out of him.

As it turned out, my periods of observation of the wild herds were particularly fruitful at night. Mustangs fear attacks from predators mostly at dawn and dusk; at night they could afford to relax and their social interaction was more marked. It became a habit to watch them by the light of the moon, and I slept usually from about 1.30 until 5.30 in the morning.

Puzzling over what I had just seen, I began to learn the language of 'Equus', as I now call it.

Of course, my comprehension of this silent language took more than these first few weeks alone out on the high desert of Nevada, but I was to continue rounding up mustangs for the Salinas Rodeo for the next two years.

It was certainly the single most important thing I saw — this matriarch disciplining the young, adolescent horses. There was a gang of adolescents she had to deal with, and it was educational to watch her do it because a lot happened. Their youthful energy drove them to do things, and their inexperience meant they made mistakes, much like the young of any species.

It was the dun mare's job to keep them in order — and over the three-week period, I watched every move.

Certainly, she went on and made a Christian

out of that sugar-coloured colt. Often, like a child, he would re-offend immediately after being let back in, to test the disciplinary system and gain back the ground he'd lost. Maybe he'd start fighting with another colt or bothering the fillies.

The dun mare came right back and disciplined him again. She squared up to him and said, 'I don't like your actions. You're going away.'

He sinned a few more times, but she always drove him out and kept him out there before letting him back in and welcoming him into the group with extensive grooming. The third time he sinned, he practically owned up and walked out there by himself, grumbling about it but accepting his fate.

Then he came back in and stuck to the group like glue. He was a positive nuisance; he turned out so nice and co-operative, wandering about and asking everyone, 'D'you need any grooming?' when all they wanted was to be left alone to eat. For four whole days the dun mare had made the education of this awful brat her number one priority, and it had paid off.

As I watched the mare's training procedures with this and other adolescents, I began to cotton on to the language she used, and it was exciting to be able to recognise the exact sequence of signals that would pass between her and the adolescents. It really was a language — predictable, discernible and effective.

First and foremost, it was a silent language. It's worth dwelling on the silent aspect of her commands because it's easy to underrate a language which uses a different medium from our own.

As I was to learn much later, the most common form of communication on this planet takes place silently — in the dark of the deep sea, where animals use bioluminescence, intricate lighting systems, to attract mates, ward off predators, attract prey and otherwise convey all the signals necessary for their existence.

Body language is not confined to humans, nor to horses; it constitutes the most often used form of communication between animate objects on dry land, as well.

And here, moving as close as a quarter-mile from a herd of wild horses, I learned that the dun mare was constantly schooling the foals and yearlings without the need for sound. In their turn, they were reacting to the matriarch without the need for sound either. The stallion was operating his security system with a distinct need for silence, and meanwhile he was also investigating the potential for mating.

They were happy with one another, upset with one another, guiding one another and advising one another, and it was all done silently.

I was to realise that nothing was done by accident. Every small degree of a horse's movement occurs for a reason. Nothing is trivial. Nothing is to be dismissed.

Lying on my belly and watching these horses with my three different pairs of binoculars pressed for hours at a time to my eye-sockets, straining to see all I could in the moonlight, I began to log their vocabulary.

124

I discovered that the key ingredient to the language 'Equus' is the positioning of the body and its direction of travel.

The attitude of the body relative to the long axis of the spine and the short axis — this is critical to their vocabulary. It *is* their vocabulary.

The dun mare squared up, eyes on eyes, with spine rigid and head pointed directly at the adolescent to drive him away, and he knew exactly what she meant. When he was malingering in his purgatory 200 – 300 yards away, he would know by her body position whether or not he was to be allowed back in.

If she was facing him, he wasn't. If she showed him part of her long axis, he could begin to consider himself invited back into the group. Before this act of forgiveness, she waited to see signs of penitence from him. These signals he gave — asking forgiveness — would later be fundamental to the development of my technique.

If he walked back and forth in his isolated position with his nose close to the ground, then he was asking for a chance to renegotiate his position with her. He was saying, 'I am obedient, and I'm willing to listen.'

If he showed her the long axis of his body, then he was offering the vulnerable areas to her and asking to be forgiven.

Their eye contact also spoke volumes. When she was holding him out there, she always kept an eye directly looking at his eye, sometimes for uncomfortably long periods of time. When

125

her eye slid a short distance off his, he knew he might be allowed back in.

I came to realise that their reading of eye contact was extraordinarily subtle. Even when I was familiar to this herd, I could cause a horse to alter its direction and pace of movement by changing which part of its body I looked at — even from quite a distance away.

When the colt trotted out to suffer his exile, he'd be throwing his nose out in front of himself in a circular motion, which would mean, 'I didn't intend to do that, I'm sorry, it wasn't my idea, it just happened, it was the other guy's fault.'

Then the dun mare made a judgement as to whether she believed him or not. I could see her thinking about it. Sometimes she believed him, sometimes she didn't.

The licking and chewing action of the colt's mouth that I had observed was a signal from him that he was penitent. He was saying to her, 'Look, I'm a herbivore, I'm no threat to you, I'm eating over here.'

Observing these signals that passed with absolute regularity and predictability between the adolescent and the matriarch, it became clear to me that the pattern of behaviour set up within the group accounted for the 'yo-yo effect' as described to me by my Uncle Ray.

Press the young horse away, and his instinct is to return.

The dun mare advanced on him, then she retreated.

When I made this connection between the

mare's disciplining of the adolescents and Uncle Ray's story, I can remember it was as if the synapses in my brain all clicked at the same time to tell me I'd found what I was looking for. A name sprang to my head — 'Advance and Retreat'.

After a time spent observing these signals, I could see how exact a language it was; there was nothing haphazard about it. These were precise messages, whole phrases and sentences which always meant the same thing, always had the same effect. They happened over and over again.

Perhaps I could use the same silent system of communication myself, as I'd observed employed by the dominant mare. If I understood how to do it, I could effectively cross over the boundary between man — the ultimate fight animal — and horse, the flight animal. Using their language, their system of communication, I could create a strong bond of trust. I would achieve cross-specie communication.

'Advance and Retreat' also seemed to me to provide a psychological explanation as to why horses are 'into pressure' animals. If you place a finger against a horse's shoulder or flank and push, you'll find the weight of the animal swing against you, not away from you. To understand this phenomenon is to be halfway to achieving good results as a trainer of horses.

Over the years I would be able to add to my vocabulary in the language of 'Equus', but the more refined definitions — important as they'd become to my techniques — would all be contained within this overall, most important concept of 'Advance And Retreat'.

While Brownie and I were trekking over the high desert for days at a time, and I was learning all these things, I felt compelled to offer him an apology for what he'd suffered. The vicious sacking out which meant he always panicked at just the sound of paper, this was a human fault — our fault. Someone had to apologise to him and put things right. We'd abused his status as a flight animal and — what was worse — there had been no need to do that.

Oriel and Sergeant tagged along behind us, performing duties as a pack-horse and saddle-horse well enough, but Oriel also unconsciously providing a lot of diversion. He was an accident-prone, affable character who always got into trouble but somehow always made it seem funny.

Once he spiked himself by walking into a shard of wood. I'm not sure exactly how he did it — and only he could have done it — but he ended up with a two-foot-long splinter which was driven through his nose and the roof of his mouth. It was a painful sight: not at all funny, I'd agree. But this was Oriel we were dealing with.

He was most apologetic and sorry for himself and allowed me to pull out the splinter, which was a grisly task. He was then left with a hole the size of my thumb in his nose, pouring blood.

I took off the bright red bandanna I customarily wore around my neck and plugged the hole with that, to stem the bleeding. So here was Oriel with the tail end of a red bandanna sticking out of his nose, and every time he took a drink of water it would soak up through the cloth and dribble out via the tip of this red flag he had flying in the middle of his face. It was a sorry sight, but we had to laugh at him for it.

Then I witnessed the fight between two stallions.

Water was in short supply that year and I watched, fascinated, as the matriarchs were making frantic efforts to get their families watered and fed. The different family groups were queuing up at this water hole like airliners in a holding pattern. They had to keep their distance because the stallions couldn't tolerate the groups being too close. Their territorial instincts were in conflict with the matriarchs, who wanted to get closer to the water, and this caused an unsettled atmosphere over the whole area.

There was also a bachelor group in the holding pattern — young males who'd left their family groups and were now hanging out together and scrimmaging, practising their fighting skills ready for the day when they'd make a challenge for a herd of their own.

Then the inevitable happened. A member of the bachelor group got into a fight with the alpha male of a family group waiting in the queue for water.

The noise was tremendous — squealing and screaming — yet the mares took no notice of what was going on at the perimeter of their group. And this was serious; it wouldn't be a draw, someone was going to win this fight. The two males reared at each other, plunged and kicked and bit. It went on for five or six hours, well into the night — and although my eyelids were drooping, I had to watch. Every now and again it seemed like the stallion had won as the bachelor hobbled off; but then he came back, his leg torn and bleeding from the teeth raking his hide. Limping towards the stallion, practically carrying this hind leg, the bachelor tried again.

This time, when he left, he could not have lived. I knew it was all over, that it wouldn't be long before the predators gathered around him and he would be their meal for the next day or two. He knew it, too, you could tell. The vanquished male often commits a kind of suicide, deliberately seeking the areas where he knows the cats are, almost offering himself.

Even the victor, on this occasion, was a sorry sight. He was left battered and limping, and walked like he was 100 years old for the next day or two. If he'd met another challenger, he'd have had it, but he nursed himself back to strength.

It took Brownie and me about three weeks to gather the different family groups.

When we were five miles from the trap in the barranca with one group, the day-hands on the ranch were ready to help; a team of about a half-dozen would ride out, circle around the mustangs and help drive them into the enclosures.

Then they would tell me where the second

group had been last sighted, and drive Brownie, Oriel and me as close as the dirt roads would allow, which might have been a distance of 15 – 20 miles. Then they'd leave us.

Driving back, they dribbled a trail of alfalfa every mile or two back to the trap, to help me establish a direction for the group. Also, they were feeding alfalfa to the horses who were already waiting in the corral.

Even at this young age, I knew I was learning something important and I was full of excitement about it. I was looking forward to telling my mother and brother about my new discoveries; I was exuberant over what I'd found. I felt I had a special affinity with horses and, now that I was beginning to understand their silent language, I could look forward to making plenty of progress.

In only a few weeks' time, I'd be able to put my theories into practice, as I was going to be starting about 100 of the colts that I was presently following.

I felt impatient to see what I could do. I was certain that I'd come to an understanding with these wild animals which would enable me to change the way men related to horses. I had seized on a way of fulfilling my ambitions.

It seemed to me that Brownie was the magic ingredient in all this. It was because of him that I'd wanted to find out at all. He'd brought me here, to the very ranges he came from. He'd carried me and I was lucky to have received the message.

At the end of the three-week period, we had

around 500 mustangs corralled. We separated out the lactating mares, the breeding stallions and the older animals; we singled out the young colts and the fillies who weren't pregnant, until the numbers reached approximately 100 head. Then we loaded them up in the trucks and drove them back to Salinas as before.

This year, they had a much better Wild Horse Race. The horses were suitable for the task in hand, and there were fewer injuries among the animals. Once again I watched from the grandstand, but I couldn't take any pleasure in the experience. I vowed to train myself to communicate with horses at the greatest possible speed; it seemed like there was a lot of apologising to be done.

After the Wild Horse Race was over, the mustangs were returned to my care at the Competition Grounds, just like the year before. My task was to 'start' as many as possible within the two months, ready for the sale ring in September.

It was only a little more time than my father would have taken to break just half a dozen horses, using conventional procedures.

As can be imagined, I was forced into learning fast. It was the ideal testing ground for the new ideas I had gathered as to how to form a natural bond with a wild horse — how to step over the barrier from being a predator, an object of fear, to being on their side; how to cast myself as the dominant matriarch and speak her language.

All this I had to try and accomplish with one eye on the whereabouts of my father, as I didn't want him to interfere. However, underneath it all, I still sought his acceptance and approval.

And as it happened, I discovered something so exciting that I began to be sure that I could persuade even my father to see things my way. I'd identified a phenomenon which I called 'join-up'. As I lay in bed at night I could hardly sleep, I was so convinced I had stumbled on something which would change the way we operated with horses. It was 100 per cent proof, as far as I was concerned, that I was on the right track, that the efforts I was making were worthwhile.

I was so excited by it, and so sure of it, given what I had accomplished in the concentrated atmosphere generated by having to start so many horses in a short time, that I knew my father would latch on to it as well. He was too experienced a horseman not to.

However, I wasn't going to go to him and show him directly, after what had happened before. Instead, I settled on showing Ray Hackworth, in the sure knowledge that Ray could prevail over my father because he had his respect.

Ray Hackworth leased some of the facilities at the Competition Grounds. He was a noted trainer and a gentleman: soft-spoken, but also a disciplinarian. I asked him to come and watch what I could do. I told him I had discovered a new phenomenon which I could explain only in terms of the horse's own language. I promised him it was true, that I could dissolve the natural barrier between horse and man, flight animal and fight animal.

He reminded me that my father had often warned me over the years that my ideas could be dangerous and I should stick to the conventional ways of doing things. But I continued to ask him to come and watch what I could do. I was certain I could impress him enough to talk to my father in a positive way about what he was about to see.

Eventually he agreed to come and watch.

When we arrived at the round pen, Ray strolled up the ramp on to the viewing deck and positioned himself leaning against the fence. 'OK,' he said, tipping his hat to the back of his head. 'Go ahead. Let's see it.'

I stood in the middle of the round pen, together with a yearling colt who'd not long escaped from the trauma of the Salinas Wild Horse Race. The colt was wearing no head-collar, rope or restraint of any type. The door to the round pen was closed; it was me and him.

From practising this a hundred times over, I knew what to do. I had developed a confidence in my attitude.

I waited a moment or two to allow this un-named, perfectly wild mustang to become accustomed to the round pen. He was too nervous to take a single step towards me, although his attention was on me as the main threat currently confronting him.

'What I'm going to do,' I said to Ray Hackworth, 'is kind of use the same language as the dominant mare in his family group.'

There was silence from Ray up on the viewing deck, so I figured I was here to explain myself

134

and I'd better get on with it. He wasn't going to stop and ask questions.

'And that language is a silent language, a body language,' I continued, 'and the first thing I'm going to ask him to do is to go away from me, to flee. I'm only doing this because then I want to ask him to come back and join-up with me.'

I moved — quite abruptly — towards the colt. I squared my shoulders and fixed my eye on his eye. Straight away, he went into flight, taking off in a canter around the perimeter, staying as close to the wall as he could — and as far from me as possible.

I continued to press him into flight, in the same way that I had observed the matriarch driving away the adolescents in the wild. I remained square on to him, I maintained direct eye contact. To look at, it was like I was long-lining (or lunging) him but without any ropes.

For Ray Hackworth's benefit, I continued to explain what I was doing. 'In his own language I'm saying to him "Go ahead and flee, but I don't want you to go away a little. I want you to go away a lot. For now, I'll call the shots, until we can form a partnership. You see, I speak your language."'

I had a very light sash line, and I pitched it at the colt — not to hit him, but to encourage him to go away from me.

And he continued to flee. As he cantered around the round pen I maintained the use of the line and my body posture to cause him to remain in flight; my shoulders were parallel to his long axis. I was facing directly toward his

135

head and pressing with my body, so to speak, for him to go away. My eyes were locked on his eyes.

For a few minutes, this continued. I was watching for the signals — the same signals that I'd observed in the wild, when the adolescents were asking the dominant mare if they could be released from their enforced exile.

Meanwhile, just to try him out, I allowed my eyes to drop back to his neck. When I did this, I noticed a slowing up on his forward movement.

I let my eyes come even further back to his shoulder . . . and he slowed a bit more; his head started to come off the rail a bit to look over at me. When I let my eyes drop back on his hip, I saw a further reduction in speed, and he began to angle off the wall even more.

Then I took my eyes back to his eyes, and his speed increased immediately; he locked himself against the wall and was in full flight again. He was reading me. He knew I was talking his language.

I maintained him in his flight. Each revolution of the round pen took him beneath Ray Hackworth.

I called to Ray, 'Just to let you know, I'm waiting for his ear to open on to me, for him to start licking and chewing, and then for him to duck his head and run along holding it a few inches off the ground.'

I hoped he could hear what I was saying, because it was important that he realised I could *predict* what would happen.

136

'Here's the first one, now!' I called. 'See?'

The colt's inside ear had opened towards me and stayed fixed in that position. The outside ear was tuned to the surrounding areas, flicking forward and back. The colt was saying, 'I know you're there, I know you're important, I give you respect. I don't really know what this is all about, but I'll pay attention to you and we'll see where it goes from here.'

The colt had taken approximately eight revolutions of the round pen before the ear closest to me was adequately locked on.

Each time his circuit took him underneath Ray Hackworth's position, I was acutely aware of him watching us. I knew he wouldn't interrupt, and I wouldn't know what he was thinking until it was over.

At this point, I pitched the line in front of the colt and stepped a bit to the front of his action, keeping my eyes locked on his eyes to prevent him coming off the wall towards me.

Quickly, he reversed and fled in the opposite direction. Again, this would be a familiar sight to anyone who's seen long-lining, except I was doing it without ropes, using the enclosed structure of the round pen to keep the colt within range of my influence and my body language to control his speed and direction.

In a moment or two, the ear closest to me was locked on to me as before. It was going well — right to pattern.

Although Ray Hackworth couldn't know what to look for, and so it was important that I was telling him, I suddenly sensed it might be a mistake. The 14-year-old was explaining things to the older man? I was only telling him what I was going to do next and what I expected to happen, but it might be counted as arrogant. However, I thought the value of what I was doing would counteract that.

I began to take the pressure off the colt. First, I reduced the number of times I cast the line at him. Then I coiled the line and held it in my hand, slapping my leg with it to encourage him to continue. The colt came back to a trot. By this time he had made twelve revolutions of the round pen.

The next signal came dead on time. He started to lick and chew. His tongue actually came through his teeth and outside the mouth, and then he pulled his tongue back and chewed with his teeth. There was a ripple effect across the large mandibles.

'There!' I called to Ray Hackworth. 'You see that chewing action with his mouth? That's exactly what I saw them doing out on the range. It means he's ready to discuss this situation. He's gone away and I've pressed him away further. He's recognised my desire to communicate with him, and now he'd kind of like the chance to re-negotiate.'

I hoped that Ray Hackworth wasn't losing what I was saying because by necessity I was turning in a circle to follow the colt, so half the time I was facing away from him.

I continued declaiming to Ray's silhouette on the viewing deck, 'So this licking and chewing action the colt is doing here is a message to me, it's saying something like, "I am a herbivore, I am a grazer, and I'm making this eating action with my mouth now because I'm considering whether or not to trust you. Help me out with that decision, can you, please."'

Then came the final signal I was looking for. As the colt trotted around, he dropped his head so his nose was travelling only an inch or so above ground level.

'And there you go!' I called to Ray. 'His head's dropped, and I can't tell you the times I've seen this out there in Nevada, and it always means the same thing — it means "Let me back in, I want to come back, I don't want to flee any more."'

It was time for me — just like the dun mare had done — to turn passive and let this colt come and join up with me.

I allowed my eyes to come forwards of his body and travel to a point maybe 15 – 20 feet in front of him. I moved my shoulders round to follow my eyes until they were on a 45-degree angle to his long body axis. I was avoiding eye contact and showing him my flanks, as it were.

Immediately, he stopped. He came off the wall and faced towards me. I maintained my position, my body and my eyeline at 45 degrees to his.

He took a step or two towards me. I waited.

Then he walked right up to me, not stopping until his nose was inches from my shoulder. He was right there, next to me.

I couldn't speak. I wanted to shout to Ray Hackworth, 'Look, this is what I mean. How *about* this? Isn't it fantastic? But I couldn't afford to break the spell. And that's what it was, it was like magic: this colt trusted me. Now I was part of his group. I had turned from being a predator to being on his side. I was his safety zone. The moment of acceptance — this phenomenon — I call 'join-up'. This is what I'd discovered, it was my achievement, and I felt a vibration of heartfelt emotion move me then, as I have done since with every one of the 9,000 or more horses I've started this way.

God, I hoped Ray felt the same way!

To test the strength of the join-up, I took a slow right turn. The colt followed me into the circle, his nose to my shoulder. Then I took a left turn. He hesitated, and looked to be going the other way.

Immediately I knew to return to a dominant stance, and I began to drive him away. He didn't like that, and before he'd completed one circuit of the round pen he was flicking his nose out and apologising, asking to be let back in.

Sure, I allowed him back and gave him a good stroke between the eyes, standing up close. While I don't think it's essential to use the area between the eyes as the stroking point, it seems to me to be more effective than other parts of the body. I've asked people who are expert in animal behaviour why this might be, and there's a general consensus that if a horse allows you into a part of his anatomy that he can't see, it's the ultimate expression of trust.

Now I had the colt walking comfortably behind me and I knew Ray Hackworth would be amazed, watching from the viewing gallery above the fence. I imagined him telling my father how much I had accomplished. 'I tell you, Marvin, that boy of yours had a wild horse walking along behind him like it was his best friend after only twenty-five minutes. He's on to something. Come down and see for yourself.'

Then my father would walk over with Ray Hackworth and ask what all this was about. I couldn't help predicting his amazement.

Now I walked to the centre of the pen with the horse behind me. I soothed him and talked to him for a while, testing how receptive he was to my touch.

I called out to Ray — as quietly as possible now the colt was standing next to me, 'Ray, you know, now that he's joined up with me and we're on the same side, it's pretty much of a formality.'

When I was confident the colt was fully trusting me, I went and brought in a long-line, a saddle, bridle, and a saddle-pad, as well as a long stirrup leather.

With the click of the gate, the colt's adrenalin rose immediately. He saw something different — a pile of equipment — and became frightened. He had justification for being sceptical, so I waited.

I allowed him to choose between me and the equipment which I'd now put on the ground in the middle of the round pen. He chose me, he calmed down. I sensed his adrenalin level dropping.

141

He stood — still with nothing on his head — while I carefully lifted the saddle-pad and the saddle on to his back. He let me fix the girth — slowly, smoothly — with his only taking a step or two away before he steadied and let me continue.

He was wearing his first saddle — before any rope or lead had been attached to his head, let alone a bridle. He was asking me lots of questions, his ears flicking back and forth and his nostrils blowing, but he trusted me.

At this point I stepped away from him and squared up to him, driving him away, not aggressively but with the confidence I'd developed over the last 200 or so horses. He went into flight and began to canter around the perimeter of the round pen.

I wanted to familiarise him with the saddle, before a rider was on it.

He went away and bucked hard for several minutes, which I was glad to see because I didn't want Ray Hackworth to think this was a fluke. I had difficulty believing it wasn't a fluke myself, but I had already 'started' nearly 200 horses and I'd refined this down to exactly the same sequence of events.

Yet within a couple of minutes the colt was cantering steadily around, not bucking at all.

I saw the same signals — the licking and chewing, the inside ear settling on me, his coming off the wall a little way to get closer to me. In addition I could smell his sweat now, as he was working quite hard and was expending a lot of nervous energy.

I didn't observe the head lowering, but from experience I knew this wouldn't happen now. I put it down to the fact that with the saddle on, the mustangs didn't feel comfortable lowering their heads. There was something odd going on, and they weren't sure if it was safe to lower their heads.

For a minute or two I worked him around the outer limits of the pen, and let him find comfort in carrying the saddle — first one way, then the other.

Ray Hackworth's silhouette was immobile, and with the late afternoon sun slanting in from that side of the round pen I couldn't read his expression.

After three or four revolutions of the round pen in each direction, the colt was telling me he was ready to come back in.

I let him join-up with me, with the saddle on. I made some adjustments in the girth and generally soothed him with my voice. He was doing fine, he was an OK horse. There was nothing to be frightened about, if he stuck with me. I loved him, like I loved all his brothers and sisters. I was looking after him. He'd have fun with me. We'd find him a good name.

Next, I took the bridle and lifted it over his ears. The colt accepted the snaffle with no more than a brief lift of his head. I secured the reins under the rear portion of the saddle and took the stirrups down to prepare for long-lining.

I looped the long-lines through the stirrups, making sure they wouldn't flap on the colt's sides. Then I sent the colt back to work, cantering him around the perimeter. He was fully tacked-up, wearing a saddle and a bridle and the long-lines.

I called out, 'We're thirty minutes into the starting procedure, now.'

Although I was talking to him, I didn't dare glance at Ray. I felt his eyes on me, and I knew he could not fail to be impressed at what he was seeing.

I long-lined the colt in both directions.

I said to Ray, 'I want to gain his confidence and make him happy to follow the bit and bridle — as he'll be doing just that for the rest of his working life. I want to make it a happy experience for him.'

I probably turned the colt six or seven times before stopping him and reining back one step.

I adjusted his girth; I brushed the saddle with my hands, rubbed his neck and belly.

Then I put my left toe in the stirrup and prepared to lift myself on to his back. I felt the strain in my thigh muscle as I asked the colt if I could put my full weight into the stirrup, testing for his reaction. He took a sideways step to help redistribute the extra weight, but he held firm.

I lifted myself up.

I didn't swing a leg over, but instead lay across his back for a while, waiting to see if he was comfortable with this. Any questions he had, I hope I was answering with the things I was saying to him. We'd find him a good home. Perhaps he'd enjoy being a ranch horse, or maybe he'd go into a Western show, in the pleasure-horse category. Perhaps he'd end up

144

with some kid like me, learning to ride.

I let him catch sight of me out of both eyes before very calmly swinging a leg over and sitting up.

I was riding him after only 40 minutes.

Looking up at Ray Hackworth, who was staring at me with a concerned look on his face, I was sure he realised what an incredible discovery I'd made, and that subsequently my father's opinion could be turned around by this man whom he regarded as his equal.

I was an idealistic child of 14 and as I sat there in triumph on the back of this horse, I believed it was only a matter of a few weeks before I would be enjoying the respect and admiration of my elders and betters all over the county.

Instead, from his position on the viewing platform, Ray Hackworth barked out, 'That was a fluke!'

The sound of his voice coincided with the colt's first steps and I didn't try to stop him. We just walked around together while Ray continued calling out to me, 'You're very wrong to go against your father's advice. If I were you I'd cease messing around like this, it could end up with you lying seriously injured in the middle of that round pen there. I wouldn't like to predict what the injury will be, but for a start you'll be trampled or kicked, even before you get to be bucked off.'

He continued in this vein as he walked from the viewing deck and disappeared from sight. I could still hear him making disparaging remarks as he went across the yard to the barns he leased from the Competition Grounds, which were adjacent to mine.

I was left riding the colt around, crushed by disappointment at the very moment when I should have been triumphant. The people whose respect and guidance I needed were refusing to give it.

I vowed never to mention my ideas to anyone again.

MOST rodeo events have evolved from common working practices on the ranch. In team roping, a pair of day-hands would rope the cow's head and her hind feet and stretch her out on the ground in order to treat her in some way or other. They'd carry a medicinal kit on their saddle, and the two of them might have to deal with a hunk of barbed wire around her leg or a foxtail in her eye. Their horses were trained to maintain the tension on the rope until the job was done.

I was to win the National Intercollegiate Rodeo Association world championship at this event — team roping — in 1956. It's a title which takes a whole year of effort to make your way towards; and sometimes you scored points, sometimes you didn't.

Once, in Scotsdale Arizona, Jack Roddy and I had drawn a perfect steer. You would have bet money on this one. He was steady and moved in a straight line. If we were going to win any points during the year, it was roping this steer, in this event, today.

The steer was in the middle chute, the header — Jack Roddy — was in the chute to the left of him while I — the heeler — was in the chute to the right.

A little piece of string is attached to the steer so that when he takes off, he's given a certain distance before the string trips the latch which holds a cord across the front of the header's horse — and it's a ten-second fine if the header breaks through the barrier too soon. The art of it is to have the horse moving forward at precisely the right time so that he takes up the tension in the cord just as it's being released anyway. On this occasion Jack Roddy timed it perfectly. He was moving through that cord and it was about to break; then the latch tripped and he was on his way already. He threw a great rope and the championship trophy appeared like a vision in front of me. If I could do my bit all right, we'd certainly score below ten seconds for this one. I was on a horse called Berney, and we shot off after the steer which Roddy was drawing across our path. I leaned out, my loop built and whirling above my head, well within range — and suddenly I had no horse. Berney took a dive and somersaulted, throwing me on to my chin just as I was throwing my loop. So, I didn't have a horse but what I did have was a rope in my hands with a steer's hind feet in the loop at the other end of it — and that rope cooked my hands. The steer pulled it through with this neat little bucking action he had and the palms of my hands were like hamburgers, practically smoking. I had to apologise to Jack Roddy. No score!

At Albaquerque, New Mexico, it was a different story. We drew a steer that was a blue screamer, a racehorse, not a bovine at all. Jack Roddy wasn't put off. 'Don't worry,' he said, 'we'll beat these potlickers.'

So this blue roan steer was in his chute wringing his tail, he was so anxious to run out of there, and Jack and I were lined up on either side of him. Jack was on a horse called Chango and he had Chango backed all the way up in the chute, ready to try to time it so that he pushed through the cord practically at a full gallop.

That blue roan steer lit out of the chute like it was on fire, and Jack rolled Chango forwards just as the string was tightening. He had Chango flat out after only a couple of strides clear of the chute, and Jack roped the steer's head with a superb long throw. However, the long rope meant it was more difficult for me — the heeler — because the steer was swinging back and forth in a long arc. I had Berney after his tail and I could see his hind feet going quicker than I thought was possible. Berney was practically scratching his inside ear on the ground, leaning that hard into the corner to try getting me close enough to rope this critter's heels, and it was an 18 – 20-foot throw instead of the usual 4- or 5-foot distance. It was the only chance I was going to get, and I didn't even have time to make my loop any larger. I threw the rope and both the steer's hind legs ran into the coil — and never in 100 years would I have believed it. We had that racehorse steer laid out flat on the ground and the field judge dropped the flag. It was somewhere near the eight-second mark, and we'd stitched up the world championship even before the last fixture was held.

During my years in the rodeo ring, I did

more calf-roping than I care to admit. In the calf-roping event, a small, 200-pound bovine scatters from the gate, moving more nimbly than the bigger animals. A cowboy charges out after him, dexterity the name of the game now. His loop is built and he's closing on him; the calf knows he's there because he's ducking his head and flattening his ears, expecting his pursuer — as a predator — to catch him on the back of his neck. The cowboy throws the loop around his head. The other end of the rope is tied around the horn of his saddle. The cowboy dismounts, the horse stops hard jerking the calf off its feet. He lands with a thud on his side, but the cowboy's running at him with a small length of rope in his hands, waiting for the calf to get to his feet. It's the cowboy's task to throw the calf to the ground again and then wind the rope around any three of his legs — usually the one front leg and both his rear legs — and the minute the cowboy's on his feet and both his hands are thrown in the air, the field judge drops the flag and the clock stops.

It's not a very nice event, and bears no comparison with what happens on the ranch. Roping calves on a ranch is a very necessary practice — for branding, castration, and medical purposes — but the calf is allowed to run with the rope and is brought to a halt slowly. Usually they are roped by a team, so there's less stress on the calf. I personally did a day's roping on a neighbouring ranch quite recently and my horse, Dually, a champion reined cutting-horse, never broke out of a walk during a whole day's work.

And that's how ranchers prefer it — after all, these babies are their livelihood.

Protests against calf-roping on the rodeo circuit increased to such an extent that now it is virtually never seen, as an event, by the paying public. It takes place in the 'slack' — the hours before, after and in between when the paying audience take their seats.

In 1949, when I was 14, I began to practice the rodeo event called 'bulldogging', which would prove to be the one at which I was most capable.

Bulldogging started as a working practice on ranches in Texas. Cowboys would have to hold herds of cattle together for hours at a time while various animals were singled out and roped — either for veterinary treatment or for branding or whatever reason.

Once in a while a grown animal would run out of the herd, and the cowboys would have to chase after him to turn him back. For their own amusement during the long hours, they started to compete among themselves to effect this. Eventually, they'd try to jump from their horses on to the animal's neck and turn him back using their bare hands.

Then a black cowboy by the name of Bill Pickett rode after a steer, jumped on its head, leaned over and grabbed its upper lip in his mouth and bit down hard. The animal was so surprised by the pain that it fell. This was the method that the English bulldog used to drop deer.

Bill Pickett would then turn the animal round

and drive it back into the herd. The ranch put him on a tour to demonstrate his talents, which evolved into the event that we know today as bulldogging.

In the modern version, two men on horseback chase like crazy after a fully-grown bullock. One stays on the right and hazes the animal to keep it going in a straight line. The other runs alongside it on the left-hand side and leaps off.

As long as he doesn't miss and crash to the ground, he'll land on the steer's neck. He'll want to stick to the animal like glue to prevent falling underneath his hooves, and his priority now is to 'throw' the steer.

He wraps an arm around the animal's horns and takes its nose in the crook of his elbow, then gives an almighty twist to the steer's neck. The impetus of the animal means it flips onto its side — it's like performing a wild judo throw with an 800-pound cow at full pelt. Its flanks hit the dust and the clock stops. The injuries to the animals are virtually nil. The injuries to cowboys are numerous.

I won the NIRA bulldogging world championship in 1957, the year after Jack Roddy and I won the team-roping. This time, however, I had to go to the final event — and not only that, I had to do well if I was going to win it. There were people on my tail and it was their chance to pay me back, because generally the rodeo championships are 'owned' by the inland states such as Texas, Idaho and Montana. These boys from the Pacific coast needed to be taken down a peg or two.

My first steer was a very bad draw. He was a big, slow handling animal and by the time I'd thrown him I was placed seventh in the event, with a time of 6.2 seconds. This was OK; it meant that I'd win the championship as long as I was placed in the second round, the score being worked out over both rounds and the average time taken together. It wasn't a winning hand quite yet, but I remained the target for everyone else to beat.

I drew for my second steer, and got myself perhaps the best on offer. Drawing this animal was going to win me the championship. However, I drew in the 'slack', which meant I'd have to wait for my second round until the public had left the rodeo arena, and it would probably be quite late at night. None of the audience would know the outcome of the bulldogging world championship before they went home, which seemed a little crazy — but there it was, I'd drawn in the slack and that was my lot.

This turned into the most horrible set of circumstances, because as people were going home at around 10 p.m. a cold, sleety storm blew up and worsened rapidly. I hung on to my one piece of good luck — drawing the right steer — because there sure as hell wasn't any more. There was wind and rain and particles of ice dripping off our hats. There was no cover for me as I hung around, waiting. I had to pile whatever I could find on my horse and myself, to keep body and soul together. Every now and again, I would run around in circles for ten minutes to keep my muscles warm. A while later I'd take my horse, called Miss Twist, and trot her around in circles for the same reason.

Just past midnight, there were two more bulldoggers to go, and then I was up for my second round. My college crew were all drinking hot coffee, and they swore it was the best thing for me in these crazy conditions so I took half a cup and drained it, even though I knew coffee and me didn't get along too well.

The bulldogger before me was in the chutes and ready to go. With the steer set on its way, the hazer's horse slipped on the muddy ground and failed to keep up, so this kid, the bulldogger, found himself galloping alongside the steer with no one on the other side to keep it in a straight line. The steer peeled off to the right and the kid mashed his horse over as best as he could, to keep alongside it. By now the steer was running alongside the fence and just as the kid leaned out to pitch from his horse, the steer carved a line to the left, towards the horse, and the kid was upended and found himself bounced over the top of the steer and into the metal pipe-and-rail fencing. He hit his head on an upright stanchion and lay completely still where he fell.

People ran over immediately, the ambulance was called and there was a sorrowful delay as can be imagined. I think we all realised there and then that he'd died instantly — the sound of his head hitting the upright had been ominously final. As the young lad was carried away I thought, there goes another injury common to young men in the rodeo.

God willing, I won't ever be among them. Our thoughts were cast in a sombre mood and the toughness of the weather blackened the occasion further. Suddenly, this event was a life-and-death struggle for all of us.

To add to these increasingly desperate circumstances, I began to feel nauseous; the coffee was working away in my gut and producing the allergic reaction which I subsequently came to know should be avoided at all costs.

I backed Miss Twist into the box and threw off all the sheets, keeping her more or less out of the sleet and rain, meanwhile feeling my stomach churning. I signalled to my hazer, Jack Roddy, that I was ready.

The steer was let out and I blew after him as fast as I could, Jack Roddy's horse keeping his grip in the mud to haze the steer in a straight line for me. I leapt from my saddle on to the steer's neck and with a giant twist of his head I brought him down in 4.3 seconds. I knew as soon as I felt this 800-pound bovine hit the turf that this great score, taken with the average, meant I'd earned myself a world championship in bulldogging.

When my college crew ran over to applaud me they found me staring very closely at the ground, in an odd kind of way. The allergy had taken effect and I was being more sick than I would have believed possible. I threw my heels up, it was that bad.

They all thought it was from the over-excitement of course, and I couldn't draw a breath to tell them it wasn't and could they stop pounding on the back of such a sick, sorry man!

I felt like I earned those 4.3 seconds, every bit of each and every one of them.

However, of all the events performed in the rodeo, perhaps the most dangerous is bull-riding. Each contestant has eight seconds to enjoy trying to stay right side up on a professional rodeo bull. Bulls are more ferocious in their tactics than bucking horses. The horses arch their backs, curl their heads between their front legs and jump, stiff-legged, in a po-go-stick type of action which is difficult enough, but the bulls have this extraordinary strength and traction in their cloven feet which allows them to dive, then twist up to the left, come down again, crack into a right spin and so on like some kind of hairy, snorting rollercoaster. And of course, once you've had your eight seconds holding on to the braided rope around their middles, and you either jump off or are thrown, then the bull straight away turns around and heads for you, making his intentions very clear indeed: he wants to see you as dust under his feet. The so-called 'clowns' have to run into the ring and distract his attention, which they do with any number of humorous antics. The clowns are amazing athletes and bullfighters who risk everything to entertain the crowd.

With the bull-riding, the draw is everything: — your life depends on which bull you draw to ride. After your eight seconds, the bull receives a score between one and fifty for his efforts and the rider receives also a score between one and fifty for his efforts. You might even call it a team event . . .

When I got married, my wife Pat asked me to give up the bull-riding as competitors were particularly prone to serious injury. And, she argued, my other rodeo events would improve if I wasn't undergoing the stress and strain of bull-riding. I agreed to give it up, and it didn't take more than one rodeo event to prove her right. I had strange flashes of bull-riding, and constantly stopped and found myself worrying about which bull I'd drawn — only to be able to relax and tell myself I wasn't in the draw this time. Without knowing it, I'd been suffering from enormous tension from bull-riding, and my other rodeo events improved dramatically once I'd given it up. It was a good piece of advice.

As for the broncs — of course, we've all seen them in the movies. I should say here that the bronc is not just any wild animal; he's a highly prized specialist. There are not many horses that can hope to be a bronc. Far from being a cruel sport, this is a competition event where you can be sure the horse is enjoying himself. The champion bronc is a valuable animal, kept to a high standard of care and given the best nutrition. He's not bored with repetitive exercises like many horses working in the other rodeo events or in the Western show-horse categories. He's respected as a bronc and not allowed to get spoiled. He's a wild thing, and nobody tries to spend hours at a time bending his will.

Then he's taken into the squeeze, and a man gets on him and the gate opens, and he can do what the hell he likes. It's a good life.

★ ★ ★

In 1949, a group of amateur state associations banded together and established the regulations for a new amateur contest called 'Horsemastership', which was to be for anyone under the age of 18.

They laid a grid on the United States and each state was divided into districts. After the district contest it graduated to a state competition, then a regional title. At the end of this long trail of hard work the reward was to be invited to the international final of the 'Horsemastership' contest, held in New York.

Parents up and down the country entered their children. The number of man-hours taken up with tending to all the young people's efforts in this enormous and comprehensive horse competition must have lowered the United States GNP in the few years it ran.

In 1949 my brother and I entered the competition; I remember it well. It was one hot day in Santa Rosa, California, and we were roasted in more ways than one. We wondered what hit us. There was nothing funny about that day. We were unprepared, we didn't do well and came home as out-and-out losers.

Almost the day after we'd been so roundly defeated in the 1949 'Horsemastership' contest, my brother and I started to prepare for the 1950 event.

I graduated to the state level competition at Palm Springs very confident that I could win; I can still remember some of the questions today.

They had numbered the parts of different bits and bridles and ancillary equipment, and one of the questions involved answering which were the most important facets of this equipment. For every bit and buckle and strip of leather, I answered with the same cryptic reply. It could have been judged as a touch patronising to the judges, and perhaps behind it was a lad who didn't know the right answers, but in the event they liked the philosophy behind this phrase that I repeated over and over, and they gave me full marks. My answer was, 'The most important part of any bit or headgear are the hands that hold it.'

I won the Palm Springs contest; and it wasn't a surprising victory. Again — I had to remind myself — I'd been training horses for this event obsessively for two years in the manner of an adult professional, yet I was pitched against young people who undertook their horsemanship more as a hobby.

I'd reached my fifteenth birthday by the time I travelled to New York to win the final event with points to spare. Nearly all the other 20 finalists were on the maximum age of 18 years. Fifteen of them came from various states in the US; the rest were from Canada, Mexico, Panama, Puerto Rico, South Africa and Argentina.

In between the rodeos and the showgrounds and the 'Horsemastership' contests, and all the travelling on the railroad car, I did manage to fit in a little bit of time at school, but I have to say that my attendance record was slimmer than average. It consisted mostly of turning up

161

on days when tests were required, to prove that I was up to standard.

However, I was registered with the local Catholic school, administered by Notre Dame nuns. They'd been assigned special names when they'd joined their order, and always wore full habits.

The most influential teacher in my educational career was a nun by the name of Sister Agnes Patricia. The thing I will always remember about her is that she taught me about teaching itself. It was her belief that no teacher could ever teach anyone anything. She felt her task as a teacher was to create an environment in which the student can learn.

Her opinion was that knowledge needs to be pulled into the brain by the student, not pushed into it by the teacher. Knowledge was not to be forced on a student. The brain has to be receptive, malleable and most importantly desirous of that knowledge.

I apply the same philosophy to training horses. To use the word 'teach' implies an injection of knowledge, but it is my opinion — garnered from Sister Agnes — that there is no such thing as teaching, only learning.

★ ★ ★

The Laguna Seca Ranch is just 15 miles from the Competition Grounds, south of Salinas. It comprises about 6,000 acres backing up to Fort Ord Military Reservation.

The ranch was purchased in the late 1940s by

162

a lady named Dorothy Tavernetti, who around the year 1950 took a live-in boyfriend named Trevor Haggeman; he was an enthusiastic rodeo cowboy specialising in team roping and she became his financial backer. She bought batches of 'Mexican Corianti' steers with long horns on which Trevor could practise his roping. My brother and I would go over three times a week to practise as well.

Within three or four months the steers became too heavy and stopped running because they were tired of being roped all the time. Instead of selling them, Trevor would turn them out on the ranch and Dorothy would buy another batch of steers for him. The cattle lived on the ranch and grew bigger and bigger.

In 1951, Dorothy Tavernetti became somewhat disenchanted with Trevor and asked him to leave. She then decided to sell all the steers that had been put out on her ranch over the years.

The first group of 400 steers weren't difficult to round up, and they were shipped off to market without further ado. The remaining 100 head were perhaps a bit more disenchanted with Trevor than Dorothy Tavernetti was, and were now wild to the point where you were lucky to glimpse them in the daylight hours and only sometimes at night.

Dorothy's hired hands concluded it was impossible to catch them. She didn't agree with this defeatist attitude, however, and instead she contracted a man named Ralph Carter to come at night and try to catch these renegade cattle. Mr Carter was closely associated with us, and since we'd roped the steers dozens of times earlier in their lives it was natural to ask Larry and me to come and help him. For us, then aged 15 and 16, it was going to be an unusual nocturnal experience.

The first few nights we went out, we were able to gather about 40 head without too much difficulty. After that, it was a different story. The remaining 60 head were now professionals.

Mr Carter came up with a plan. First of all, he would drive out with a load of hay in the pick-up and feed them on some open, flat areas along the south side of the ranch.

It was high summer and food was in short supply, so the cattle quickly found this new source of food and they started to listen for the pick-up as it came to deliver the hay at around 9 or 10 at night. They grew to like the sound of that 4.5-litre engine.

When this routine was established, Mr Carter had my brother and me fully rigged on horseback, hiding in the trees on the border of this open area. When he'd delivered the hay and the steers were eating, we were to break from the trees and gallop through the darkness to head them off from reaching the safety of the brush. We were charged with roping a steer apiece in near pitch-darkness.

When it came to it, it was hair-raising to be riding hell for leather over broken ground, trying to see enough by the scant moonlight to rope some of the wildest steers known to mankind. You only knew you'd caught one when you felt the sudden yank on the line.

Then we'd have to hold the steer with a dally round the horn of the saddle until Mr Carter came with the truck and trailer. We passed the ropes through the front of the trailer and pulled the steers into it. Mr Carter drove the pick-up, while Larry and I rode the 5 – 6 miles back to headquarters.

Over six nights, we captured 12 steers in this fashion. Then the remaining 48 animals cottoned on to what was happening and they couldn't be tempted out from the cover of the brush to eat the hay at all. So Mr Carter had to devise a new plan.

This time, Larry and I left headquarters on horseback, heading north for 5 – 6 miles, putting us to the north of the cattle. We then pressed south, driving whichever cattle we found ahead of us and into the open areas.

The moment we arrived at the line dividing the brush from the open areas, we ran the horses flat out to catch the steers before they thought to circle round and head back to cover.

I was chasing a steer that I could barely see in front of me when it ran into a small clump of oak trees. I was concentrating hard on not riding into a limb hanging low. Unlike me, the steer obviously knew that in the centre of this clump of trees there was a deep pit. I didn't know about the trail that skirted round the edge of it either, and neither did my horse, but the steer did and it scattered safely off to one side while my horse and I went airborne.

I was thrown over his head and accidentally

165

caught my hand on the crown of the bridle as I passed over his ears.

I found myself in the bottom of a 16-foot pit, standing in sand up to my knees. In my left hand was the whole bridle and part of a rope; in my right hand was my loop, still built. My horse was standing there in sand up to his knees and hocks.

Outwitted by a steer! I felt sore about this — but not as bad as when I found I couldn't easily get out of this pit which was 4050 feet across. I'd run at it and scramble up the side, hang on for a while by the tips of my fingers — and then slide back down again. Once or twice I reached the top, but then couldn't persuade my horse to come with me. I was spitting dust and my boots were full of stones.

It took me a half-hour to fight my way out of there, horse included. Back at the pick-up, they were wondering what had happened to me.

Perhaps it was this incident which led to us making some enquiries as to our salary, and whether or not some danger money ought to be paid on top.

It transpired that Mr Carter was getting half the value of the steer at market — around $100. He judged we might fairly expect to earn a whole $10 for every steer.

We carried on anyway, because we were having fun. Finally, there remained around 20 steers to capture, and Mr Carter had another new plan.

We had learned that they were only scared of the horses, which they could smell from way

166

off. The horses were their nemesis. However, they still liked the sound of that pick-up and they certainly wanted the hay. So Mr Carter stowed me in the back of the pick-up, well hidden from sight but with a loop already built. The other end of the rope was attached to the trailer hitch. Then he drove slowly through the steers, while I tossed flakes of hay over the side from my position lying down in the bed of the pickup.

Mr Carter would be muttering in a low voice out of his side window, 'Three coming up now on the left side . . . '

At the appropriate time, I leapt from my hiding place and roped a steer. Mr Carter put his foot flat down on the accelerator and jerked the steer to the ground. Larry and I then jumped on the steer and held him down while Mr Carter got a rope round his horns. We then tied him to a tree, to wait for us to be able to come back round with the trailer. We were doing very well with this method until the accident.

I was thinking the steers were going to be on the right of the truck, but they'd made a turn and were approaching from the left-hand side. I jumped up as usual, but then had to face in the other direction to throw the loop.

I didn't stop to think about where the rest of the rope was lying. As Mr Carter put his foot on the gas pedal, I suddenly realised it was caught around me. I didn't have time to do anything before the rope whipped up, crossed over my left cheekbone and slammed my head into the tailgate of the pick-up.

They dragged the steer for 30 yards with that rope coming from the trailer hitch, up to the tailgate, across my head and out to the steer. It's not a recommended form of employment. I was unconscious for several hours; I awoke in the hospital with bandages covering my head and wondering what had happened.

Eventually we caught all the steers and made a fair amount of money for those nights' work. It was a lot of fun. We were lucky to live through it, but it taught us to see in the dark.

★ ★ ★

During my trips to Nevada, I had become acutely aware that Brownie was due an apology from us, as I mentioned earlier. Up there on the high desert, I'd seen how he himself must have been brought up during his first couple of years. It had looked to me, I have to say, idyllically happy, notwithstanding the threat of predators. He'd been raised in a close family group where affection had been tempered by discipline and where he would have enjoyed all the security of a large extended family communicating effectively with one another.

Then he'd been taken from that into an alien environment, and one of the first things to happen to him was that he was beaten and frightened into submission — and so I took it on myself to try to make up for the sacking-out procedure Brownie had gone through at the hands of my father. I'd talk to him all the time, listen to him, try to excel in the level

168

of care I gave him; I wanted to do everything right for him. His health was always good; I thought carefully about his diet, I read his every mood.

And he had responded. He'd become as close as a brother to me and we lived and breathed the same air, it seemed to me. Except for his phobia concerning paper — which would be with him to his dying day like a shadow of the fear cast by that terrible event — he was a steady and well-adjusted horse. In short, he'd recovered as well as could be expected.

However, around the year 1952 I began to notice a sorrowful air come over him in the stable, and a certain reluctance when I swung into the saddle. To try solving the problem, I spent some time messing around with diet and exercise and so on.

One of Brownie's favourite exercises was to run at a group of steers in a corral, splitting them up and sending them in all directions. This was a necessary requisite in working-horse competitions, as a cutting horse is required to single out a steer and the challenge is then to keep that single animal from rejoining the herd. It's equivalent work to that demanded from a sheepdog, and cutting horses have a particular affinity for it similar to that of the sheepdog. Horses do possess a canine tooth, the purpose of which has never been adequately explained, and it's my pet theory that this canine tooth is tied in with the cutting horse's predatory instinct when asked to cut a steer out of a herd.

In any case, Brownie loved running at steers

169

and having them scatter from under his feet. He was like a puppy chasing birds, at this game.

However, when I included a touch more of this favourite activity in his training schedule, his apathy seemed worse rather than better. I couldn't figure it out.

Suddenly, it hit me what was happening. He was bored with me, he needed a holiday. A young person as driven as I was will almost always overwork their horses, and for all the attention I was giving him it was too much. I was overworking Brownie, and he wasn't giving his best. I'd crowded his life with my own life and attached my ambitions to his ambitions. I was certain I was right about this.

However, at the same moment as I realised it, we were into the last few weeks before the biggest horse show in Salinas in 1952, that would require the best — both from Brownie and from me. We would be up against some tough competition.

Were we to duck out of it, and give up all we'd worked for? I couldn't believe this dilemma we were in.

More than ever, I wished that we could share the same language. Then I would have learned about this months ago, and together we could have sorted it out. I'd been blindly carrying on, trying every which way to find the answer to our problem by trial and error.

Brownie's stall was on one side of a partition, with horses on either side all the way up the length of the barn. I leaned my elbows on the partition and had a conversation with Brownie.

He was right in front of me and I spoke directly to him.

I made an agreement. I said, 'Brownie, I will love you from Monday to Friday; I will feed you and exercise you from Monday to Friday, but I won't badger you or fuss you. You can do what you want from Monday to Friday. In return, can you give me everything you've got on Saturday and Sunday?'

Knowing he couldn't understand, and fresh with the knowledge I'd gained in Nevada, I made a promise to him that I would dedicate my life to understanding his language.

This was just as much a promise to me as it was to him. It was a goal-setting conversation, from which point I can see how my ambitions became focused and my life took its course.

Brownie won everything in sight at that Salinas show; he gave me 100 per cent. It was as though he *did* understand.

★ ★ ★

Meanwhile, every summer I was on the railroad car, travelling to horse shows all over the country with Miss Parsons, a groom, Brownie and up to eight more highly trained horses.

Miss Parsons had already taught me mathematics, grammar and so on. She had also been intent on teaching me how to use a library indexing system, which I thought was a horrible thing to have to learn. There was no escape, though; she was as dedicated to it as she was to keeping the mice out and the dust at an acceptable level. If I were to meet her today, it wouldn't be a happy task to have to tell her that no one ever did ask me to set up and run a major library facility.

The groom meanwhile looked after the horses and slept; more often than not, if he wanted human company he climbed up through the roof of the car and walked down the top of the train to the caboose at the end. The railroad crew hung out in there, and he spent his time with them.

The shows themselves were a flurry of activity and dedicated hard work.

My father employed an advance man whose job it was to sort out transport from the railroad yard to the showground, to identify where we could restock with provisions and — more importantly — to sell as many tickets as possible to a 'clinic' which was run by me after the shows — often on the Monday night.

The advance man (whom I seldom saw) also secured the venue for the clinic. Often the tickets were sold to club groups and schools. The idea was, 'Monty can show you how to win like he does.'

Looking back on it, I can see that my father hit on this initiative to help cover the considerable outlay involved in running this railroad car around the country with all these horses in it and two people employed full-time. He would have needed more than the prize money to keep that show on the road.

So, we'd arrive in a town say on a Thursday and leave the railroad car in its siding. I would do the necessary schooling to be ready for the show on the Saturday and Sunday.

At the show, I would generally win everything in sight. And why shouldn't I? Not only did I have Brownie, but I also had with me up to eight head of highly trained horses to mop up any prizes that were left over. I was a professional with years of experience behind me. The American Horse Shows Association recognised me as a professional, but they didn't exclude me from entering amateur competitions as long as they were within the qualifying age. And I was competing against kids who might go to two or three horse shows over the entire summer and only ride at weekends, who had fun with their horsemanship without thinking of it as their life's work.

So, in a way, I was a freak occurrence on the show circuit in those years, and that's why my father could set up these clinics at which the secret of my success would be revealed to an enthusiastic audience, it was hoped.

Those who'd bought tickets turned up with their trailers. Some didn't bring horses, but came simply to watch. Miss Parsons took the gate money and banked our share of the takings at the local bank. She kept accounts in a steel box which would then be pored over by her and my father when we got home — although I was never privy to any of that.

So, some time after the show was finished, I'd be faced with a string of young people who all had some questions or other to ask me. I'd have Brownie on hand just so that they could see this famous, multiple-championship-winning horse.

I went along the line and listened hard to everyone, and concerned myself with giving as much advice as I could. The voice of an adult came out of the body of a young kid as I spoke about equipment, about work ethics, about training. I watched their horses and gave advice as to what should be done with them next. I learned to project my voice and speak clearly. I took each person seriously, however small the question or however impossible the situation. I did feel the responsibility keenly, because I knew they'd all paid to get in and deserved the best attention.

However, as I worked my way down the line I knew — of course — that no one was going to dedicate 6 – 7 hours a day to riding, nor would they have parents who would share that devotion to a single aim, so the advice I was giving was not going to turn anyone into Monty Roberts. In that sense, the premise of the clinic — to allow other young people to become as successful as I was — could never be achieved.

Sometimes I felt sorry for them, but quite as often I felt sorry for myself. I could liken my lifestyle during those summers to that of the young evangelists who travel the country preaching; in many ways it was a trying existence. I was a young person who'd never really been given the opportunity of behaving as a child. I was separate from everyone else, and occasionally I felt this isolation. I became aware that I had a completely different set of values from most people. I hadn't ever visited a toyshop, for instance — something that didn't strike me as odd until much later, when I saw how common an experience it is for a child at some stage to go into a shop, point at a train set or a Barbie doll and say, 'Can I have that one, please?'

And because my world was focused so tightly on horses, I was ready to drift into the attitude that I was better than anyone else and that I possessed qualities which no other person had.

After all, I was the high-profile junior horseman in the show ring on the north American continent. I was competing successfully in professional competitions, primarily in the western division. Also, behind my father's back I had secretly started to investigate the silent language of 'Equus', and I couldn't wait to be free from him and to start using my own methods which I was sure would bring world-class success. I had some reason to be arrogant in this area.

Luckily, Miss Parsons kept me on the straight and narrow, and allowed the whole circus of our operation to become a tremendous adventure and an education. She pointed out to me that I was only this far advanced in my career because of the many hours of work that I had put into it: time that hadn't been made available to other young people of my age.

So even back then I knew what I know now, that the results I have achieved have come from year after year of hard work, study and practice. There are no inherent mystical qualities involved. Other people want to attach those qualities to me, but I won't accept them.

★ ★ ★

At the age of 17, I was closer to being a man in his twenties in terms of my experience of life and my education, which made the relationship between me and my father increasingly difficult. As a boy reaching manhood, I had good reason to believe I should be testing my wings.

I remember a whole string of conversations with him, when I was asking if I could start to train horses using my own methods.

He'd ask what was wrong with his own methods, he'd done pretty well with them — and what was there to change? He wanted his ways to be my ways; he never allowed in his own mind that there was any potential for me to do anything except what he had taught me. The mere thought of it created immediate anger in him.

Also, I wanted to play American football and try for the wrestling team, but he wasn't having any of it; I might as well have been asking to go to the moon. Anything that took me away from the life he'd made for me was impossible for him to think about. He'd given me the breath in my body, so he had the right to determine what I should do with each and every breath I took thereafter — that's how he reasoned it.

I asked him, 'Maybe you could release some of the income I earned from the motion pictures I did, so I could buy some equipment?'

'What money? You used that up long ago.'

'OK, what about the clinics we just held?'

He replied with a question of his own. 'Who paid for your education, who paid for your room and board, who paid for your upbringing?'

'You did.'

Then he made the point even clearer. 'I, as your father, am responsible for everything you've done and you owe me, not vice versa.'

His interpretation was that I should never waiver from the operation which he had set in motion. I was to carry on from where he left off. I would therefore reap all the benefits of what we achieved together, and so I wasn't to take anything out of the business or do anything else with the money. However, my intention was never to cast the same shadow and be just an extension of his work. I wanted to cut my own path.

I gave up on him, and confided my dreams only in Brownie. 'This issue isn't going to go away,' I told him. 'We'll get ourselves out from under him, you'll see. Hang around. We're getting ourselves a new life.'

The next time a row started, I was in the house talking with my mother.

'You know, Ma, it really taught me a lot, working with the mustangs over the last few years.'

'Like what?' she asked.

'It's something real important. For instance, I just know, I *know* one hundred per cent, that no one should need to sack out a young horse any more. You don't need to go through all that

177

stuff. I'm doing it a different way. I don't even hit a horse once, not ever, Ma — not the way I do it. I don't even tie a rope to their heads before I ride them.'

'Well, that sounds like a lot happier way of doing things.'

'It *is*, I'm telling you . . . '

Just then, a movement caught my eye and I turned and saw my father. He was staring at me from the other side of the doorway, and I knew from the look on his face that he must have caught the edge of this conversation I was having with my mother. As he stepped forward wearing this hard, unforgiving look in his eye, I felt the blood drain from my body into my boots. I knew what that look meant.

He stepped in front of us, his colour heightened by his terrible fury. The veins stood out in his neck as he shouted, 'I don't want to hear any more of this sort of talk.'

'Dad . . . '

He shouted louder, one of his hands curling into a fist, the other jabbing at my chest. 'You are ungrateful to me.'

'I'm not.'

'You are too stupid to do anything without my help.' I swallowed hard, knowing what was coming, as my mother interjected, 'Marvin, please . . . '

'You owe *everything* to me!' With that, he raised his fist to his opposite ear and brought it back across my face, knocking my jaw hard. It was a familiar shock and at the same time I registered that my mother had screamed, briefly.

I was thanking God that she was there, since in her presence he wouldn't dare go as far as he normally did.

Sure enough, as he advanced further on me, I heard my mother say to him, 'Marvin, stop at once.' She caught hold of his arm.

I stood with one hand to my jaw, waiting to see what would happen. My mother was staring at my father so hard that it looked like she wanted to turn him to stone. She said to him, 'Listen to him for once. Let's just see what he has to say. He's seventeen years old; he's not a child.'

I watched as my father's pulse rate dropped, and with it his temper fell to a lower level. 'Listen, uh?' he said, with some sarcasm, as though anything I said wouldn't be worth much.

Nevertheless, because my mother was there and he couldn't just lay into me the way he might have done otherwise, he went quiet and gave me a chance.

We moved to the lounge and I can remember he sat on a couch by himself while my mother stood closer to me to protect me.

Something clicked; I recognised my opportunity, and this wasn't just a conversation now — I was telling him what was going to happen.

'I want to start up on my own. I figure there're people who will give me work training their horses, and I want to be left to do as I think fit. I want a chance to prove I can do it. It's not much to ask, it's only what every other citizen in Salinas could do — that is, come to you and

179

ask to lease some facilities so they can work with horses here at the Competition Grounds. Same as Ray Hackworth or anybody else.'

There was a moment's pause while my father digested what he'd just heard. I watched as a look of disbelief stole over his face and then he said, 'Good! You can do just that! I'll rent you barn number eight, course I will. And we'll see how you get on.' Then he stood up and pointed a finger at me. 'And while you're about it, since you're so darned grown-up all of a sudden, you can pay us money for your board, you can buy your own vehicle and your own clothes.'

As a parting shot he added, 'The rent for your room here is $35 a month!'

Although he was telling me what I wanted to hear, the truth of it was that he was telling me I'd fail. The house in Church Street had been $35 a month for the whole house, so that's probably why that figure sprang to his mind. He wanted to show me the kind of payments he was having to deal with.

I eagerly accepted the arrangement. He outlined the details and told my mother that she would be the administrator for all the various charges. He told her on which days she was to expect rent, board and so on.

So I took him at his word, which I think half surprised him. I leased barn number eight, and opened for business as a trainer of show horses and cutting horses. I made it quite clear that I was now in charge of my own destiny. I didn't only do rodeos now — I went all out for American football at school as well, catching

180

up with the other members of the team who'd been training for four years already. I also went in for wrestling. I began to spread my wings.

As far as making a living was concerned — well, I was a world champion horseman, wasn't I? Surely there'd be more than enough work training other people's horses to give me a decent living. I thought there'd be no problems at all.

The reality struck home pretty quickly: there wasn't nearly enough work for me. If it hadn't been for my mother helping me out in the background most of the time, forgetting a month's rent here and there and slipping me some cash when she saw I needed it, I would certainly have crashed quickly and had to find myself a job digging ditches somewhere.

She cheated all over the place. She even bought pants for my father that were in my size, so she could give them to me instead. Without her adjusting the accounts in this way, my father would have been right and I wouldn't have survived.

But, thanks to her, I was out from under him for the first time in my life. It was a start.

★ ★ ★

I was mounted on Brownie, standing in one corner of the corral. In the other corner stood a bunch of steers. While Brownie jigged on the spot, wanting to be set loose and to run at them as he knew he would be doing in a moment, I counted the moments and judged when to give the command.

I gave a chirrup and he jumped forward in the usual way; this was his favourite exercise. He'd already run at them a few times and they knew what was happening, so they were already splitting every which way like balls on a pool table.

Brownie dived in, rolling the last calf out of the corner and bouncing it out from along the rails — which was his particular skill. You had trouble keeping him away from doing this.

Suddenly, he felt all wrong underneath me. It was as though his nervous system was plugged into mine and I felt the sharp, fearful breakdown in his system at the same time as he did. Sure enough, he stumbled and made a crashing fall. This wasn't a horse tripping over a piece of rough ground; this was the rug pulled out from under his feet.

By the time I stood up, I knew he was dead. It was too quiet. He was lying on the ground, not moving a muscle.

A terrible sadness overtook me. I couldn't imagine not having this horse as my friend and companion. It was a true bereavement, as bad as any I've suffered. I stood there for a long while in dumb silence, not doing a thing.

As I stood there, it was like I watched his life flash before my eyes. I remembered my first sight of him — he had that single white dot between his eyes — and hearing his name. Brownie. Standing nose to tail with Oriel in the pale moonlight up on the high desert in

Nevada. Rocking back and forth in the railroad car, keeping his balance. Walking forward to collect many, many championship trophies as a working horse. Spinning calves out of the corner of the corral . . .

I hoped he'd understood my apology to him last year. Certainly, after that show in Salinas we'd enjoyed a better relationship. I'd given him time off work, away from me and my concerns, so he'd come back to me fresher and with renewed enthusiasm over the last year.

I thought now, 'Rest in peace.' I really meant it; that's what he should do.

★ ★ ★

Mr Fowler paced back and forth at the head of the class, while we students waited with our pencils sharpened and our paper at the ready. A tall man with an erect bearing and an olive complexion, he always dressed immaculately.

'I want you all to think about this very carefully,' said Mr Fowler, waving his long, elegant hands. 'It should be like painting a picture of your lives in the future, as if all your ambitions had been realised.'

A voice piped up. 'How much detail d'you want, sir?'

'As much as possible. It should be a complete portrayal of what you envision for yourselves in the future.' He turned to gaze at us calmly. 'And my last instruction to you is perhaps the most important: this vision of the future that you're all going to paint for me should be a realistic one. I don't want to hear about some crazy, off-the-wall plan. I don't want to know about any Hollywood dreams, either.'

There was a smattering of laughter at this idea. We were in California, after all.

He finished by saying, 'It should be a fair and accurate assessment of where I might expect to find you if I were to visit you in your mid-thirties. It's to be called "My Goals in Life" and should be returned within three weeks.'

I was in my last year of high school, and this was one of the first projects we were set to do. It was an easy start for me, because I knew exactly what I wanted to do in life. In fact, it was a continuation of a useful exercise I'd already been doing for myself over the years. I'd started doing drawings of stables and training facilities when I was nine years old.

Given my subject matter, I didn't have to worry about Mr Fowler's final instruction either, as mine was no Hollywood dream, even though I'd been in countless films by this time. So I pressed ahead with the assignment and I turned in what I thought was a good paper on the subject. It was a ground-plan and associated paperwork for the running of a thoroughbred racehorse facility.

Five days later the paper was returned to me with a big red 'F' printed across the top of the page. Also written were the traditional words: 'See me.'

This was a shock, because I was accustomed to achieving good grades. I went immediately to see Mr Fowler after class, showed him my work again and asked him what in the world I'd done wrong.

He leafed through the pages and said, 'You know that my last instruction to you was to be realistic in this projection of your future?'

I replied, 'Yes, I did realise that.'

'Do you realise what the annual income of a person in the United States is?' he asked me.

I replied, 'No, I'm sorry but I don't.'

'Sixty-three hundred dollars!'

I waited for him to continue, but I had a clear idea of what he was going to say next.

'So how many years would you have to work and save up to earn the amount of money you'd need for your plan?' he asked me.

'I don't know.'

He tapped his finger against the red 'F' and advised me, 'It is a wild, unattainable dream. That is why I gave it a failing grade based on the instructions that I issued at the outset.' Then he handed me back the paper. 'I know your family and background; it would just not be possible. Take it home, think about it, change it to an appropriate level and hand it in again. The last thing I want is to fail you based on a misunderstanding.'

It felt like he'd driven a knife into me — his reaction was that unexpected. I was suddenly awakened to the reality of finance and I faced the prospect that my dream could never be realised.

The next two or three days were depressing. I was at home, agonising over what to do. I couldn't figure out how I could change it. My mother saw I was troubled and asked what was wrong, so I confided in her.

She read my paper and suggested, 'Well, if that's truly your life's dream, then in my opinion you can achieve it. I think you ought to consider turning the paper back in just the way it is, without any changes.' She added, 'If you think it's unattainable, then you can change it yourself. But I don't think it's for a high school instructor to set a level on your hopes and dreams.'

I recall feeling renewed at that point.

I returned to school and handed the paper back the same as before, except with an additional note written on it that his perception as my instructor that it was unattainable was fair enough, but my own was that it was attainable as a life plan, and that I didn't think he had a right to put a cap on my perceptions. He should grade the paper as he thought fit.

When the grades were mailed to us, I did get an 'A' for that particular course. I never did find out to what extent he changed the mark, but I couldn't have achieved an 'A' overall if he'd left that paper with an 'F' grade.

I didn't know it then, but I was to come into contact with Mr Lyman Fowler much later in my life, in 1987. Then, the boot would be firmly on the other foot.

* * *

One night in the summer of 1953, I was in the railroad car, winding through the Imperial Valley in California.

186

It was still a little strange, not having Brownie with me. That brown gelding with the dot of white between his eyes was like a ghostly presence, we'd spent so long together in this rattling wooden structure as it rolled around the vast country of America — and this was especially true at night.

On this occasion, however, I'd gone back over the roof of the train to the caboose where the railroad crew rode. Nothing much was happening. The cards were put away and no one was drinking or eating. As I recall, I was looking out of the window into the desert of southern California, or as much of it as could be seen from the square patches of light thrown by the railroad car and by moonlight.

Quite suddenly the image of a young lady named Patricia Burden came into my mind as clearly as if I'd invited her to sit by me. It just hit me that she was going to be a major factor in my life.

Pat Burden was a girl who was just one year behind me through primary and secondary school. Her father was the owner of a company having to do with the drilling and installation of water wells. She had relatives who were involved in the horse business and rodeo as well.

With her just walking into my head like that, the thought of what I should do next preyed on me. It wasn't like a decision I had made; it was as though someone else was pulling the strings.

As soon as I returned I went up to her in the corridor of Salinas Union High School

187

and simply informed her — by way of an announcement — that she was my 'chosen woman'. She didn't have the same reading of the situation, and shooed me away.

Later on she was with some friends of hers, Sally and Jim Martins, who also happened to be related to my family. She told them that I was pestering her every day for a meeting of some sort and suggesting no end of things we might do together.

They dared Pat to go out with me just once. Not being the type to turn down a dare, she said she would.

The next day, I made my usual trek to ask her to go somewhere with me. This time, she said yes.

We went to dinner and a movie. From that date, we've been together for more than 40 years.

★ ★ ★

A major Hollywood picture was scheduled to shoot in and around Salinas in the summer of 1954.

It was to be called *East of Eden* from the book by John Steinbeck, who had been a Salinas resident in the early years of the century. I had gone to school with members of his family.

The director was to be the noted film-maker Elia Kazan. He had cast a young kid from a New York stage school to be in this movie, but naturally the producers were worried at the differences the actor would encounter when he was put down in California and asked to play the part of a Salinas resident.

Our old friend Mr Don Page was the first assistant director on the film, and he suggested to me that I take this young actor under my wing and show him around, to help him soak up the atmosphere of this part of the world.

I thought this was a terrible idea. I didn't want some type from a drama school slowing me down! But Mr Page pointed out that there was a $2,500 payment for the three months, plus food allowances, whereupon I agreed wholeheartedly that it was a sensible plan of action!

Mr Page continued, 'Now, I want him to become familiar with the whys and wherefores of life in Salinas.'

'Fair enough, I can show him around.'

Then he asked, 'Can I go one step further than that, and ask if he can live with you for a while?'

I agreed to the arrangement and asked him, 'What's the actor's name?'

Mr Page answered, 'James Dean.'

So I was given the job of providing a lifestyle barometer for this young unknown actor.

He turned up at the Competition Grounds with a little suitcase, wearing jeans and a T-shirt and a leather jacket. He was dishevelled, careless, goofy, irreverent, unstructured and confident.

He was 23 to my 20 years, but it seemed like it was the other way around; he was young for his age.

I took his bag and showed him to the pair of

bunk-beds in my room, where I gave him the top bunk.

Then I noticed his boots. They were a city-slicker's idea of cowboy boots, with the jeans an inch or two short to show them off — terrible!

I didn't say anything for a while, but then I couldn't bear it any longer. We had a clothing allowance for him from Mr Page, and I suggested we go to the Garcia saddlery store to buy him some real boots.

Jim was stoic about it, though he wanted to hang on to his original pair. But I told him, 'If you don't burn them by the time we're through, I won't have done my job properly.'

A little while later, when he was acclimatised to his new footwear, he admitted to me that he'd given the original cowboy boots away.

It was the fulcrum of our relationship; after that, we tipped into a firm friendship. He would sit on the fence and watch Pat and me riding, either at shows or in the practice corrals. We went to Mac's café and had dinner; we introduced him to everyone we could.

Jim would melt into corners and sit balled up, running his fingers through his hair. I advised him to straighten up, to come out of his shell, not to slink back all the time, if he wanted to appear like a Steinbeck-type Salinas resident.

Jim replied, unconcerned, 'Yeah, yeah. I'll do that.' Then with real interest he'd ask, 'Can you show me how to spin that rope?'

We sat up 'til three in the morning teaching him to do a 'butterfly' — which is a particular pattern made by spinning the rope this way and that.

He thought being able to do this 'butterfly' spin on the rope would be his ticket to social acceptance in the environment in which he found himself — and he was right. He did it everywhere, showing off his new trick and having the assembled company nod in approval.

He also wanted a pair of chaps. Often I'd find he'd borrow mine, and I'd catch glimpses of him at the shows we went to, wearing them. This wasn't done, so I gave him an old pair of my father's which he was pleased with.

Also, he fell in love with Pat and followed her around like a puppy. He was never a threat because he never advanced his case. He simply looked at her all the time, and wherever she went he'd go too.

After my three months were up, Mr Page and Elia Kazan called me in for a meeting. They were close to shooting now, and they wanted to know how their young prospect had fared.

I told them that I really liked this guy. He was like a brother to me, and I was impressed with his character and everything about him.

I had to add that I thought he'd never be an actor, though. I knew plenty of actors from my film work; and Jim wasn't like a John Wayne or a Roddy McDowell. He wasn't gregarious, he didn't engage people in conversation, he didn't evoke enthusiasm or participation. He just didn't seem like an actor to me.

They thanked me for my report and I went away to prepare for my various functions on the shoot itself. I was to be the wrangler — that is, looking after the horses my father had provided for the movie — as well as a stunt-man and an extra.

The crews turned up. Jim moved out of my bedroom and into the hotel with them. Nonetheless, we were out together every night and in a general sense still made up our threesome: Pat, Jim and myself.

Filming started and after two days Elia Kazan and Mr Page asked me if I would attend what's called the 'dailies' — a viewing session, to check what they'd shot from the day before. They wanted me to comment on the environmental aspects, and ensure everything looked authentic.

I felt a certain dread because I was sure Jim's acting abilities were about to be cruelly exposed. I pictured the scene: They'd be saying, 'What are we going to do to save this movie?' I'd have to stop myself from saying, 'I told you so.'

Anyway, I attended the dailies.

As I watched Jim larger than life up on that screen, I told myself to keep my mouth firmly shut. I went right back to my position as environmental consultant, and I never breathed a word about Jim's acting abilities again. He had a whole new kind of magic and it was immediately obvious. He was electric.

When we were out together at night, Jim would run through a couple of scenarios and act them out for our amusement. First of all he'd pretend to be on the telephone to someone, telling them that he was a wild success. He acted like he was going to be a Hollywood star. He didn't know what to do with all his money; there were girls beating at the door to see him; he wanted to buy everything in sight; he was going to buy a huge ranch in the area, and Pat and I were going to manage it for him. He'd fly in from whichever part of the world he was shooting in.

Then he'd take the opposite tack and pretend this film was going to be a terrible failure. No one was watching it; the studios wanted their $150,000-fee back; they wanted the clothing allowance back; they came and took the boots off his feet.

None of us knew which it was going to be.

History relates the phenomenal success of James Dean. I was with him when he shot *Rebel Without A Cause*, as well as *Giant* with Elizabeth Taylor and Rock Hudson. As it turned out, he was the Hollywood star and he had the fortune to go with it.

As he used to say when it was make-believe, he wanted to buy a ranch and have Pat and me manage it for him. It turned out that he really did want that; and so did we.

There was a property for sale near Salinas. Mr Pedrazzi senior had died, and some time previously we'd even driven out and looked at his land.

Jim was due to take part in a road race in Salinas. He was going to drive up with his mechanic in the Porsche Spyder, and would be staying with us at Pat's parents' place. We would be looking at property in earnest. Pat and I felt our future was secure. Through our friendship with this young man, we were following a new track in our lives. It was full of promise.

On 30 September 1955, we were waiting there for him as he was driving up to join us. We'd told him to call us when he was near and give us his estimated time of arrival; we'd be ready for him.

The mechanic, Wolf Weutherich, had our names and numbers in the pocket of his overalls and was getting ready to stop.

As everyone knows, they collided with another car. The other driver walked away with a bruised nose. Weutherich broke a leg and his jaw.

James Dean died of a broken neck.

After the accident, the mechanic was so dazed and traumatised that he went right ahead and the first call he made was to us. Through his broken jaw, he mumbled that James Dean was dead.

It was a freezing experience. In particular, it was difficult because Pat and I were alone with our grief. We'd known him for only a year. We knew none of his family, and they weren't aware we existed. His body was taken back to the mid-West and we never attended the funeral.

The life that we had been expecting to lead closed down in front of us.

We simply went back to school.

★ ★ ★

I won a full-ride football scholarship to Cal-Poly in 1955 — meaning not only my tuition would be paid, but also my living expenses.

Again, it wasn't surprising because of the level of experience I'd attained, but I was the only freshman to go straight to the front of the college rodeo team.

By the following year my football career was over, as I couldn't straighten out my knee injury sufficiently to continue playing. I did, however, do some wrestling.

I'd registered for the draft but they hadn't called me up yet, beyond giving me a physical and noting that I was completely colour-blind. This was the first time I'd had it confirmed for me, and I was glad to have been proved right. I did see differently from other people. I perceived movement more clearly and from a far greater distance. I could see better at night. Very much later, when I was 61, I went to a specialist in Britain who gave me a contact lens which offered some insight as to what it's like to see colour. I was amazed. A vibration of energy entered into the middle of me and caused me enormous agitation. I thought, if that's what normally-sighted people have to put up with, no wonder they're so distracted and nervous. It was a revelation, and I know I couldn't have done all the things in my life which I have done if I'd been able to see colour.

At Cal-Poly, I was taking a triple major: in biological sciences (specialising in psychology), animal science and agra-economics.

Woody Proud, who owned the Proud ranch right near Cal-Poly, was keen to have me come and live there while I attended college. He judged that my reputation would bring him significant business and for this reason he allowed me to occupy a house free of charge, as long as I could share it with two other men also attending Cal-Poly who would be paying rent.

It wasn't so much a house as a hut. They had recently torn up a freeway nearby, and Woody Proud had bought several redundant motel cabins and parked them on his land.

Nevertheless, it enabled me to keep my three rodeo horses — Miss Twist, Finito and Hyena — and afford to go to college. I practised hard with the college rodeo team from the outset. It was good news for them that I was a four-event man and we were getting along fine.

One of the early rodeos which the team attended was during October 1955 in Eugene, Oregon. The drive took us over vast tracts of deserted, mountainous terrain. I was becoming interested in the way horses travelled in trailers — how they countered the stress and strain of road travel. A year or two later, I was to team up with Sheila Varian and make an in-depth study of it, hauling horses over very twisty roads for sustained periods of time. We chose to use an open truck with no partitions in it, the idea being that if the horses were loose, they'd be free to find the most comfortable position to travel in.

Nearly one hundred per cent of the time, they chose to arrange themselves not facing forwards, not facing backwards, but standing at forty-five degrees to the roadway. They were better able to brace themselves against the stopping and

196

starting and against the pull of the corners. I subsequently took my old trailer to a welding shop and had them change the partitions so they were all hinged to the one wall and would swing open, so I could haul my horses at forty-five degrees. This would be late in 1960 and to my knowledge it was the first trailer adapted in this way. I never thought much more about it, until everyone started building the design into their commercial trailers. I'd say eighty per cent of show horses are now hauled at forty-five degrees.

Anyway, at this time, back in 1955, we were in a conventional, three-rig convoy on the way to Eugene in Oregon, and we made the outward trip without incident.

On the way back, however, we were caught in an early winter blizzard blowing in from the north-west. We crept on slowly through the mountains of south Oregon. It was passable, and we were pleased to be gaining ground and heading for home.

I was driving with Don Switzer in a pick-up with a trailer behind. Inside the trailer were Miss Twist and Don's horse, fresh from their successes at the rodeo. In the pick-up the heater was going full blast, and we were making slow but steady progress through terrain which was now a featureless white blanket without a house or another vehicle in sight.

Then the trailer blew a tyre. I looked at Don and asked, 'Spare?' He shook his head.

We got out of the pick-up and looked at the flat tyre, the dry snow billowing around us, already knee-deep. There was nothing we could do but unload the horses. Don would have to drive to the next town, Weed. We weren't sure how far away it was.

We backed the horses out and I waved Don off, watching his tail-lights disappear in the blizzard, the pick-up sliding this way and that.

Miss Twist was fairly unhappy about the snow and didn't know what to make of it. She kept on trying to circle round and aim her rear into the wind, to gain some shelter for herself. I wondered what I could do to keep her and Don's horse all right during our wait for the return of the tyre. So I decided to walk them on down the road and, even if I didn't find any shelter, we'd run into the pick-up a touch sooner.

A short while later, looking down the road, I was glad to see an isolated gas station already well banked with snow. There was no sign of Don, so they couldn't have stocked tyres — that would have been too much like good luck. However, beneath the canopy there was a dry square of ground where I could wait for Don's return. It was a godsend.

Leading Miss Twist and Don's horse, I plunged through the deep drifts. The blizzard was stinging our faces and it took some courage for any of us to look into the wind and see where we were going.

In a few minutes we reached the haven of the gas station and slithered down the slope to shelter under the canopy. With the snow building up on all sides, it was like being in a cave. All of us were glad to be there, and Miss Twist settled down pretty quickly now she was out of the wind. I counted myself lucky, and began to take stock of where I was.

The building itself was frozen up. I peered through the glass, but couldn't see a sign of life. I guessed there was no one there; they wouldn't have sold any fuel right now, there wasn't a soul on the road.

So, five minutes later I jumped out of my skin when the front door banged open and quite a senior lady rushed out of the building yelling at me at the top of her voice and waving a broom. In an instant the horses reared up and pulled away, bashing through the snow and scattering to the south-east. The lady continued to attack me with her broom, shouting, 'You're spoiling my business!' Then, as quickly as she'd appeared, she was gone.

I was amazed and I guess my jaw dropped open in astonishment. I was used to visiting some pretty out-of-the-way places, but this was the first time I'd met such a hostile reception.

I had to fetch my horses so I started out, following their tracks, which was easy enough in the snow. They'd travelled down a gentle slope at the back of the gas station and I followed.

I just couldn't believe that woman. Couldn't she see I was no threat to her, but simply sheltering from the snow? She probably could have made me her best friend for the rest of my life if she'd offered me half a cup of hot tea.

Arriving at the bottom of the slope, I could

see the horses' tracks rising on the other side and I pressed on.

Unknown to me, there was a stream in the dip here which had iced over and snow had fallen on top of the ice, completely obscuring it from view. Perhaps I would have been all right if I'd avoided following the horses' tracks, because the ice might have taken my weight.

However, I plunged on and of course, where the horses had gone through, they'd broken up the ice. I fell through into the water, up to my waist.

There was nothing to do but carry on. Their tracks bent right — and I followed, walking fast to retrieve my body warmth.

As I worked my way up the slope, I pictured myself telling Don about that woman: 'She was like something out of a horror movie, Don. She just came at me with that broom and beat me out of there. The horses took off like they knew she was the devil incarnate . . .'

Eventually I caught up with the horses, picked up their lead ropes and turned them round to head back for the road. I had to return as quickly as I could to be sure not to miss Don and the trailer. In the near-zero visibility, I followed the tracks back the same way I'd come.

'You're spoiling our business,' she'd said — what kind of crackpot was she? She probably hadn't seen a car in there since before the war.

At the bottom of the slope I plunged through the water again; I was soaked to the skin anyway, so it couldn't matter.

When I reached the road, I contemplated

heading for the service station again and trying to present my case to the lady. I couldn't see her being the listening type, and I could quite easily picture the same sequence of events happening all over again, so when I saw a large pine tree beside the road I chose that instead. It was more inviting. Better company, all round. It had wide-spreading, needle-filled limbs and was offering just as good shelter as the canopy of the gas station.

When we ducked underneath it, the horses were literally scraping their ears against the lower limbs. We were safe — and right by the road.

I sat against the trunk and looked at the horses' leads in my hands. As long as those two leads were there, we were OK. I couldn't actually open my hands, but that didn't seem to matter. Apart from the occasional spell of shivering, I began to feel almost euphorically warm. I didn't care that I seemed unable to move a bone in my body; I was fine, no thanks to her. Who was that woman? Not to worry; I was surprisingly happy now, just a little tired.

I slipped into unconsciousness.

I was half aware of a rumbling sound, and I felt the two ropes leave my hands as though of their own accord. I couldn't do anything about it — and everything returned to black.

When Don came back with the trailer fixed, he spotted the horses standing next to a tree. He stopped and caught hold of them and looked around for me.

No sign.

Then he recognised that the tree had

undergone the equivalent of an avalanche; the snow on the upper branches had dropped on to the branches below, and so on, which created an avalanche effect. The tree's entire load of snow had been dumped at the bottom. Far from being a shelter, it could have been a tomb.

Don knew enough about snow to realise what had happened and after quickly hitching the horses he began to poke around, calling my name. He found my black hat — and started digging hard.

He carried me out of the snow and took me to the pick-up. My clothes were frozen on me, but he got them off and rolled me in horse blankets. Then he loaded the horses and started driving for the hospital. He undoubtedly saved my life.

I woke up in the emergency room, attached to a drip and wearing thermal protectors on all my extremities. I had trouble with my fingers and toes for some time, and my ears shed all their skin. I was lucky not to lose my toes; they brought them back from the dead.

I still wonder about that woman, though. Where is she now? If she went to heaven, she'd be running a little sideshow where eminently deserving souls call by for help and she gets to turn them down — she'd enjoy that for eternity, all right.

★ ★ ★

On 16 June 1956, Pat and I got married and together we moved to something that was a little closer to being a real house on the Proud Ranch. Our first child, Debbie, arrived less than a year later. That day was the greatest in our lives, to be matched only with the births of our other two children, Lori and Marty.

Suddenly, money disappeared more quickly. I watched it run out of my pocket and waved goodbye to it . . . and wondered where the next few dollars were going to come from. I just couldn't win enough at competitions to pay for the upkeep of the horses and for our own needs. I brought back prize money on maybe four days a month in the summer, but in the winter this dropped to perhaps one day per month.

Either side of taking her business qualification Pat opened a shop, to which she was able to give the famous 'Garcia' name; it was something like an early franchise operation. Garcia made the best saddlery in western America, and her store was conveniently located in between Cal-Poly and the Proud ranch.

However, towards the end of our college years, the economic climate looked like it was going to brighten for us with the arrival of one Homer Mitchell.

He'd put a horse or two my way for training, and he'd been impressed. Now he wanted to find a property near the ocean — near San Luis Obispo — and he was proposing that I should help him build a training facility on it which I would then manage for him. When he was older, he would retire there.

I found him an 80-acre property near Edna, California — 5 miles inland from Pismo beach.

In those days Pismo beach wasn't as developed as it is now, and the whole area was as beautiful as you could find along that coastline.

The property was called Laurellinda, and Homer Mitchell agreed that it was perfect.

Pat and I sat and watched Homer in the escrow office as he stood at the desk, reached into his coat pocket and took out a cheque-book and a pen. It was a simple thing to do and he just went ahead and did it: he wrote a cheque for $160,000 — but to us he might as well have been walking on water in front of our very eyes. We didn't think that kind of money existed, even in a bank.

We signed an agreement with him, to lease the property for a certain amount per month. At the same time, he signed an agreement with us — to put three horses into training for a fixed amount per month. It meant that we started out already half-way to covering our costs.

We counted ourselves lucky. By now our second daughter, Lori, had been born. We were about to leave college, and now we were going to make a living at what we loved. We were young, and rightly optimistic. All was set fair.

★ ★ ★

The 1960s prompted an era of change. Young people started leaning far to the left of the political spectrum. Men were burning draft papers and women were burning bras.

I have to say that these changes passed us by. Our values were rooted in a different system, and we regarded the new way of thinking as a fad which would soon be over.

I can't say we were right in that prediction, but we were too busy to notice that much. We had two infant daughters, Debbie and Lori, with our son Marty on the way. We had a 2,000-sq-foot ranch-house and the outbuildings to finish constructing on Homer Mitchell's property, Laurellinda — and we had our horses.

What we didn't have, however, was money.

When we moved to Laurellinda, there was just 80 acres with a couple of broken-down shacks on it. Homer pointed at the shack and said, 'A nickel box of matches will do the job here.'

Pat and I asked, 'So where will we live?'

'You'll have to rent a place in town and drive out here to work. Money dictates that we shall have to build the horse facility before we build the house.'

Pat and I didn't want to rent a place. We didn't have the money, and we didn't want to have to run back and forth. Horses aren't a 9-to-5 job; they're all hours.

This little pair of shacks was standing right where the training barn was going to be built, so we moved them away a short distance. One was a very old, very small railway car, and the other was a sort of garage-shaped box. We bumped them up together and plastered over the holes.

This was a temporary arrangement because I believed that, with my reputation, there'd be a lot of horses arriving at any minute. As far as I was concerned, they were already in vans and on their way over. As soon as they arrived, we could hire a big trailer until the house was built.

However, they didn't arrive. Not only that, but Pat had given up her saddle-shop franchise now that our third baby was on the way.

We did not have two cents to rub together.

I didn't know what to do about all these horses the owners weren't sending me. I had a few mares to breed and I was giving a few lessons, but it didn't answer the question what to do next. I had only four paid horses in training with me, and I was desperate. I was trying hard for prize money in rodeos, but the figures just didn't add up. I had to find more work.

Someone then gave me a piece of advice: 'Go live with Don Dodge for a while.'

I knew Don Dodge of course — everyone did. He was possibly the most successful trainer of horses around, and he really did have a line of vans waiting to turn into his place.

The advice given to me was, 'Study your ass off with Don. Give him 100 per cent. If he believes in you, you'll have it made. He'll recommend people to you.' Then came the warning, 'Remember he's impossible to impress!'

What did I have to lose? I called him up and asked to work for him for a while.

'Yup. Come up if you want. Prepare to go to work, though. You can bring a couple of your own horses, and when it's time for you to leave I'll figure out what you owe me. 'Cos I'm going to teach you something. God knows you need it!'

'OK, Don. Look forward to it.'

'Oh — and, Monty?'

'What?'

'You have to promise to do exactly as I tell you. OK?'

'I promise.'

So I took two of my horses in training, Selah Reed and Finito, and drove up to 3400 North Del Paso Boulevard, North Sacramento, California. The address is still engraved on my memory.

Don Dodge had about 40 horses in training for some of the best owners in the world. He was about 44 years old, 6ft tall, with dark hair. He had a slim build, and this beaky nose and close-set eyes which gave him an intense look which women loved. He cut a good figure on a horse, too.

I'd no sooner pulled up in his yard than he had me working. 'Glad you're here, Monty, Billy Patrick here could use some help.' He waved at a red-haired kid running back and forth carrying water buckets.

So I backed out my two horses and they were allocated a couple of open booths of distinctly inferior quality to the box stalls occupied by Don's horses.

I helped Billy feed all 40 of them and top off their stalls. In addition there was more bucket-carrying because Don didn't believe in automatic watering. After that, we had to clean all the tack that'd been used.

At around 7 p.m. Billy and I were through, and I went indoors. I was looking forward to a wash and brush-up, changing into some clean clothes, then maybe having dinner with Don. I imagined we'd share a drink and a chat, and during the meal I could begin to cultivate his friendship.

When I went inside Don asked me, 'Where you going to stay?'

My jaw fell open. 'I thought you might have a bunk room for me, Don, somewhere.'

'Nope.'

My heart sank. 'Oh.'

'You can go down the road a way, and there's a sort of rooming house. Old Mother Harris.'

Don went to the telephone and called Mother Harris to tell her I was coming. He added, 'She'll fix your meals for you.'

Cursing in disbelief, I drove down the road a way and came to Mother Harris' place. She told me that a room with my board included would be . . . well, it was a figure I couldn't dream of paying.

A room without board was $2 a night, and I had to go for that; I had no other option.

I rang Pat, who had the children crying in the background and the shack falling down around her ears, and I asked her if there was any more money. She replied no, of course, and we had to get on as best we could.

In short, the only thing I could afford to eat was a product called MetraCal, which was an all-in-one glue type of substance for people who wanted to lose weight. It cost 90 cents a can, and I lived off it for 10 weeks.

Just to look on the bright side for a moment, there were different flavours — I had a choice

208

of Chocolate MetraCal, Vanilla MetraCal or Strawberry MetraCal. You made your decision, and then you had to punch a couple of holes in the top and suck it out of the can.

I had to show up at Don Dodge's at 4.30 in the morning and feed the horses and attend to their stalls. Don would appear at 7.30 and start barking orders. I'd ride a minimum of 10 horses for him during the morning. Then I'd crack another can of MetraCal and keep going.

At some point in the afternoon, he'd always spend time with me as I worked on my two horses. He'd shout at the top of his lungs — he was a hard taskmaster. I bit the bullet; I didn't breathe a word about what I thought, and I just did what I was told.

I learned a lot.

Whenever he was around my two horses, Don Dodge would ask a lot of questions about the other two which I'd left at home. Surrounded by the number he had, it sounded pitiful to talk about the four I had in training. I told him about one of them, a stallion owned by Lawson Williams called Panama Buck, who tried to mate with his reflection if he caught sight of himself in glass. I told him many other details, including who their owners were and how much I was charging for their keep and training. I remember thinking, Why's he so interested? Does he like hearing about how badly I'm doing?

Then, for the rest of the afternoon Billy and I would be finishing the chores and topping off the stalls and cleaning the tack. We'd be through by 9 p.m.

I'd swallow some more MetraCal and carry on back to Mother Harris' place. Occasionally, Don asked me in for a meal and I fell on the food like the starving person I was. Once or twice we went to a rodeo and I won enough for a few meals, but basically I was on a MetraCal diet.

This went on for 10 weeks and I turned into a skeleton; my ribs popped out and I had a deathly pallor. My hands were calloused from the hard work carrying all those buckets, and I was worn down by the constant shouting.

As the time for my departure drew near, Don invited me into his office for a formal meeting to re-cap on my visit — and he warned me he'd be telling me how much I owed him. After his stern treatment of me and my unflagging slave labour for him, I looked forward to the pay-off. Here we go, I thought, he's going to recommend me to everyone he knows and I'll have earned it.

He sat down on the opposite side of the desk, stared at me and said, 'Well, Monty, I have you figured. You have a little talent, which maybe you could build on. But it's a lot different now. No college bullshit rodeo team.'

'No, I realise that, but I hope I'm ready to do it on my own.'

'You're going to have to work a lot harder than I've put you through if you want to make any progress at all.'

I could not believe he'd said that. Suddenly, I was so tired and dispirited I could have beaten him with my fists.

'Now then,' he went on, 'there is this matter of your promise to do exactly what I instructed.'

I nodded in agreement. 'Sure.' A promise was a promise.

He leaned forward and spoke slowly and precisely. 'What I want you to do is to go home and call Lawson Williams, and tell him his horse is no good and you're wasting his money. Tell him he's to come and pick him up immediately. Then do the same with that other horse you got back there.'

I went into a tailspin, hearing this. 'How can I do that? I've only got four horses, and you're asking me to cut my income in half? Why? Why on earth should I do such a thing?'

'I don't owe you an explanation, but seeing as you ask — you're going to do it for a very good reason, you're going to do it because he'll be impressed with you. That horse of his isn't going anywhere. You know it; I know it. You'll tell him the truth and he'll respect you for it and send you five horses right back again.'

I let this sink in. I could see his psychology, but it seemed too risky for someone with only four paid-in-training horses to send two of them away.

'Now,' he added, 'the reckoning.'

I waited for him to congratulate me on my hard work, and he might even judge the poor straits I was in compared with him and press a few dollars into my hand. Instead he said, 'You owe me $50 dollars per day; that's a total of $3,200.' And he wrote out a bill. 'Pay me just as soon as you can. You'll some day realise it's the best bargain you ever had.'

I drove home with my tail between my legs.

When I showed the bill to Pat and told her the story, she was as disappointed as I was.

However, maybe it was because I'd paid so much for this advice that it began to sound good. I started to like the feel of it. It would be a brave thing to do, but I didn't have a lot else to turn to.

I delayed for a while, trying to work out the best way of saying it, but there was no other way but head on. I rang Lawson Williams.

'Mr Williams?'

'Yes?'

'It's Monty Roberts here.'

'Hello, Monty. How're things going?'

I hesitated, then plunged on. 'Mr Williams, I don't want to waste your money, and it's my judgement that Panama Buck isn't worth spending any more on. I'd like you to come down and collect — '

Lawson Williams interrupted me, 'You useless son of a gun, you wouldn't know a good horse if it leapt up between your legs. That's the last horse you'll ever get from me!'

Then he slammed down his receiver, and the next day a man arrived to take Panama Buck.

Great! Now I really couldn't feed my wife and children. We'd all be on MetraCal now.

Shortly afterwards Selah Reed, the one paid horse-in-training I had with any promise, broke her hind leg and had to be put down.

I was running on empty. I was so low that I literally walked about the place thinking about suicide the whole time. It was going badly wrong and I was letting my family down. It

212

wasn't worth carrying on.

Then I received a telephone call.

'Hello. Mr Gray here, Joe Gray. I'm a contractor laying pipelines.'

'Hello, Mr Gray.' Who was this guy?

'I was having lunch with Mr Williams yesterday. He was complaining about you, but from what I heard you must be about the only honest horse trainer I ever heard of.'

A wave of emotion overtook me. I remembered Don Dodge's intense stare, and his advice and the MetraCal. Everything came flooding back, and I sensed it was all going to pay off.

'What can I do for you, Mr Gray?'

'Well, I know that Panama Buck horse of his wasn't any good, and I just want to take a flyer on you. I have this horse I want to send you; it's called My Blue Heaven.'

The feeling in my heart was that I'd turned a corner and I could glimpse daylight.

Joe Gray continued to explain, 'I'm a little worried for the safety of my daughters, you see. I have this small six-year-old, grey quarter-horse mare, believing her to be a good show horse for them, and she has been trained extensively. But she went wrong, and no one can stop her now.'

'Is she dangerous?'

'Extremely. They can't pull her up at all now.'

Apparently, when his daughters attempted to show her she would take the bit between her teeth, run away and crash into fences or try to avoid fences by turning very sharply and falling down at high speed.

He sent the mare to me with the instruction that she should be sold. The family was going on a three-week vacation to Lake Shasta and, regardless of how low a sum I had to take for her, I was to find a buyer for her by the time they returned.

When she came out of the van I saw she was a pretty mare with a good action and a lively eye. I couldn't wait to ride her.

She proved to be highly sensitive with the bit and bridle, and I remembered Mr Gray saying they'd used fiercer and fiercer bits to try and get her to stop. I put on a hackamore, which doesn't have a bit, and rode her in the arena.

To my surprise, I discovered that My Blue Heaven was a well-trained mare. When she was frightened, yes, she would run out of control — I discovered that right enough — but she would also perform better than any horse I had ridden in the show ring up to that time.

I took off the hackamore and the saddle and turned her loose in the round pen. She wasn't wearing a single line, not a stitch of leather. I wanted to earn her trust like this, then perhaps I could begin to encourage her to enjoy stopping and cut her out from this vicious circle of crime and punishment which she presently found herself in.

I squared up to her and sent her away. I cast the light sash line in her direction and pressed her away harder until she was travelling at a smart canter around the perimeter of the ring. I fixed my eye on hers.

She began to drop the odd signal that she

was prepared to talk. I saw her tongue briefly, and her large mandibles rippled, showing the chewing action. She was keeping one ear fixed on my position. She dropped her head.

After one more turn of the round pen, I turned my shoulders through 45 degrees to the front of her action. She stopped immediately, and my eyes left hers. Although I wasn't looking at her I could sense her waiting, and I could hear nothing but my own heartbeat.

She was wondering whether to trust me or not. She was asking herself, where would this lead her?

Moments later, she took her first step towards me. Then another one.

She was tentative . . . and all I could do was wait.

Eventually she was there, standing by me. I soothed her and told her I wouldn't abuse her trust. Together we'd work it out, we were going to help each other. She would help me make a reputation as a trainer; I would help her to escape from those harsh bits in her mouth.

Her early training for stopping had been conventional; that is to say, if enough pressure is put on a horse's mouth, it can be forced to stop. As they'd become increasingly frightened of her, so they'd used increasingly severe bits to pull her up. It was an unhappy progression — the worse the bit, the worse she'd got.

My intention with her was to get her to like to stop, to be happy with stopping and to school her with signals from my body and voice, causing her to ease into them. I tried to put as little pressure on her mouth as I could. I created a situation whereby she herself wanted to stop — by pushing her on until it seemed like stopping was her idea. The word 'Whoa' and my weight pressing down into the back of the saddle began to be welcomed by her.

Once she learned that she could avoid the pressure, and that it wouldn't be applied at all if she made the stop comfortably and without any resistance, she then started to like it. Even though her problem was deep-seated and fairly long-standing, she was smart enough to sort it out and she became extremely effective at stopping.

About two weeks after the Grays left for their vacation, there was a show at the Alisal Guest Ranch in the Santa Ynez Valley. It was a popular, high-quality show, and I decided that if I put in a good performance there, she would reach a better price for Mr Gray and his family.

I couldn't get in touch with the Grays because they were in the mountains near Lake Shasta, where there were no means of communication. Therefore, I made the entry myself and continued to school her.

There was a fair bit of money for the winner, but more importantly there was a Jedlicka saddle, a Western saddle with hand-tooled leather, and the letters depicting the trophy were on the fenders. This saddle would be valued at $5,000 today.

There were close to 20 good horses in the class. My Blue Heaven performed like a

Monty and James Dean on the set of *East of Eden*.

James Dean with
Monty's chaps.

Pat and Monty, in costume,
on the set of *East of Eden*.

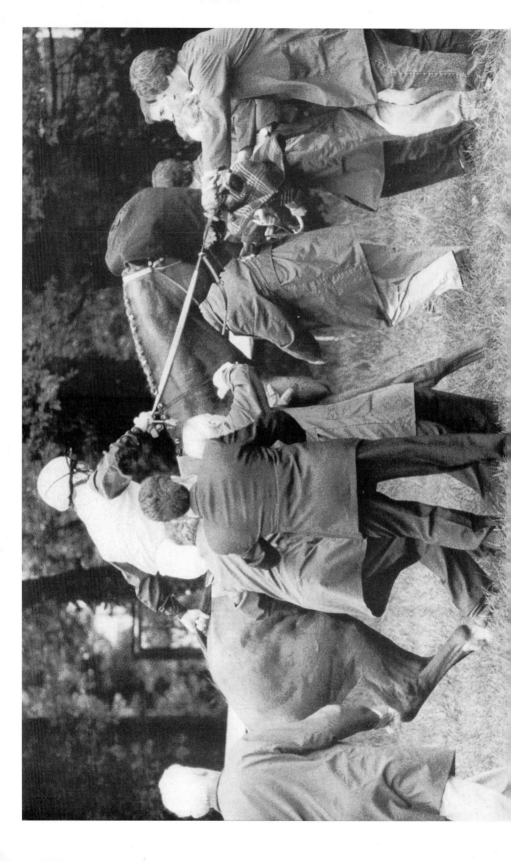

Opposite page: Lomitas refusing to enter the starting stalls the day he was 'banned for life' at the end of May, 1991.

Right: Lomitas, with Monty leading him to the starting stalls 23rd June 1991 10 days after he met him. He went in like a lamb got the best start, won the race and was reinstated.

Below: This is Lomitas on winning form in the following months.

Above: Jonny Tivio winning
a world championship with
Monty up. Jonny Tivio
won four world titles in the
Western division .

Right: Jonny Tivio at home
on Flag is Up Farms, 1967.

Monty on Ginger, June 1939, aged 4, Winner of the Junior Stock Horse Class.

Monty's father in police force uniform.

c. 1949 Monty aged 14 with Brownie aged 9 or 10. They are rigged up for roping.

MONTY'S FATHER'S METHODS OF BREAKING A HORSE.

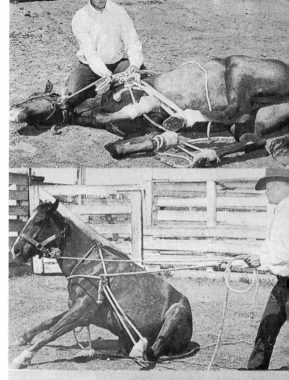

Top two photographs: Tying a horse down to gain supremacy.

Sacking out an eight-month old foal with hind leg tied.

Mounting a three-year-old with leg tied up.

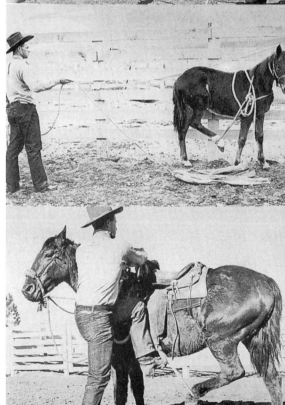

MONTY DEMONSTRATING JOIN UP

Starting 'join up' with a young unbroken horse; flicking a long rein allows its instinctive initial flight of panic to peak and then subside as it realises there is no immediate threat.

Along with the gradually subsiding fear comes the telltale lowering and stretching out of the horse's neck. It is now saying 'OK, I'm willing to talk'.

Avoiding eye contact repeatedly walk up to the horse, reassure it, then walk away again. The horse is left to make its own decision on whether to follow this intriguing new 'leader' or resist.

Won over, the horse follows. Subsequently it allows itself to be saddled, bridled and ridden.

Monty receiving awards for National Intercollegiate Rodeo Association Bulldogging Championship 1957.

Below: 1963, Monty bulldogging on Bar Flash at a Professional Rodeo Cowboy's Association event, Clovis, California.

Dually and Monty in competition, January 1996.

Dually with Monty up, working cattle at home, April 1996.

With Kelly Marks demonstrating the Monty Roberts blanket, April 1996.

Monty joining up with deer on Flag is Up Farms, January 1995

Monty with Her Majesty The Queen at Windsor, April 1989.

Lester Piggott and Alleged winning the Prix de l'Arc de Triomphe. As a team, they won in 1977 and 1978.

Monty with one of Her Majesty The Queen's horses
at Windsor, April 1989.

professional and won the competition.

I wasn't surprised, but there was a fair bit of magic to this situation now. Don Dodge's advice was working well. I was getting what I wanted, so was My Blue Heaven, and I also thought I saw a chance that the Gray daughters might get what they wanted too: a top-flight show horse.

I called some friends of the Gray family in Santa Maria and was able to get into their house via the arrangements they'd made to care for the pets and the plants. I put the saddle in their dining room, with a note on it that I needed to discuss My Blue Heaven with the family before selling her.

When they returned, Joe and his family were elated with My Blue Heaven's win. The daughters particularly were excited and the family agreed that she should stay in training.

The following year, she was second in the world for the reined cow-horse division. Twice she finished second in the world — and only because she happened to come up against Mona Lisa, one of the greatest reined cow horses of all time. Mona Lisa was owned and shown by none other than Don Dodge.

My Blue Heaven represented the first horse I campaigned in open professional competition. She was a big break for me and a significant part of my learning process. One year she had the best stops at Monterey, California, and was the supreme champion reined cow horse of the show.

After I showed her for two seasons, she went on to compete under the two daughters, who were successful on her throughout the western United States.

I did pay Don Dodge's bill eventually. I wrote and thanked him for the best advice I ever had. Within six months I had fifteen horses in training.

* * *

In 1961 the ranch house at Laurellinda was complete, and we moved out of the shack in which we'd been camping and into the main house.

On 1 February our son Marty was born, so it seemed a good time for my mother and father to visit. They drove down from Salinas to see us and the three grandchildren.

My father viewed the horses I had in training. As we walked around the property he was singing the same old song: 'You wait, I'm telling you, that bastard horse is going to go the other way with you. He's going to come loose and get you. You've got to keep them tuned up.'

He couldn't hurt me any more. I looked at the lines carved more deeply into his face now, and told myself that I was 26 and he was nearly 54. I'd escaped from him, his opinions were beginning to be irrelevant. Even so, I felt anger as new as the day it was first created in me by him. I never wanted any horse of mine to suffer that same anger, fear and resentment.

Later on in that visit, he played with his

grandchildren. Debbie was five, Lori was three and Marty just born.

Debbie and Lori had their small responsibilities around the house like keeping their room tidy. They had a horse each which they mucked out every day.

My father said, 'You know, Monty, you're too tough on these kids.'

At that point my mother walked out of the room; she couldn't believe what she was hearing. The world stopped turning — it was such a thing for him to have said that.

'Me, tough?' I replied. 'D'you by any chance remember how tough you were on me?'

He replied, 'I know, but these are good kids.'

I was startled. 'And I wasn't?'

He added, 'And they're little girls.'

What deflated my father more than anything was the undeniable fact that my method of training horses was working. It was especially effective in dealing with remedial horses.

Hey Sam was a thoroughbred who came to me in 1961. He was raised on the Parker ranch in Hawaii and purchased by Robert Anderson. I started him and gave him his pre-track training before he went to Hollywood Park for racing.

Hey Sam started well and went to the racetrack in exceptional form, but he was then sent to a trainer who was not Anderson's first choice.

Something was going wrong.

I was called to come and see the horse at Hollywood Park about three months after he'd

219

arrived, and I quickly identified the root of the problem: the rider had been pulling up Hey Sam on the racetrack at exactly the same place every day, so the horse began to anticipate that this would happen.

Hey Sam started to know when he was due to be pulled up and would do it anyway, thinking he was going home. Now he was pulling off the track in the most dramatic fashion, whether his rider wanted him to or not.

He did this at the half-mile pole, which meant that there was about a half-mile left to the finish line. Hey Sam would run up against the outside and almost bury himself in the hedge, ending up a quivering wreck.

The rider thought he could correct this habit by severely whipping Hey Sam before he got to the half-mile pole so as to beat him past the troublesome area.

Then, when the horse started going to the outside of the track to pull himself up, he would whip him on the right side to drive him back down to the inside rail.

These methods appeared to work for a while, but by the time I got there to see him, all that had been accomplished was that Hey Sam would quicken his pace when approaching the half-mile pole. As soon as he saw his chance he would duck outward violently and stop at the hedge on the outer side, waiting for the whip but refusing to go anywhere.

It was a very dramatic exhibition, and the stewards ruled him off the track.

This was disappointing to me. I had given the

horse his pre-track training and had sent him from my establishment in good order and ready to race. My reputation as well as the trainer's was at stake.

There was no choice other than to take him home and re-train him, so we transported him back to Laurellinda and went through the whole process of re-establishing communication.

Once again I harked back to the lessons I had learned from other horses like Brownie. Horses don't move away from pressure, they move into it, particularly if the pressure is applied to their flanks. The wild dogs which prey on horses on every continent attack the horse's belly, aiming to tear a hole in the stomach wall so as to allow the intestines to drop out. The dogs can then fall back and track the horse, confident that it will soon die and they can eat. The best defensive tactics the horse can employ against this form of attack is not to run away but to turn into the onslaught and kick — because if they run from a bite, then it's more likely that their skin will tear. It's my belief that this causes the phenomenon which is recognised by all good trainers: that if you poke a forefinger into a horse's side, he'll move against the pressure rather than away from it. It's perhaps the single most important thing to remember, in training horses. '*Horses are into pressure animals.*'

I knew that the whip inflicted by Hey Sam's riders on his outside flanks was causing him to go the opposite way to the one that might be expected, and we had to change that.

I worked for about six months, taking all

221

pressure off the outside. Instead, I started to use my leg well back on the inside, schooling him to bring his head more towards the rail and to be happy doing it.

He was not a bad horse and had no evil in him. He learned, and he changed significantly. When he went back to the track I was able to send him to Farrel Jones, whom I had known for many years. This was the best thing that could have happened to him.

Farrel watched me ride Hey Sam on the racecourse at Golden Gate Fields in northern California, and then he put a rider on him who employed the same techniques.

Soon enough he was entered for his first race and he won at odds of fifty to one. My heart lifted; he was on his way. I also felt a personal triumph.

Hey Sam ultimately went on to win 12 races, and earned his owner more than $100,000.

It was a success story, and this was the start of my love affair with the American racing industry.

★ ★ ★

Perhaps the horse I loved most in my life had the all-boy name Johnny Tivio. He was a registered quarter-horse stallion, 14.3 hands high and weighing 1,200 pounds. He was a light bay, but his coat had this coppery sheen to it that almost made it glitter.

I'd seen him around at the showgrounds, glimpsing this brilliant coat he had. Even though he wasn't kept in top condition it seemed to outshine any other horse's coat, as though the polish came through from the very heart and soul of him rather than from constant grooming. So I'd had my eye on him for a while.

He was trained by Harry Rose, who enjoyed a lot of success with him. Harry was a rough, tough kind of man who lived hard and played hard.

Pat and I were driving just down the road from the Competition Grounds when we saw a trailer parked outside a scuzzy, honky-tonk type of bar. Inside the trailer I could see Johnny Tivio and another horse.

I said to Pat, 'There's Harry, drinking the town dry again.'

We were back on my home ground — the Competition Grounds in Salinas — not for a visit but to take part in a show for working horses. It was quite a premier event, as befitted the status of the Grounds.

We unloaded Fiddle D'Or and My Blue Heaven and put them away for the night at the Grounds, then drove back the same way. Harry Rose's trailer was still there, parked outside the bar, and so were the horses.

The next morning we turned up early to prepare our two for the eliminations for the show that was being held that day. Two blocks away from the bar, the trailer was parked outside a little house — still with Johnny Tivio and the other horse inside. They'd been standing there all night.

We ran through our preparation with our

horses as usual, which included an exercise or two to warm them up and so on. We were ready for the 8 a.m. start.

Minutes before that time, Harry Rose came tearing down the hill way too fast with his trailer swerving around behind him, the horses clamouring and struggling to keep their balance. He jerked to a halt and dragged out a girl of some description who was flitting about while he backed the two horses out of the trailer.

He threw a saddle on Johnny Tivio and sprang onto his back; then he hauled the girl up behind him and the pair of them started prancing around.

When the contest began, Johnny Tivio won everything in sight. He'd been locked up in a trailer all night and hadn't had a moment's preparation, yet he beat our two horses for fun. He walked into the arena as if he owned the place and we were lucky just to rub up alongside him.

I was half-amazed and half-angry at Harry Rose for treating such a wonderful horse so badly. I said to Pat, 'That horse is solid gold. Some day he'll be mine.'

Only months later the local humane society received a telephone call because a horse had been left in a trailer outside some woman's house for two days.

The horse and the trailer were impounded and the registration number led the police to the home of the owner, Carl Williams. They attempted to arrest Carl for cruelty to a horse called Johnny Tivio, but he soon put them right and set them on the trail of his trainer, Harry Rose.

Meanwhile, Carl Williams rang me because he knew I'd been angling for this horse for a while now. He asked me for $6,000 — and I could take Johnny Tivio away.

I leapt at the chance and replied, 'Done deal.' I didn't have the money, though, and I had to call George Smith, a customer and an old friend, to put up half.

Johnny Tivio had foundered, he was in bad shape and his shoes were grown in, but he was mine. We looked after him and straightened up his feet. He was always a willing animal, but he grew stronger and better with every kind word spoken to him and every kind deed.

Mind you, from the minute he joined us at Laurellinda, he was in charge: we were kind of working for him, and not vice versa. He had several complaints about his stall, and we had to shift the bedding around so he could drop his faeces in one particular corner. He kept us up to the mark all right with his fastidious stable manners and his superior attitude. He was quite the best horse he himself had ever seen; he'd allow, yes, that other horses could exist, but only on his say-so, and not palominos — no sir, he didn't like them. He'd had a palomino as a stablemate early on in his life, and he'd taken against it, and as far as he was concerned they were all tarred with the same brush. They were barely allowed in his sight.

Johnny Tivio turned into a monster success; I could enter him into whichever category of working-horse event I wanted, and he'd win. He was one of the few horses on the show circuit whom everyone would agree was the best on the face of this earth. He won everything in sight for me, year after year.

★ ★ ★

'Hey, Monty, look at this!' called Slim.

'What?'

'Isn't this the cutest foal you've ever seen?' He was toying around with a stick and a little palomino foal was trying to nibble at it.

'Watch this,' said Slim. Then he tossed the stick into the air and the foal turned and ambled over to where the stick lay and picked it up in his teeth. Then he wandered back, chewing the stick, to where Slim was standing.

'Incredible,' I agreed. I knew Slim Pickens from when I was a child, and he was like an uncle to me.

'He's like a little puppy,' said Slim. 'Watch this as well.' He turned to the foal and slapped his own chest, calling, 'Hup! Hup!'

The foal jumped up and put his front legs on Slim's shoulders. 'See?' said Slim. 'Ain't this going to be the brightest Walt Disney type of horse you're ever going to see?'

Slim Pickens was an actor, and a movie studio had hired him to feature in a movie called *The Horse With The Flying Tail* for Disney. It was about a palomino jumping horse.

They wanted to use this foal to depict the early years of the palomino, and were here at his farm in Soledad to shoot a lot of the footage with Slim Pickens as the principal actor.

The foal's name was Barlet.

While it seemed to be cute at that time, Barlet thought it was fun to perform the same kinds of tricks when he was a two-year-old.

Martin Clark had been showing Barlet throughout the western United States and he was virtually undefeated as a halter horse — an in-hand competition judged only on conformation. He was in line to be the national champion that year; it was almost a certainty.

The next time I saw Barlet was at the championship show in 1962 held at the Cow Palace in San Francisco in late October. When I arrived there with my horses — My Blue Heaven, Midge Rich and one other — I found that Martin Clark had Barlet in a box stall in the stabling area within the Cow Palace building itself.

He had wired this stall with an electrical circuit. Not only was there a wire all the way around, half-way up the wall, but in addition there was a wire around the top. If the electric current was switched off, Barlet would climb right over the wall.

Having learned that while the charger was going he could hear a pulsating sound, he would cause no problem at all while it was on.

When Martin wanted to take him out of the stall, he had to turn off the charger so that he could open the door. As soon as the switch was thrown, Barlet became more like a tiger than a horse. He literally attacked him.

After a day or so of preparing for competition, Martin could not get Barlet out of the stall; he couldn't catch him or handle him.

He came to me and made an offer: 'If you can catch Barlet in the stall and get him through the show ring and win with him, I'll give you a half-interest in him, then you can take him back to San Luis Obispo with you and put him in training.'

With Barlet a heavy favourite to be the national champion stallion for the year, his value had to be in the $30 – 40,000 range. It was no mean offer. This was an exciting challenge to me, and I just didn't believe there was a horse I couldn't handle.

When I arrived at the stall and saw the wires and the security arrangements, it was disconcerting. We shut off the wires, I opened the door and Barlet bolted towards me from the rear of the stall with his ears back and his teeth bared. He wanted to hurt me.

I jumped back and closed the door before he got hold of me. Unable to get near enough even to look him over, I had to reassess the situation. This horse was too far gone to even ask for his trust. From a very young age he'd been spoiled — not through cruelty in this case, but because of unintentional maltreatment. He'd been trained as a lapdog, and somewhere along the line the psychology of it had gone wrong.

I went to my tack-room and got a lariat rope. I came back and was able to swing the rope around in such a fashion that it kept Barlet at sufficient distance.

I got him roped in the stall and was able to put on his head the piece of equipment Don Dodge had taught me to use; we call it the 'come-along'. It's a way of twisting the rope over the horse's head so that you can control it easily with a line that travels over certain nerve ganglia.

I led Barlet out of his stall and started schooling him, using the methods I have described earlier in this book, trying to restore his trust. It took a good deal longer than it did with My Blue Heaven, and the results weren't as consistent, but he did eventually come to trust me to some degree.

As a result of winning his trust, I was able to show him in hand at that show. He took me up through the ranks until he'd achieved the target set by Martin Clark; Barlet became the national champion and I became half-owner of him.

I took him home to San Luis Obispo, from where he went on to win extensively over the following years.

While I was able to show him in ridden competition in the reined cow-horse division, I have to admit he was never a mentally balanced horse after being spoiled as a foal. As is so often the case with horses made mean, even by well-intentioned people like Slim Pickens, they can seldom be trusted. This type of chronically distrustful horse should only be handled by professional horsemen who are fully aware of just what they are dealing with. Failing this, the consequences can be too high.

Barlet was a truly mean horse the entire

time I worked with him, attacking me on several occasions. He was severely troubled, and one can only guess at what triggered his disappointment with human beings. He and I had an understanding based around a well-developed discipline-and-reward system, so I was able to control his neurosis for three or four years.

Sadly, his problems got the better of him in the long run and he eventually died in a fight with a gelding on my farm in San Luis Obispo. He broke down the fence to get to the other horse, and during the skirmish he broke his front leg.

III

The Sandcastle
Syndrome

IN 1964, when I was 31 years old, I encountered a man who would change our lives for ever. He would take my family and me to the heights of success . . . and then bring us way lower than we'd ever have imagined possible.

At that time we had a veterinarian by the name of Dr Jim Burns, who came to me one day and said that he had attended a quarter-horse sale in the Santa Ynez Valley near Solvang. Apparently, a man there had been buying many horses; he was very wealthy, with property in the Santa Ynez Valley and in Montecito, which is one of the four most expensive areas of California — comparable with Beverly Hills.

Dr Burns said that the man's name was Hastings Harcourt, son of the founder of the publishers Harcourt Brace & World.

Married, with a grown son, Mr Harcourt was in his sixties and was considered to be an eccentric millionaire.

Dr Burns said that he had been doing the veterinary work for Mr Harcourt's son and daughter-in-law, and that the many new horses he'd just bought had been sent to their property in the Santa Ynez Valley. He felt that Mr Harcourt would be interested in having some training done on a few of these new purchases — and he, Jim Burns, would be happy to recommend me to the family.

A few days later I received a telephone call from Mr Harcourt, and he indeed asked me if I would be interested in training his recent acquisitions. I replied in the affirmative, and within a day or so I was transporting three young quarter horses the 60 miles from Santa Ynez to Laurellinda.

After about a week, I gave Mr Harcourt a call to report on their progress. I told him that there was one three-year-old gelding in the group which impressed me as having significant talent to go into competition in an event in the Western pleasure-horse category. He seemed pleased with this report and invited me to meet him in person.

Pat and I drove down to the Santa Ynez Valley where Mr and Mrs Harcourt were basking in the sun at a property they owned there called Juniper Farms.

My first impression of him was that he was an unfortunate-looking man. He had a skin condition which meant the whole surface of his face was marked and pitted. In addition, he was overweight, and I was aware that his smile touched only his mouth; it never reached his eyes.

Mrs Harcourt seemed uninterested in our arrival, and I read her attitude as someone saying in response to her husband's new enthusiasm, 'Here we go again!'

Mr Harcourt said that if possible, he would like me to show a horse for him in the Santa

Barbara horse show which was only three months from that date.

Despite my first impression of him, he came across as a nice man enjoying the first flush of excitement at becoming involved in the horse business. Certainly, he was quick to admit that he knew nothing about horses.

I was grateful to him for his interest. He was sending me work that I needed badly and — according to my veterinarian — he had the wherewithal to become a significant owner.

So, the very next day I started to work towards showing his gelding, Travel's Echo, in that Santa Barbara show he'd mentioned.

It was difficult to expect a horse to compete favourably in a very high-calibre horse show with no more than 90 days' training, but I didn't let that thought dissuade me. I worked with a positive attitude and Travel's Echo responded in kind.

Both Pat and I had some nice horses to show in that particular event, so at least the Harcourts could see three world-class horses that his trainers were competing on even if his 'green' baby wasn't a great success yet. I had Johnny Tivio of course, who'd no doubt pull his usual trick of organising all the major trophies for himself, before he gave his attention to who should fill the reserve positions. Pat had Julia's Doll, already a well-established mare competing in the pleasure-horse division.

On the day itself, Mr and Mrs Harcourt turned up at the Earl Warren showground and hired an exclusive box seat in 'ring centre'. They had brought along a party of friends, and their position in the very middle of the arena gave them an intimate relationship with the ring. There were about 8 – 10 of them: mostly well-known faces in the Montecito society circuit. Certainly, they were as much on show as the horses.

Johnny Tivio put in his usual great performance, and I am sure the Harcourts were duly impressed. Night Mist was her sterling self, winning both her events. Pat's mare, Julia's Doll, was in top form and won with Pat in the saddle.

I was due to show Travel's Echo, the Harcourts' horse, in the Western pleasure-horse division which is open to horses of four and under.

Entering the arena, I was stunned when I saw that we were up against more than 50 competitors in that class. But Travel's Echo seemed to understand the importance of the day and performed as if he had had two years of concentrated training.

Watching us go through our paces, the Harcourts were talking to their friends, who understood the horse business better than they, referring to them for advice as to what was happening and how well their horse was doing.

As the event progressed, these friends apparently told them that they — the Harcourts — should not expect too much, since Travel's Echo was a young horse with only three months' training.

As it turned out, Travel's Echo defied them and he made the ten-horse final, which thrilled his owners and surprised their guests.

In the final run-off, he finished third to two of the nation's top competitors, defeating some horses who had already won many championships.

As I was riding forward to collect the trophy and the rosette for third place, I was square in front of their hired box. Their friends were all standing and applauding, while Mr and Mrs Harcourt were smiling from ear to ear and accepting the moment with great happiness.

We arrived at the 'out' gate almost at the same time. Pat and the children were there, and the Harcourts and their friends came to stand with Travel's Echo and pet him. Because of Mr Harcourt's standing in the community and the sums he'd given to charities, many photographs were taken. Journalists crowded around to report his enthusiasm. When they discovered that Travel's Echo had achieved his win with only 90 days' training, their pencils raced across the paper.

The success of Travel's Echo set up a mood of acceptance I had not experienced before.

Mr and Mrs Harcourt flew to San Luis Obispo within three days in their private plane, a 'taildragger' DC3. He wanted to see our operation and discuss a further involvement with us.

He said that he already owned a few thoroughbreds, but he had the feeling they weren't of the quality they needed to be. From behind his thick, black-rimmed glasses he asked me; 'Have you got any experience with the thoroughbred racing industry?'

I replied, 'We always had a few thoroughbreds in training, from the time I was growing up to the present day, but I've never been given the opportunity to get involved with the class of thoroughbred needed for top racing performances in California.'

Mr Harcourt made arrangements for me to be picked up by his plane within two days and flown to three different locations to see a selection of brood mares, three foals, two yearlings and two horses in training. He was right; as I reported back to him, they were not the kind of thoroughbreds that would give you an optimum chance to succeed on the California racetracks.

Shortly afterwards, Harcourt made his next move. He proposed sending me to the Del Mar thoroughbred yearling sale, and told me that I had a budget of $20,000 to buy a couple of yearlings of my choosing to race on the California scene.

He was offering me a chance in a lifetime, and I was incredibly excited. I had been purchasing a few thoroughbred yearlings for other clients who gave me limits of around $2,000 each for horses to run at the fair-tracks, extremely low-class racing. My purchases had done fairly well considering their breeding, and I was pleased that it seemed I had the ability to choose horses that could run and stay sound.

This prospect that Harcourt was now offering me, however, was in a different league, but I felt that Pat and I had the necessary talent and

238

he was a man who could give us the chance we needed to prove ourselves.

Mr Harcourt entered his name with the sales company, naming me as his agent in the normal way. He fixed the credit figure for $20,000 as agreed.

I went off to Del Mar, and will never forget the moment when I saw a chestnut colt walk by about 50 yards away. He caught my eye as no young thoroughbred had done previously. He had perfect symmetry and balance when he was stationary, and when he moved that symmetry and balance stayed in place in a way I hadn't seen before.

I went immediately to the stable where the chestnut was kept. I asked to see him, and on close inspection he proved even more impressive than I'd thought.

No one else seemed to figure him as that important. He was brought into the auction ring and I won the bidding at just $5,000. He didn't yet have a name. The hammer came down . . . he was mine.

The sales company representative brought the box round and I signed the receipt, 'Monty Roberts, Agent'. One copy of the receipt was kept by myself, the other went into the box.

For the first time, I was in business with Hastings Harcourt.

Soon we had a name for the chestnut colt: Sharivari, which in Gaelic means 'wedding celebration'.

In addition I'd purchased a bay colt for Mr Harcourt, which we called Bahroona. As it turned out, the bay was the more precocious of the two and was ready to run by June of the following year — 1965, when he won his first start at Hollywood Park by 15 open lengths.

Mr Harcourt was dizzy with excitement, though I wasn't at the race-track because I was competing at a rodeo event further up the country. He had provided me with his private plane and when he called to report Bahroona's success, he demanded that I fly directly to his home in Montecito because he was holding a party to celebrate his win.

The pilot and I took off, settling into the journey. Flying over Lake Cachuma, the engine died and we immediately started plummeting towards the water. I was certain we would die.

The pilot switched over to the second fuel tank and started the engine again, and we pulled out of the dive. This incident did nothing for my nerves, but it was curiously fitting. I did feel like I was riding a roller-coaster at this point.

I was picked up by the Harcourts at Santa Barbara airport and brought to their house where there was a party in full swing. Pat was already there.

There was the buzz of people talking and Hastings and his wife Fran were revelling in the many admiring glances they were receiving. Through the noise and laughter he shouted to me, 'We must have a major operation!'

I listened — the noise of the party seeming to recede as I latched on to his every word. 'I have property in the Santa Ynez Valley. What do you think of that area for creating a full-scale thoroughbred facility?'

It had been my life's dream to be a part of a horse operation in the Santa Ynez Valley. Feeling rather out of key, talking so seriously amidst the general hilarity of the party, I told him that the climate and the soil there were — in my opinion — superior to any place in the United States, and it would be a wonderful choice of location for a thoroughbred breeding and training farm.

Mr Harcourt was full of plans. 'Start studying the area,' he advised, 'and I will purchase enough property to encompass a world-class facility.'

The party was rolling and he was riding high on this early success. I responded immediately and went at it with the youthful enthusiasm you might have expected from a 31-year-old who had dreamed of doing just this for as far back as he could remember.

I had been educated for the task in hand from top to bottom. With my own extensive experience and with a triple major from Cal-Poly in just these subject areas, I knew about soils, forage grasses, fertilisation, facility design, conformation, pedigrees and, most of all, training techniques.

After only a few days of looking around the various properties Harcourt already owned in the Santa Ynez Valley, I knew none of them was right. One had too many trees on it, another was too stony, a third didn't have the water supply.

I advised him that for a top-flight operation we

needed to get alongside the river; I pinpointed an area just outside the town of Solvang and explained my case to him. It was a micro-valley 3 miles long by 1¼ miles wide. The bottom of the valley was almost dead level, and the topsoil averaged 17 feet in depth.

Even more importantly, underneath the topsoil was a generous layer of diatomaceous material — that is to say, a layer made up of microscopic sea-shells or crustaceans compressed and made into a chalky type of earth. Part of the valley had formerly been under the sea, thousands of years ago. This parent material released into the topsoil a considerable amount of calcium and other minerals.

In addition, underground aquifers — essentially fissures in the subterranean rock which held water — meant that from wells drilled only 55 feet deep, we could look forward to pumping up to 600 gallons of water per minute — an extremely desirable condition.

The climate also was perfect. There would be virtually no intolerable days. It's dry, and the influence of the nearby ocean kept it cooler in summer and warmer in winter.

Mr Harcourt began buying. He started off with only 100 acres from Mr Jacobson; then he began spreading out and making offers the neighbours couldn't refuse. He bought another 100 acres from Mr McGuire, a further 50 acres from Mr Petersen and so on.

Within 90 days we were surveying the parcels of land and initiating the design concepts. Mr Harcourt was as enthusiastic as I was and

242

devoted his considerable resources to making this facility happen as fast — and as big — as possible.

I visited Johnny Tivio in his stall at Laurellinda. 'OK, Johnny Tivio, you can start to live in the style to which you'd like to be accustomed. How about you draw up a plan for your own little palace?' If ever there was a working horse who thought he deserved to live on a classy thoroughbred establishment, he was the one.

In the middle of this frenzy of activity, I had a meeting planned with Mr Harcourt at his home in Montecito, Santa Barbara. But the day before the appointment was scheduled, I received a phone call from his private secretary. In a roundabout way, she indicated that he had had second thoughts about building the farm, and advised me to consider him out of the picture, so far as plans to develop any sizeable horse operation were concerned.

This was quite the strangest thing. Naturally, once it had sunk in I was devastated — I simply couldn't understand it. Only hours before, we'd been racing ahead as if his life depended on it.

I spent that night trying to figure out my next move. Whichever way I turned, there seemed to be no way ahead. Then I realised that the secretary hadn't said that my meeting with Mr Harcourt was cancelled — not exactly.

Since he hadn't contacted me himself, I decided to go to his home at the designated time as if I hadn't spoken to the secretary at all. At the very least, I would hear an explanation of his decision to withdraw from the man himself.

The next day I drove 100 miles to Montecito, Santa Barbara, with my heart in my mouth. I wasn't sure what was waiting for me at the other end of the journey.

Montecito, as I have mentioned, is as grand as Beverly Hills, and I was sweeping through tree-lined streets of unreal beauty.

When I stopped at the gates to his house to speak into the security intercom, I half expected to be refused entry, but the voice at the other end buzzed me through. I drove down the heavily wooded driveway, the gravel crunching under my tyres. This opened into a circular drive around a large fountain.

Everything was quiet. I had time to look around and see the place as though for the first time.

On the left was a guest-house, which in itself was nice enough. Centred on the south side of the circle was Harcourt's house — an example of the 1920s, early-Californian style. Looking at it more closely, I observed it had undergone many modifications and additions. It was an impressive residence.

I parked my car outside the guest-house and from there walked across to the front door of the main house, where I rang the bell and waited.

I had been let through the gate, so patently someone was in. I reminded myself that it was quite a long way to get from one end of such a large house to the other, so I waited longer than usual before ringing the bell for the second time.

No one came. It was deathly quiet.

After some minutes, I gave up hope and began to wander back to my car. I had one hand on my car-door handle when a sudden movement caught the corner of my eye.

I turned — and saw Mr Harcourt scuttle across an open area of ground on the other side of the fountain. I'd no sooner caught sight of him than he was gone, disappearing through a side door.

I was alarmed, because the pace of his movement implied that he was deliberately trying to avoid me. Then it occurred to me that perhaps he was hurrying into the house to be punctual for our meeting, so I approached the front door again and rang the bell. There was no answer. The house remained as silent and uninviting as before.

Bearing in mind the conversation I'd had with his secretary, I concluded I was *persona non grata*: it was all over. I got back in my car and drove 100 miles home to Laurellinda.

I had done everything right, but we were on a dead stop. I tried to call him that evening, but I received answers only from a maid who said he was not available.

Pat took the philosophical attitude that we should get on with our lives as if Mr Harcourt and his wife had never existed. Even if he did call to apologise, he was patently unstable and we should ignore him.

About four days later, as I was working horses, I got the message that there was a telephone call from Mr Harcourt. I dismounted and immediately went to the telephone, my intestines tied in knots.

He gave me a cordial greeting and apologised — he had been through a down-turn psychologically, and something untoward had happened in his family's publishing business.

However, he had sought professional counselling and now he'd fully rectified his negative experience and was ready to proceed with the farm again — at full throttle.

He asked me if I would fly to Europe to see the best horse operations there, and with the knowledge I'd gain I was then to press ahead with planning the facility as quickly as possible. Once more, he was very anxious to get up and going.

He also said, 'I want you to be more than a manager, more than a horseman. I want you to become the managing partners of Flag Is Up Farms, and for your input you should be entitled to five per cent of the operation going in and have the right to buy deeper into it as we progress. I will create a contract with you, and I will pay for the legal work. You should go to the offices of Anthony Romasanta and outline for him all that you want in the contract. I will read it, but you can create it.'

I did as instructed and outlined a contract which I believed to be fair and equitable to both sides.

Our whole family plunged into the effort to create the best thoroughbred facility anywhere. The sudden emotional shift was enormous. We were back on track again.

I got on a plane and flew to England, to hook up with Tim Vigors. He was a bloodstock agent and a gentleman farmer from Ireland and England, who had also been a fighter pilot in the Second World War.

The plan was that he would fly us to the best properties we could think of, for which we had at our disposal a 'Baladue' aircraft with the call sign GATSY.

We flew to Newmarket and landed on the gallops there, staying nearby as guests of Sir Noel Murless at his home, Warren Place. Then we flew to stud farms all round Britain and landed on most of the major racecourses. I made notes on the design and operation of the facilities we saw, and also took photographs.

Then we hopped across the Channel and landed in a little field near Paris, from where we made our way to Chantilly. We saw about ten different yards and naturally we were both amazed and impressed. The expanse of these places was amazing, and so was the attention to detail.

Next we went to Normandy, to a farm owned by Alec Head and Roland de Chambre, and we also visited the Guy de Rothschild breeding farm.

It was a whole university course in the design and management of racehorse facilities.

Then we flew from France to Germany, and on to Ireland. I'm not sure all this flying was strictly legal, but we did it anyway.

After about a week in Ireland visiting many of the race-tracks and breeding farms, we returned to London and from there I flew back to California, where I reported that it had been a very worthwhile experience.

While I'd been away, Mr Harcourt had been reading about operations in other parts of the world, so the next thing I knew I was going to Argentina, Australia and New Zealand on the same mission.

When I got back, I made a further report and final recommendations to him. I was ready now to sit down and design the property in earnest.

Both Pat and I prepared ourselves and our family for a 12 – 18-month cyclone of activity to plan, construct and open the operation of Flag Is Up Farms Incorporated, Solvang, California.

The property had four main areas.

First, there was a breeding and foaling facility with a stallion barn, breeding pens, a laboratory, a round pen, an office complex, an 8-stall foaling barn and residential quarters for up to 8 employees.

The second area was a training and starting facility for adolescents. This incorporated a covered riding arena, two covered round pens, box stalls for 80 horses, a practice race track, a 2½-mile cross-country gallop, three large hay and straw storage barns, a feed mill to make our own feed, a main office and residential quarters for up to 50 employees.

Thirdly, there was a hospital and rehabilitation area, which included space for 40 horses, a swimming pool for water therapy, an X-ray therapy facility, an office complex and turn-out paddocks, plus residential quarters for 6 employees.

Last of all, there was the main house which was sited on top of the 'mesa' or 150-foot rise on the north end of the property. It was designed in the early Californian tradition, though with much more glass than usual. From its position looking over the valley, it enjoyed extensive south-facing views, and all the principal rooms were sited on that side of the house with large windows.

Not only was my life's ambition taking shape in front of my very eyes; it was also a perfect home for my family. We were up and running!

We moved the first horses on to the farm in July of 1966. Johnny Tivio strolled in and booked the best room in the place, of course. He wasn't worried about it in the slightest; everyone else would have to fight amongst themselves.

Bahroona and Sharivari paired up and took second place — ornaments to any thoroughbred yard. Bahroona had proved to be a continued success — he won the major two-year-old stake at the Hollywood Park meet. He had blinding speed, and would later become a significant sire.

Sharivari entered the racing scene now as well — a bit later than Bahroona, but in fact he was the superior racehorse. He won his first start, won a stake in his second start and was the best three-year-old in California prior to the Kentucky Derby where he was the early book favourite. He would later become a champion sire many times.

In October of the same year our family moved into our beautiful new home overlooking the farm and the Santa Ynez Valley. As far as we were concerned, we'd stepped into paradise. Fortune had smiled on us and we'd grasped the opportunity to live this life with both hands. It was very hard work, but we were all happy doing it.

Around this time, a young man called Hector Valadez was sent to me. Eighteen years old and weighing about 80 pounds, he looked as if he might make a jockey.

I put him on his first horse that year and he has been riding 8 – 12 horses a day for me ever since, with the exception of a couple of short periods when he worked for friends of mine. As it turned out, he wasn't motivated to be a jockey.

He would go on to start a family in 1975, and he was always going to work hard at being a father. Now he has two grown sons, and he still weighs only 107 pounds.

Hector has spent more time with me in the round pen than any other person. While his size kept him useful on the training track, he has probably been the first rider up on about 1,500 horses during the nigh-on 30 years he's been with me.

Not long after we moved in, my father and mother visited us to inspect our new circumstances. I gave them a guided tour.

My father didn't like the fencing: 'Should have got oak from Kentucky and made plank fencing.' He also disapproved of all the trees I was planting: 'These trees are a mistake. Get in the way if you want to move anything around. You wait. They'll just knock your hat off every time you ride underneath.'

He thought the race-track should be bigger, and in his opinion the loft in the training barn was built wrongly. There should have been dirt underfoot in the aisle of the training barn, and too much money had been spent on the round pens.

Before he left, he advised me on my career. 'Keep a foot in the show-horse business; this racehorse thing will eat you up.'

Our horses were performing well and we won our share of the good races, mostly from horses which I had selected as yearlings. Gladwin, a beautiful First Landing colt purchased at Saratoga, was a Group I winner. Aladancer, from the first crop of Northern Dancer, also purchased at Saratoga, was a Group I winner too. Cathy Honey, a talented daughter of Francis S., was a high-weighted three-year-old filly in the US. *Petrone was purchased as a three-year-old in France for $150,000, later won over $400,000 and retired a multiple Group I winner.

The years from 1967 to 1970 were to be successful ones for Flag Is Up Farms.

One day, Mr Harcourt came to the house and started to confide in me about his psychological problems. He'd had a drink — and the talk turned into a real heart-to-heart.

He took off his thick-rimmed spectacles and suddenly his eyes were naked, watering with emotion. 'It's no way for anyone to live, having

251

this disease,' he exclaimed, striking his own chest. Then he described to me the effects of what he termed his 'bi-polar disease'. As a result of this condition, he'd suffered from manic depression from a very early age.

I felt sorry for him, but I didn't know how I could help. He went on to explain to me that it was this psychological problem which had driven him out of the family business and broken up countless business partnerships. People weren't willing to cope with him.

I sensed he was asking me to take him on, to look after him and understand his every whim, however illogical.

He continued with his morbid introspection. 'D'you know what,' he said to me, 'I've had thirty years of therapy? How does that sound?'

'Expensive.'

'It's ridiculous, a man of my age in therapy still.'

He also gave credit to his wife Fran for learning to cope with him better than anyone else, saying, 'She knows how to handle me. When I swing on the moon, she knows to draw me back down. When I'm stumbling through the cellar in the dark, she knows to bring me back up.'

In his business relationships, though, he said that people bumped up against these mood swings of his and were defeated by the experience. 'They're being logical, you know, when I'm not being logical.'

'Well, I suppose business is a logical sort of thing, more often than not.'

252

'D'you know, Monty,' he said suddenly — it was as though he wasn't listening to what I was saying, he was wanting to get something off his chest — 'my relationship with your family and what we're doing at Flag Is Up Farms is the most important thing in my life, and I don't want to encounter these problems with you.'

'I agree,' I said — and I meant it. I didn't want any part of his psychological problems to interfere with what we were doing. We'd already had a hint of it, and it had been devastating.

'I want you to know how to handle me. If we can do this, I see our relationship lasting all my days.'

'Well, I'd like that, too.'

'I tell you what,' he suggested, 'I'll make an appointment for you to visit my psychiatrist; I'll pay for it. You can learn from him how to track me. I'm confident your intelligence will allow you to do that. You'll be just like Fran.'

I felt relieved that the situation was out in the open and that a plan of sorts was being made to cope with it. I also felt a weight of responsibility for this sorry man.

Mr Harcourt did as he said he would, and made an appointment for me to visit his psychiatrist in Santa Barbara medical centre. He was a man in his late forties, lean, 6ft tall, with a genuine, sophisticated and soft-spoken manner.

The psychiatrist wasn't pleased to be holding this conference, and he checked our perceptions as to why we were here in his office quite carefully; in fact, on my first visit that's all he did. I would guess he was worried about breaching confidentiality, even with Mr Harcourt's consent.

On my second visit it became clear that he knew everything about Pat and me. His knowledge of our background and our families was extensive and accurate.

Then he said a curious thing. He described Mr Harcourt's condition as 'sandcastle syndrome'. He went on, 'A child takes great pleasure in building a magnificent sandcastle just at the water's edge. But that child then reaches even greater heights of excitement when the tide comes in . . . and destroys it.'

He waited as I took this in; then he added, 'And the larger the sandcastle, the more excitement there is for Mr Harcourt in seeing it destroyed.'

Standing on the terrace later that same evening, I looked down on the barns and other facilities carefully positioned on a broad stretch of flat land in the valley, caught now in the last rays from the sun lowering over the mountains beyond, and I remembered Mr Harcourt's wild enthusiasm and his total dedication and absorption in the project as we'd planned and built every part of it — and then I knew we'd built a sandcastle for Mr Hastings Harcourt.

In September of 1971, I was at the racecourse in Del Mar, California, 250 miles from Flag Is Up Farms, when I received a call saying that the plane would pick me up and fly me back to the farm. Mr Harcourt wanted to see me that afternoon.

I arrived at Flag Is Up at about 2 o'clock. Mr Harcourt and another man called Osborne T. Brazelton III were already waiting for me in a car outside my house. Pat was out with the children, so I was to face them alone. The lady who was helping us with house duties fixed coffee and tea and served it on the back patio overlooking the farm.

They seemed to choose the seating arrangements carefully. I was alone on one side of the table, while they were sitting together on the opposite side. Harcourt was in a stern, sombre mood, the impression aided by the thick-rimmed black spectacles he wore and his terrible skin condition.

Osborne T. Brazelton III was a brash, show-business-type attorney. Like Harcourt, he was a huge man, standing about 6ft 5 inches, with blond hair carefully groomed and sprayed to a lacquer finish. Dressed in a custom-made suit cut from modern materials with glittering threads pulled through, he was young — only about 30 years of age.

The pair of them faced up to me from across the table. Harcourt then produced from his jacket pocket a silver pill-box which he placed on the table between us. He opened it to expose about 20 tablets of varying colours, shapes and sizes.

He looked at me . . . and the hairs stood up on the back of my neck. It was a piercing, cold and ominous look which chilled me to the bone. I realised that what we'd been dreading was about to happen.

Harcourt said, 'I just want you to realise that it takes me this many pills to get through a day. You know my doctor and you know my problems. I won't bore you with a lot of the details, but I am sure that you realise I am in a grave condition.'

He paused, but I made no response, and he continued, 'I must sell the farm and all the horses as soon as possible. It is devastating to me, but it must be done. I am saddened to give up my farm and my horses, but particularly it is painful to give up my relationship with you, Pat and your family. You have been an important part of our lives for almost six years now, but where my health is concerned I can let no one get in the way.'

I knew the signs. Mr Hastings Harcourt was about to go into free fall.

He went on with his pronouncement. 'Os Brazelton here has taken over my legal problems, and he will co-ordinate with you over the disposition of all the assets. If you can find someone to buy the farm, obviously then you could remain here under similar circumstances and possibly that same person would be interested in buying some or all of the horses. Whatever I can do to assist in your quest to keep the farm together, I will do, so long as I can get out of everything very soon. I will leave you now and wait in the car for Os, who will explain to you some of my ideas for disposition.'

Having delivered his speech, Hastings Harcourt stood up and walked round the table towards me with his arms outstretched. I stood and waited while he threw his arms around me and squeezed me, saying, 'I'm sorry. I have failed you and your family, but this must be done.'

Then turned and disappeared through the house, leaving his coffee untouched on the table.

I felt sorry for this poor old man. I experienced an inexplicable wonder — awe, even — that such a destructive psychology could exist and continue to take effect, even in a man who knew himself and could afford the best possible treatment. As far as I was concerned, though, perhaps it would be better working for a different owner who hopefully wouldn't bring such a complicated psychological infrastructure to what should be an enjoyable professional relationship between owner and manager/trainer. All this might turn out for the best, depending on what this lawyer, Os Brazelton, had to say.

Brazelton now ordered me to sit down in no uncertain manner. 'I want to go over a few things with you.'

I complied, feeling like a student in the principal's office — a weird feeling for me, since he was about six years my junior.

Brazelton announced, 'I'm getting Mr Harcourt out of this thing in short order, so don't get in my way. We can work together on this, and I can help you make the transition.'

I waited to hear his suggestions.

He continued, 'Mr Harcourt has made it clear to me that he feels the people in this industry would be more responsive to buying the property and horses if you remain involved in the sale. Your reputation and approval will bring significant value to the deal and increase the speed with which we can push it through.'

'Fair enough.'

'He would like you to explain to any potential purchaser that you have a five per cent interest in the property, money they wouldn't have to come up with. You should also say to them that you will buy in on the horses to at least ten per cent, and then Mr Harcourt would not require you to pay that ten per cent. So you would end up with ten per cent in the horses as a commission.'

'That's fine, thank you.' I prayed it was going to be as easy as this — it looked like we had our escape route and Harcourt was acting sensibly.

Brazelton added, 'He might even consider fifteen or twenty per cent, depending on price and conditions.'

'That's fair.'

'Meanwhile,' continued the attorney, 'we want an immediate list of horses you would not be interested in buying into, as they will be consigned to the earliest sale possible.'

'I'll do that right away.'

Then Brazelton dropped the first bombshell. 'In addition to this, Mr Harcourt has instructed me to tell you that he wants his riding horse, called Travel's Echo, shot dead . . . and disposed of.'

His words stopped me. Up to that point, I was happy to go along with the sale and hope that my professional services would be retained by whoever bought the property. Suddenly, there was a whole new ball-game going on here. Harcourt wanted Travel's Echo shot dead? Filled with disbelief and sadness, one big question came into my head: 'Why on earth — '

Brazelton interrupted, 'Mr Harcourt doesn't want anyone else to have Travel's Echo. He wishes you personally to shoot him, rather than have him go to another home.'

I didn't say anything, I remained utterly confused. This idea of not wanting him to go to anyone else was a sentimental notion, but there was such a cruel sting in the tail to it, which made it illogical — and suddenly I remembered Harcourt's words: 'They're being logical, when I'm not being logical . . . '

I couldn't bear it. I had a sudden picture of Travel's Echo doing so well for the Harcourts at that first show almost five years ago . . . and their smiles as they accepted the applause from the group of friends around them.

Os Brazelton went on, 'He also wants you personally to shoot Mrs Harcourt's driving ponies.'

Mrs Harcourt had bought a pair of driving ponies which she thought she might like to come out and use from time to time. But she had never turned up, and the ponies were kept in good condition by the Flag Is Up staff.

Brazelton repeated, 'She, also, doesn't wish them to go to anyone else.'

He paused and consulted some papers in front of him before going on, 'Mr Harcourt has also been extremely disappointed with the performance of two horses, Veiled Wonder and Cherokee Arrow. He wants you to shoot them, preferably today. He does not want you to try to sell them to someone else; he feels they have disgraced him because he had high hopes for their performance and they let him down.'

This had turned into the firestorm, the meltdown I'd been waiting for. I no longer felt amazement, or sorrow, or incomprehension. I felt anger and determination. I *wouldn't* let this happen. I'd save these horses from being slaughtered by this troubled man and his hired-gun lawyers, somehow. No horse that I looked after was going to be sacrificed on the whim of an unstable man and his capacity to buy the power of legal process.

At that point Brazelton rose to his feet and prepared to go. He finished by saying, 'I will be in touch with you on a daily basis to facilitate the disposal.'

Then he turned and walked through the house, and I heard the door shut with a click. He'd be going to the car where Mr Harcourt was waiting for him.

I was left sitting on the patio overlooking the farm I had created, feeling hollowed out with shock.

However, I knew one thing — I didn't have time to feel sorry for myself, because if I didn't move quickly things would be taken out of my hands. I walked back and forth, thinking what to do. I was empowered to sign papers, so there were options open to me; I had to figure out a way to save the lives of these animals.

Brazelton's words rang in my head: ' . . . disappointed with their performance . . . a disgrace . . . ' Cherokee Arrow and Veiled Wonder were vital, young, well-bred, stakes-winning colts, who had only 'disappointed' us because we had set our hopes extremely high for them.

I went down to their stalls and looked over them. It was painful to think how unaware they were of what was happening. I reassured them, stroking their muzzles and trying to think meanwhile what to do for the best.

I went across to the Flag Is Up office and rifled through some paperwork. Just a month before, we'd had Veiled Wonder and Cherokee Arrow appraised along with all the other Harcourt horses. I checked closely, and it was as I thought; Veiled Wonder had been appraised at $3,500 and Cherokee Arrow at $3,000.

The only thing I could do was to sell them — right now, this instant — making sure that the money was logged into the Flag Is Up accounts in the usual way, because I couldn't leave myself open to the accusation that I'd stolen them.

I called a friend immediately and asked him to send me a cheque for $6,500, naming the two horses. I promised him I'd get the money back to him. He agreed, and I immediately made arrangements to ship both horses to England where they would go into quarantine before shipping on to New Zealand, to Alton Lodge where Sharivari and Bahroona were standing at stud.

As they were taken from their stables and loaded up in the van, they naturally accepted it as a fairly routine journey. They didn't know they were going to the other side of the world, nor that they'd just escaped certain death. They were relaxed, in superb condition, walking into the van with their ears forward.

I felt renewed incomprehension at Mr Harcourt's actions. What was going on inside that man's head? And how would he react if he found out I'd refused to destroy his horses?

As a matter of ethics, although his instructions had been disobeyed there was no wrong done to Harcourt as the farm received their full appraised value. I took the position that he was a sick man making irrational decisions, and I simply could not allow the animals to be the victims of this malady.

Next, I had to deal with the driving ponies. I telephoned a lady whom I knew could give them a good home, and she was at the farm within an hour to take them away. I led them out of their stalls and into the van. They were cheerful little creatures who'd been under-used for some time; hopefully they'd have a better life now.

Then I called a nearby neighbour. 'Can I park a horse with you, in secret?'

'What's going on?'

'I can't tell you, but if you can trust me that this horse's life's in danger, then will you take him and not tell a soul?'

'Well, OK, I guess so.'

'You've saved his life.'

'Send him over, then. What's his name?'

'It's best if I don't tell you.'

I led Travel's Echo out of his stall and loaded him into one of our vans. He was driven less than a mile away, to be hidden until some sense could be made of these events.

This frenzy of activity occupied me through the afternoon and well into the night. I finished by visiting Johnny Tivio in his stall, just to touch base, to check he was still there, alive and well. As usual his stall was in immaculate condition, the dung all in a neat pile in one corner out of the way. He hardly ever urinated in his stall. I said to him, 'You're almost house-trained, aren't you, boy? You want to come and live with us in the house, a room of your own, huh?'

He regarded me silently, impassively. Often it felt like it was me working for him, instead of vice-versa.

Early the following morning, I received a telephone call.

'Mr Roberts?' It was a woman's voice, normal and unconcerned, the sort of voice you'd hear on the other end of some complaint you were making about a dishwasher you'd bought which didn't work.

'Speaking.'

'I'm calling on behalf of Hastings Harcourt.'

'Yes.'

'Can you confirm for me that the horse named Travel's Echo has been destroyed?'

I needed to lie, but I found it sticking in my throat. I'd never been in a situation where it was demanded of me to deceive anyone. Yet now it was utterly important.

'Yes, he's gone.'

'And the two colts, Veiled Wonder and Cherokee Arrow, have they also been destroyed?'

'Yes, I can confirm they've gone too.'

'And can you confirm that Mrs Harcourt's driving ponies have also been destroyed?'

'Yes. They're no longer here.'

'And lastly, I need to confirm that you personally undertook the disposal of these animals.'

'Yes.'

'Thank you, Mr Roberts.' The phone clicked and the disembodied voice had gone.

★ ★ ★

The next few months were chaos for us as we prepared brood mares, yearlings, foals and racehorses for sales conducted in a radius of 3,000 miles.

The children were now 10, 12 and 14 years old, and had a difficult time making any sense of what was going on — and I must say they weren't alone in that.

I immediately started to contact people in the horse business, endeavouring to attract a buyer for Flag Is Up Farms as a going concern. We were fighting for our lives, with Os Brazelton and the Harcourts breathing down our necks. If we failed to find new owners quickly enough, I knew Flag Is Up Farms would be broken up and sold in lots.

Although the whole family was tense and worried over what was happening at Flag Is

Up, I was reasonably confident that things were going well. I had avoided having to shoot the animals, and Harcourt had obviously believed me because no one was out looking for where they were. There was also — fingers crossed — perhaps an interested buyer who might be able to purchase the ongoing business of Flag Is Up — a Mr Greenbaum, from Los Angeles.

Meanwhile, we tried to continue with some semblance of normality, though it wasn't always possible.

Two months later, in the first week of December of that year, Rudolf Greenbaum finally agreed to buy Flag Is Up, as well as 12 yearlings, the two stallions Gladwin and *Petrone, the rolling-stock and the equipment — in other words, the ongoing business.

The price was negotiated, and by the third week in December an escrow was opened at a title insurance company in Santa Barbara. Mr Greenbaum deposited $200,000 into the escrow account; the deal was done.

We were safe — and not only that, we were on a better footing than before, since we'd no longer have to worry about the psychological problems of Hastings and Fran Harcourt.

Then the story twisted back to worse news.

On 3 January 1972, I got a call from Brazelton to say that everything was on hold and that I should be prepared to meet him in my office on Flag Is Up.

He arrived with a large briefcase and came into my office, asking me to sit at my desk while he paced the room delivering what seemed to be

265

a well-rehearsed speech.

'Mr Harcourt is very upset,' he began. 'He has discovered that you didn't shoot Veiled Wonder and Cherokee Arrow, and that you had a friend buy them only to transfer them to your name. It looks as though you stole them.'

'I paid their fair market value,' I said, 'and since he wanted to shoot them, he got $6,500 more than he should have.'

Brazelton paused and then said quietly, 'By the time I get through with it . . . I'll make you look like Jesse James.'

I saw what was happening. None of this was about the property, or the horses, or the money, or about our family. This was the sandcastle syndrome. The sale of the farm had gone too smoothly; Mr Harcourt hadn't made enough waves, yet.

I sat there, thinking how impossible it was that I had been caught up in this scenario. It really was unbelievable. I didn't want to be branded a horse-thief, I didn't want to shoot horses, and I didn't want to go to court for this man — I wanted to go for a ride on Johnny Tivio and forget all about it.

Instead, I was arrested on a charge of being a horse-thief and Mr Harcourt put all his considerable resources into a sustained persecution of myself and my family. I found myself sitting in a jail cell, my case making headline news throughout the western United States, my good name destroyed in the press coverage, my family worried sick and our future destroyed.

As I sat amongst a gaggle of other prisoners, all sticks thrown to the wind and bundled together behind bars awaiting bail proceedings, it amused me to remember the last time I'd seen the inside of a jail.

Seven years previously, in 1964, I was driving a brand-new car, an Oldsmobile 98 in gunmetal blue. I was driving with Hoss Dilday and we were hauling a two-horse trailer with Johnny Tivio and Night Mist inside. It was 550 miles from one show to the next.

This Oldsmobile was a gorgeous thing to drive. I was playing some Tijuana Brass tapes someone had just given me, and we were happy. I thought that was the most wonderful music; it was such a good feeling to drive down the open road and listen to Herb Alpert and the Tijuana Brass. There we were, just out of Huron with the two greatest horses that ever lived and this brand-new Oldsmobile. I said to Hoss, 'This must be the nicest car I've ever had, it's such a pleasure to drive. Isn't this the greatest life?'

The words were no sooner out of my mouth than there was an enormous explosion under the hood of the car. A blast of fire came out from under the dashboard and ran right up in front of Hoss and me. I looked over at Hoss, who was absolutely white with fear.

I slid the car off the road. The fire was raging in the engine compartment and flames were coming out of the hood.

The first thing I did was grab my Herb Alpert tapes and throw them clear into the desert. Hoss jumped out on the passenger side, then

I jumped out on the left side with the keys in my hand because I was thinking about the horses — Johnny Tivio!

By now the flames were building up through the front-seat area. Also, there was a trail of fire back along the highway where, I guess, we'd spilled fuel, so naturally I was thinking about the fuel tank.

Hoss started grabbing equipment while I ran around, opened the tail-gate and backed the horses out. I trotted them into the desert while Hoss was bringing along the saddles and tack.

While Hoss held the horses I ran back and unhooked the trailer, putting my shoulder to it and pushing it away from the Oldsmobile, so that if the car exploded at least we'd have saved the trailer. The wheel on the front of the trailer worked pretty well, and I was able to get it back about 10 feet from the car.

A man who had gone by in a pick-up, headed towards Huron, had yelled out that he would call the fire department. It seemed no more than two or three minutes before we had the horses safely out in the desert along with the saddles, bridles and, of course, my Tijuana Brass tapes!

Naturally, as soon as Johnny Tivio was out he took control of the situation. This entire event was for his benefit, and he'd have liked us to provide a little more in the way of refreshments. He wasn't sure he'd got the best seats, and in general there were quite a few complaints to the management.

By now the flames were really taking the car over; they were completely through the passenger compartment. The right front tyre blew, and after that the rubber really started to burn. The car became a torch.

Just after that, I heard sirens in the distance and out of Huron came the most incredible fire-truck you could imagine, although naturally Johnny Tivio wasn't that impressed with it. Probably built in the 1930s, it looked right out of a Hollywood movie, with ladders and men hanging all over it. These fellows were all just wearing undershirts in the heat and they parked the truck in the middle of the road, put the red light on and stopped any traffic. It took 4 – 5 minutes to fire up the pumps and get the water going. Within 2 – 3 minutes they had the flames out, but by this time the car looked like a marshmallow — there wasn't a lot of it left.

The fellow who'd gone by in the pick-up came back, got some of the fire department's men to help him hook up my trailer to his truck and put my equipment in the back of the pick-up. He said he'd give us a ride back to town with Johnny Tivio and Night Mist.

He'd already talked to the police, and apparently they had a vacant lot next to the police station where we could park the trailer, tie the horses to the side and give them some feed and water. We could call for help from there.

As it turned out, our saviour in the pick-up was a fan of Johnny Tivio and had seen him often in horse shows. He couldn't believe that this was the horse he'd rescued.

By the time we had unloaded the horses and unhooked the trailer just next to the tiny police station, it was late at night. We tied the horses to the side of the trailer and Hoss stayed with them.

I went into the police station, which was about the size of a box stall, and called Pat in San Luis Obispo, awakening her from a sound sleep to tell her what had happened.

After that, I asked the police officer if there was any chance of getting a room for the night. He said, 'Well, there's nothing in town except a brothel with a girl in every room.'

I shook my head.

'Well, you're welcome to sleep on the bunks in the cells here, if you want . . . '

Then he showed me to my cell.

So we slept the night in Huron jail!

The cheerfulness of that occasion — and the helpfulness of everyone around us — brought home to me how unfair my incarceration was now.

As I sat waiting in my cell, I remembered arriving home all those years ago where there was a letter waiting for me. Please could I be sure to take the Oldsmobile back to the garage for an adjustment? A fault had been found which could possibly lead to an engine fire!

Someone was saying my name now, so I was brought out of my reverie and turned to see a deputy at the doorway, 'Come with me,' he said.

As we were walking down the hallway and out of the hearing of the other prisoners, he said, 'I don't understand this. Somehow a private citizen has been able to convince someone that

270

they should get a telephone call straight through to you. Normally this is not allowed, but I have orders to let this man talk to you.'

We entered a small room, where there was a phone on the wall with another deputy holding the receiver towards me. It had to be Harcourt on the other end of the line, I thought. Only he had the power to trample through the rule book. I took the phone from the deputy's hand.

'Hello?' I said.

'Hello,' said the voice on the other end of the line. 'This is Glen Cornelius.'

'Glen!?' It was amazing to hear a voice I knew, the voice of a friend and a good man.

He didn't waste any time. 'I'm about to go to a meeting at your home. I want you to know that a group of people in the community believe in you and want to stop Harcourt.'

Then he went straight on to ask, 'Did you steal those two horses?'

I said, 'No, I took nothing from him.'

'Well, they want $50,000 bail money to get you out of there, and I am sitting here in my front room with that amount in cash in a shopping bag. I'm going to this meeting at your home, and then I plan to drive over there and get you out.'

With this sudden message of support arriving out of the blue, my heart filled with hope. The up and down of it was more than I could bear. The group of people who attended that meeting in our support included Marge and Vince Evans, George and Kathy Smith, John and Glory Bacon, Dr Jack and Cae Algeo, Peggy and

271

Slick Gardner, Raymond and Rosalie Cornelius, as well as Glen and Ora Cornelius.

These were our friends, and they fought for us.

When I got out of jail on the following day, Flag Is Up was surrounded by powerful searchlights and security guards in Harcourt's employ were posted all around the house. Our lawyers advised us to leave the property immediately.

We had no vehicles, as they had all belonged to Flag Is Up, so we were left stranded for transportation. Slick, Mrs Gardner's son, arrived within a matter of minutes; while he didn't have a trailer, he started to help Pat load the things we'd need to set up housekeeping on the Gardner ranch.

I ran down to the stables and immediately saddled Johnny Tivio, Jess and Cadillac, the three horses I knew we had to get away from Flag is Up.

While I was saddling Johnny Tivio, one of my office staff came to say that the horses should remain on Flag Is Up until everybody knew who they really belonged to.

I smiled at her and continued to saddle. She knew who these three horses belonged to . . . knew that Harcourt was trying to have animals shot and killed left, right and centre . . . knew that a whole army of people could not separate me from Johnny Tivio, short of burying me a distance from him.

I put as much of my tack and equipment as I could on my three horses. Then I mounted

Johnny Tivio and led the other two down the long straight drive, past the buildings which I'd so carefully planned and the paddocks I'd cultivated over the past six years. It looked peaceful and well-ordered, and its beauty had the usual effect on me — I was proud of it. I'd built those fences that were now like straight lines running across the pastures. I'd laid out the design of those buildings and tapped the water. Those horses grazing in the paddocks — some of them I was training, some I'd started or was about to start. I thought in amazement, They don't know our troubles, and we don't know enough about their troubles — but I wanted to, and felt renewed resolve to concentrate on my work, developing my abilities with remedial animals and refining my techniques in starting young horses.

The acres spread out on each side of me would exist long after Harcourt was dead and gone, and long after I was dead and gone too. This beautiful valley would weather all the injuries which mankind tried to inflict on it.

Johnny Tivio clip-clopped along, wondering where he was going on this unusual journey, but in charge of everyone as always, his ears flicking back and forth, half listening to me and half checking out what was ahead. Johnny Tivio's self-confidence, his belief in himself and his natural superiority to everyone around him seemed to me at that moment like gold-dust — something magical and priceless. I loved this horse.

As I rode out of the gate, I wondered when

273

this blight on our lives would end. I wondered if I'd ever turn into Flag Is Up again — a place I'd found, designed and built, taking eight years out of my life to achieve it.

I reined Johnny Tivio right on the highway, and after only a few hundred yards we ducked into the entrance to the Gardner ranch, trailing Jess and Cadillac on their lead ropes.

I rode on up the driveway feeling greater relief with each and every step that Johnny Tivio took to carry me away from our troubles, and as we neared the collection of white buildings perched on the side of the mountain which together constitute the Gardner ranch, I was grateful to Peggy and Slick for their immediate offer of a safe haven. I had no idea how long we'd be there — if it would be for a day, a week or a year.

During the following year, the case against me began to unravel. Harcourt and his lawyers could only bring misdemeanour charges against me on the issue of Veiled Wonder and Cherokee Arrow. They were still pressing for a charge of theft, but since I hadn't profited from disobeying instructions on these two animals, their case was incredibly slim, so in reality they would only be able to bring this misdemeanour charge.

There followed a long-drawn-out legal battle, with many factions lining up on different sides.

Greenbaum, the man who thought he'd bought Flag Is Up, was suing Harcourt for $10 million.

The Hollister firm of attorneys filed a law-suit on my behalf against Harcourt for $30 million, for wrongful prosecution. Pat and I had to talk to more attorneys than we've had hot dinners.

Harcourt was trying to press charges against me for theft, and paying everyone left, right and centre to ensure he won his case.

David Minier, the district attorney, having washed his hands of the whole fiasco, announced that he was a candidate for the governership of California.

Documents relating to Flag Is Up were either buried or resurrected by the two ladies in the office, at the whim of Harcourt's lawyers.

I was at the centre of litigation the likes of which I never want to hear about ever again. It is too exhausting to contemplate describing it, and certainly no one should be forced to read about it.

The upshot of all this shouting and posturing was that an elderly judge was hauled out of retirement to sort us all out.

C. Douglas Smith was a slight, grey-haired man, distinguished-looking, with a deliberate manner and a cool gaze from behind his spectacles.

As we went into the room with him, everyone was angling for their particular side.

The Hollister firm wanted their shot at Harcourt for the full $30 million.

My criminal attorney wanted a no-felony victory.

Os Brazelton wanted to retain his licence to practise law.

Harcourt had a fight on his hands to stay out of jail himself now, for malicious prosecution.

The judge listened to the shouting match which ensued, then he cut through everyone and called for silence. He announced that he had read depositions and evidentiary documents and he did not see a felony here at all — at least, not on the part of the accused.

Pointing directly at me, he said, 'I want to see that man smile.'

I liked this judge. I *wanted* to smile. It seemed like a long time since I'd last done it.

I sat back and waited.

★ ★ ★

As soon as Mr Harcourt realised how flimsy his case was, he began to panic and started selling off pieces of Flag Is Up Farms for much less than their real value.

In the end, my attorneys came to me and said that they had a deal. They weren't sure it was good enough, but they were obliged to outline it for me.

I was to plead a *nolo contendere* to a misdemeanour — not a felony — for refusing to shoot Veiled Wonder and Cherokee Arrow and signing the papers over to myself, even though I paid the full $6,500 appraised value for them. They said this had to happen if I wanted to avoid going through a full trial.

If I wanted to take my persecutors to court, I'd have to wrestle with Harcourt's lawyers maybe for a number of years.

It was agreed that the two horses in question, Veiled Wonder and Cherokee Arrow, would be

276

given to me by Harcourt, as final proof that I had committed no intrinsic wrong in the transaction, although I was admitting to a misdemeanour. When I heard that part, I felt a smile begin to creep over my expression. It had been worth it, maybe, just to see that pair of animals back at Flag Is Up, blissfully unaware of the trouble they'd caused me. I couldn't wait to give them a piece of my mind.

All other charges would be dropped and the California Horse Racing Board agreed that my licence would immediately be restored and a letter of apology be sent to me.

Last but not least, Flag Is Up Farms was ours. The compensation paid to us by Harcourt for the malicious prosecution allowed us to buy our farm back. It was all over. We could go home.

★ ★ ★

By this time a year had passed since Pat and I, Debbie, Lori and Marty had left Flag Is Up.

While we were staying at the Gardner ranch, we'd fitted out that old barn pretty well, and for Johnny Tivio, Jess and Cadillac it had been like their home. Now I loaded them up in the van, and drove them back the short distance to Flag Is Up.

Johnny Tivio was interested to see that he had his old stall back. I'm sure it didn't occur to him that he couldn't have strolled back in here whenever he'd liked, but he was definitely pleased to see the old place again, with its gracious stabling and the sense of space in the paddocks laid side by side over the bed of this beautiful valley.

When Pat and I and the children walked back into our house at Flag Is Up, it was like a big old dusty barn which had stood empty for 100 years, rather than a mere 12 months.

There was no furniture in it, and echoes resounded as we walked over the wooden floors. Cobwebs hung from the rafters, and there was the eerie presence of the events which had preceded our departure.

We switched on the electricity supply and the plumbing. We opened the windows and blew some life into the place. We rang up the storage company and arranged to have our furniture delivered.

Pat started painting pictures like mad and hung them all over the house. She wanted to bring some light and colour back into our lives.

We walked the farm, reintroducing ourselves to each paddock and building. Some of the outer reaches and the site containing the breeding barn had been sold off, but the core of it remained the same as ever.

After a while, we began to believe that Flag Is Up was ours and that we were beginning to mend, as a family. Johnny Tivio was back in his stable and we were our own bosses. This was a new beginning.

I was keen to get back to what I was good at: horses. Perhaps it was this renewed energy that led me to being over-zealous and making a crucial error of judgement with a horse called Fancy Heels.

I'd been talking to our friends Dave and Sue Abel of Elko, Nevada, about coming to the Elko horse show to look over a very large contingent of reined cow horses which compete there every year. These horses come from ranches where they work long hours each day, honing their skills without suffering the drudgery of exercises specifically geared for the show-ring, which tends to make horses resent their job. So, there are often wonderful equine athletes to be found at the Elko show, with sound work ethics and good attitudes.

I soon spotted a horse at the show who impressed me very much. His name was Fancy Heels, and he showed an enormous amount of cow sense and a good athletic ability, with a light, responsive mouth. I thought that if I brought him back to California, I could possibly improve him enough to win some of the major competitions. I didn't think he'd need a lot of work — just a touch here and there would go a long way and turn him from a good working horse to a top show-horse.

Fancy Heels won his class at the Elko show on the Saturday, which earned him a place in the championship on the Sunday, a contest held between the top horses from the different classes.

However, I was anxious to buy him before he started winning any championships outright, so that afternoon Dave Abel and I went round to his stall so that I could be introduced to his owner, Randy Bunch.

'Well, he's for sale all right,' said Randy.

'That's why I brought him to town in the first place. I'd rather be on the ranch right now, but I needed to sell him.'

'How much d'you want for him?'

Randy waited for a moment before saying, '$3,500'.

I was surprised at this low figure, and agreed immediately. We shook hands and I wrote him a cheque.

'You looking forward to the championship tomorrow, just the same?' I queried.

'Uh-uh. Hang on. You own the horse; you show him tomorrow.'

Startled, I said, 'Now wait a minute, I've never even sat on him yet, and I don't have any clothes or equipment even.'

Randy pointed his finger at me and said, 'Come here. I want to show you something.' Fancy Heels shifted to one side as we walked to the back of his stall.

Randy raked back the bedding from one corner and hidden there was a half-empty bottle of Jim Beam whisky. He reached down, picked up the bottle and held it between us. 'That's how much whisky it took to get me through the elimination classes. I don't intend to have to drink the rest of it to get through the championship. I came to town to sell him, I've sold him and now I'm going to be back on the ranch before ten o'clock tonight. Good luck with him — you're showing him.'

I looked across at Dave Abel, wearing an expression that called for his help. Dave shrugged, 'That's the way people are up here,

Monty. I guess you're gonna show the horse. We can find you a pair of chaps and a bridle.'

I rode Fancy Heels for an hour or so that night, just to get the measure of him. The following morning, also, I rode him for about half an hour to warm him up.

The next I knew, I was in the arena, riding into the herd to work a cow on a horse I'd sat on for less than two hours.

Our herd work was pretty good and Fancy Heels was leading the competition going into the single cow phase. Our single cow work was acceptable, but had some rough spots in it. After this came the dry work — the stops and turns done without working any animals whether singly or in a herd. We did OK in the dry work, and came out second overall in the championship.

I arranged for Fancy Heels to be shipped back to Flag Is Up Farms, California — and I couldn't wait to start work on him and take him into open national competition.

After about a week of working with Fancy Heels, I gained a lot of respect for Randy Bunch. It was clear that the changes necessary were going to be harder to effect than I'd realised. This was a mature, well-established working horse, and I couldn't find my way forward with him.

After a month, I would say that Fancy Heels was 10 per cent *less* effective than he was on that Sunday at the Elko show.

After two months, he was 20 per cent less effective. I thought, 'Hang on, I'm a major trainer of thoroughbred racehorses as well as several world champion working horses, including the legendary Johnny Tivio. I know I can get this job done.'

After three months of work, and then four months, I had to conclude that I'd taken Fancy Heels backwards so enormously that — for his sake — I had to tell myself I'd failed and call it a day. It was the kindest thing I could do, to sell him to a good ranch home where he could go back to the work he enjoyed.

I've no idea how many times it was, during the many hours I rode Fancy Heels, that I told myself, 'You can't teach an old dog new tricks,' but certainly it was a fair number.

In fact, you *can* teach a dog new tricks, but I just wasn't doing it the right way. I was so keen to get to work on him that I came home with the attitude that I could force rapid changes on him. I took him off his game and pressed for what I wanted, for what I perceived as a standard of excellence, without taking his feelings into account. It just didn't work.

If I had the chance to work with Fancy Heels again, I wouldn't set a time frame for making changes and demand that he stick to it. He taught me to respect horses and not to demand immediate perfection. As far as I was concerned, I failed him, but I did learn from the experience. I'm convinced that in the 20 years since then the hundreds of remedial horses I've worked with have benefited from the lessons taught me by Fancy Heels.

★ ★ ★

In 1974, I received the worst kind of telephone call.

'Monty?'

'Yes.'

'Crawford's taken a bad fall. Broken his neck.'

My old friend Crawford Hall was lying severely injured in an intensive-care unit. He'd been riding a young horse when it suddenly kicked up a fuss and had slammed Crawford to the ground, breaking his neck.

Dave Abel, a classmate of Crawford's, was at the farm when I got the news and we immediately ran to the car and drove as fast as we could to Fresno, where Crawford was in hospital.

On the journey, we went through our memory banks and dredged up all we knew about him.

Crawford Hall is the son of Clark Hall, who owned and ran a sizeable cattle operation in Shandon, California, near where James Dean was killed.

Clark was a sportsman, and the kind of man who tried a little of everything. In the late 1940s he was a good team roper who used to come to the jackpot team ropings in central California, and he entered some of the big team-roping events in the major rodeos.

I roped with Clark Hall when I was 10 – 12 years old, got to know him well and went to his ranch a few times. Crawford, his son, was growing up and just beginning to ride at that time. He was an active kid around the ranch, and would work cattle with his dad.

While at Cal-Poly, which is only about 50 miles from Shandon, I saw Crawford many times. That was in the early to mid-1950s, by which time Crawford was starting to show horses in competition and getting active in junior rodeo.

It wasn't until later, when I was out of college in the early 1960s, that he started to come by my place a lot because we had a student by the name of Sandra Lewis whom he took a shine to and later married.

It had been like a family event when Sandra married Crawford, and I got to know him a lot better through that association. They moved to Fallon, Nevada, where he ran a feed lot for his father, but we were in contact quite often.

Sadly, it just did not work out for Sandra and Crawford, and although they made several attempts to patch things up they eventually split.

In 1973 Crawford had taken a job in Tulare with a very close friend and ex-classmate of mine by the name of Greg Ward who had set up a business there training cutting horses, reined cow horses and quarter racehorses. Crawford went to work with him as an all-purpose horseman, primarily interested in the cutting horses and reined cow horses. He was also a good rider of racehorses in training.

Now he was having to face the reality of never being able to ride again.

We arrived at the hospital and were shown

immediately to an intensive-care room where he was undergoing treatment for severe spinal-cord damage.

I shall never forget the sight that greeted our eyes as we stepped into that room. Crawford had an eye bolt embedded in the top of his head and screws through his heels, and from these points he was wired to a contraption that looked for all the world like a barbecue spit. It not only provided the necessary traction but served to roll his weight around, which would reduce vital organ damage.

The doctor took us to one side, to explain his condition. Very calmly he said, 'Crawford can't feel anything from the shoulders down. This means he is going to be a quadriplegic, with I'd guess only 5 – 6 per cent use of his arms. He's been in a very serious accident and is lucky to be alive, but I'm afraid there's a long road ahead of him.'

We returned to his bedside and waited to be able to talk to him.

I remember vividly how Crawford struggled to cope with the trauma when he first talked about it. He spoke with such a mixed-up bag of emotions — half hopeful, half depressed, always shocked. 'And if I can't be involved with horses,' he said, 'I'd just as soon not live, you know?'

'I'd say the same myself, so don't you worry, we'll find a way.'

'You promise me something?'

'What?'

'If I'm good for nothing but selling pencils somewhere, you all agree to give me enough pills to put me to sleep, d'you hear?'

'You won't be selling pencils, Crawford.'

'Hell, I probably won't be able to do even that. I sure as hell won't be able to lift the pills to my mouth, even, so you do it for me if I ask you.'

'OK. We'll see just what you can do.'

'I'll do something. I'm telling you, I'm not just lying down and doing nothing. There's a spot for me somewhere.'

It was a desperately unhappy sight and our hearts went out to him.

Driving back to Flag Is Up with Dave Abel, I wondered out loud whether it would be possible to find a job for Crawford on our farm. It had always been an easy place to get around. The main buildings and offices are on a dead level and there are good surfaces between the barns, the covered riding school, the round pens and race-track.

I thought that if Crawford could learn to operate an electric wheelchair, he could be another set of eyes around the place, oversee the operation and let me know if there were things that ought to be done. Looking over the place, I found a spot where we could locate the type of modular home that was specifically designed for quadriplegics.

The idea grew and took shape: he could be employed as an observer and help me wherever possible. He would find his own role and cultivate his position as his abilities allowed.

Dave Abel also thought it would be a great idea, and was excited that his friend might have a chance to stay involved with horses and the life he loved most.

Within a couple of days I called back to the hospital and talked to Crawford about the potential job. It was only four or five months afterwards that he and a lady friend of his, Lisa Guilden (who had been with him prior to the accident) came from Fresno to Solvang to look the place over. By that time, they had a special van which was equipped to allow his chair to be wheeled in and buckled down so he could travel. It was strenuous and difficult for him. His was a cruel fate that could have fallen to any of us, but it was Crawford who was having to put up with it. This was not going to be easy.

However, there was potential for him to learn to operate the chair more satisfactorily — and the future would undoubtedly bring better chairs. I recall him saying that they were developing improved technologies all the time, and he thought that eventually he'd be able to get around the farm about as well as a normal person.

The professionals who were involved with Crawford's rehabilitation sent doctors and therapists to visit us. One after another, they tried to convince us that we were taking on a near-impossible task. The doctors explained that the human body had a great deal of difficulty adjusting to the quadriplegic state, and they felt obliged to tell prospective employers. They didn't want us to underestimate the challenge Crawford was facing and in an initial rush of sympathy to create false hopes for him.

They explained dozens of physical problems that could be expected. Finally, they told us it was likely that Crawford wouldn't live longer than 3 – 5 years, although if he did last through the five years there was a good chance that he might live close to his normal life expectancy.

Within a few months Crawford was living on Flag Is Up in a specially built modular home provided by his family which allowed him to be there, on the scene, 24 hours a day. He found himself a good chair, and was getting around the farm just fine.

I had a meeting with him and explained that all I was looking for was another set of eyes around the place. He was employed to report to me if he saw things going on that should be changed.

From the outset, Crawford insisted on complete co-operation from me in terms of educating himself about the thoroughbred racing industry. Voracious in his appetite to gather information about the business, he was learning fast. In no time at all, he became extremely proficient at understanding the needs of the horses. In fact, he had already taken over the operation without my realising it.

After only one year, I came to the conclusion that he should be running the training operation and calling the shots on a daily basis and I should step back and be the overseer.

The first year he came, 1975, I purchased a yearling I named An Act. This horse was a good school for Crawford because An Act proved to be a first-class prospect and went on to win the Santa Anita Derby.

The next year I bought two horses Alleged and Super Pleasure. The world won't know Super Pleasure as a great racehorse, although in my opinion he had as much talent as any horse I've owned or trained. Unfortunately he was later beset by a throat problem that relegated him to being a sprinter, so we'll never know how he would have turned out.

However, with Alleged, An Act and Super Pleasure, Crawford had a very solid foundation to build on and to gauge the rest of his horses by. The years have added to his education, and he has become one of the most valuable people that any owner in the racing industry could have available. His life revolves around the operation of the training centre at Flag Is Up Farms, and it is an incalculable asset to an owner to know that his horse is with someone who concentrates on the job 24 hours a day, 7 days a week.

When Crawford came to me, his approach to training horses was conventional. While he was a thinking horseman, he had been trained by people in the main stream and it was natural for him to follow the way things had been done for hundreds of years. However, over the years he has evolved to embrace a set of philosophies more aligned with my own.

Crawford is now famous for working with the young people who come to Flag Is Up and ride for us.

He'll say to them, 'Leave the horse alone, let him go on, let him explore a little and then correct him. He'll be all right. Let him go in the direction he wants for a few steps, and then bend him more towards what you want. Don't just hammer him.'

The youngster struggling with the horse will inevitably snap back, 'But he's going to run away.'

Crawford's laconic reply is, 'How can he do that? You have the Atlantic on your right and the Pacific on your left. Where's he going to go?'

If a horse can be allowed the freedom to explore before he's brought back into line, he'll listen and respond much better than a horse which is beaten into submission.

As I write this, Crawford is in his twenty-first year with us and as healthy and active as anyone in his condition could be. Hospitals and therapists have often come to videotape him at work and to chronicle his career subsequent to the accident, for use by their institutions as an educational tool for treatment of similar cases.

Crawford Hall is an inspiration to everyone who meets him.

★ ★ ★

The auctioneer's gavel came down — *bang!* — and then lifted just as quickly to wave in my direction while his patter hurried on to the next sale.

It was just another moment in Kentucky's long history of trading in young racehorses. There's plenty of promise at these thoroughbred sales; the trick is to back the winners. It's as though they're racing already, without having taken one step down a track.

I'd just bought a registered thoroughbred stallion, 14 hands 2 inches high, less than 900 pounds in weight, by Hoist The Flag out of Princess Pout, foal of 1974 and now a yearling. A bay horse with black points and both rear pasterns white, he was in horrible condition and not many people were giving him a second glance.

However, because he was so thin, I could see that he had the best skeletal balance of any thoroughbred I'd ever dealt with.

I was right — and this was borne out by an amazing coincidence some 10 years later when, in 1984, I attended a thoroughbred symposium held by a Dr Michael Osbourn, who was a world authority on thoroughbred conformation.

Towards the end of his lecture, Dr Osbourn flashed a silhouette of a thoroughbred on to the overhead projector. 'This animal,' he said, 'is perhaps the most perfectly constructed thoroughbred I've ever studied.' He gazed out to his audience. 'Can anyone name this horse, by any chance?'

I raised my hand.

'Aha,' said Dr Osbourn, 'how did you identify your horse in silhouette, Monty?'

I replied, 'You have your system of circles that you draw, to see if certain anatomical features meet or fail to meet the various points in the circle they should?'

'That's correct.'

'Well, I have a similar system involving a triangle.'

Dr Osbourn invited me to the overhead projector to explain my triangular theory, as opposed to his circular one.

I explained that my triangle seeks to discover the balance between the two major skeletal structures in a horse, the pelvis and the shoulders. These two engines, if you like, are what propel the horse over the ground, and the engineering of these two skeletal structures determines the efficiency with which the rest of the body responds to brain signals.

Dr Osbourn finished by saying, 'For those of you still in the dark, this horse was owned by Mr Roberts very early on in his life. His name is . . . Alleged.'

Pat dreamed up that name for him, and still has it as the number-plate on our car.

Alleged went on to be an incredible success story, eventually owned by Robert Sangster and a consortium of investors, and was twice the winner of the Arc de Triomphe.

This is among my favourite cuttings from the Santa Ynez Valley News on October 5 1978:

Monty and Pat Roberts of Flag Is Up Farms here in Solvang have good reason to feel proud this week as Alleged won the 57th Prix de L'Arc de Triomphe at Longchamps, France, last Sunday. Alleged, ridden by Lester Piggot, won easily by two lengths ahead of Trillion in a time of 2:36.5 . . .

292

* * *

On a cloudy day in November 1977, I was riding Johnny Tivio around Flag Is Up Farms as I often did to check on pastures, fences, horses and so on.

Most of these riding sessions would take me over the farm proper and then to the north of the property, where I would ride up a hill overlooking the farm to survey what was going on — and today was no exception.

There's a trail in a canyon on the north-east corner of Flag Is Up which takes you to a flat area 150 feet above the pastures themselves. I was riding up that trail when I noticed some activity on the face of the hill across the canyon.

As I focused my eyes, I saw that the commotion was caused by a group of coyotes darting in and out of the brush. They were obviously frantic about something.

I decided to ride my horse down to the bottom of the canyon and then up the other side so that I could see what it was that was exciting them.

Arriving near the brush, I saw that they had a deer down and were in a feeding frenzy, ripping at her hide with their sharp incisors. I ran at them with Johnny Tivio and, fortunately, I had a rope on the saddle which I took down and threw at them.

They ran off, heading northwards to a higher position on the hill before turning to look back. I chased after them so as to drive them further still from the deer, before returning to have a look at her. She was an old doe, very thin, with no teeth, and probably only half her normal body weight. She had severe lacerations from the coyotes' attack. Looking around me for any children she might have, above us on the side of the hill and a bit to the south I spotted two half-grown fawns, obviously hers. I hoped they'd fare all right — certainly they were old enough to survive once they'd found their way back to the herd.

I couldn't help but try to save the life of this old doe. So I remounted Johnny Tivio and cantered down the hill, across the farm to the shop area where I got my pick-up, some woven fencing and some steel posts.

I called to a couple of the farm-hands to come and help me, then I drove as close as I could to the doe. When I got out of the truck I noticed that the coyotes had inched back down the hill towards her, so I started up the hill yelling at them, carrying my rope with me, slapping my leg and diverting their attention from the doe while the farm-hands brought the fencing and the posts behind me.

Eventually the three of us built a wire cage over the doe about 15 feet in diameter, and closed at the top so that the coyotes couldn't climb in. I put some grain and alfalfa hay in there and a bucket of water.

As we worked around her, the doe struggled in a vain attempt to get up, but she was too weak. I was certain that she'd be dead the next day, but I had to give her a chance.

When I arrived the following morning, she

was up on her keel and had eaten and taken some water. This was amazing — wild deer don't often allow themselves to eat or drink in captivity.

I disturbed her as little as possible, and for the next 4 – 5 days I returned only long enough to make sure that she had feed and water.

It was on the fifth day that I found her standing up. As I watched, she began to take a few steps around her enclosure. Fortunately she did not have enough strength to run at the fencing and bash into it like a healthy wild deer would do.

Before she recovered any further and began doing just that, I decided the best course of action was to try to acclimatise her to my presence so that she wouldn't panic at the sight of me.

I started by going into the cage, bending over, working gently with her using subtle, short non-threatening movements in the same communication system I've called 'Equus'. Amazingly, I was to find that the two languages were almost identical.

Saving this doe started an adventure for me which has spanned nearly 20 years. It's been one of the most gratifying experiences of my life.

I called her 'Grandma'.

She was only two or three weeks in the cage before she was strong enough to take a chance on going outside. When I opened it up, she walked off in that stately fashion that deer have, but you could tell she wasn't intent on putting much distance between herself and me.

I returned the next morning and found her 100 yards or so away from the cage. I put some more grain and alfalfa there and rigged up a watering device so that she could have water without travelling too far.

Each day I went to this area and began to work with her, using the concepts of 'Advance and Retreat'.

Whenever she acted as though she didn't want to be with me, I'd deliberately push her away and walk behind her for as many as two or three miles. When I felt her circling and showing me her flanks, thinking about re-negotiating with me, I would turn and walk in the opposite direction, away from her.

I was squaring up, looking her in the eye, driving her away, then dropping off and turning from her, in order to invite her to join up with me, just as I did with my horses.

I found I was able to coax her back towards me.

I did not do a perfect job of 'join-up' — it seemed more tentative, not as solid. In fact, it would be several years before I was able to get her to come out from the herd and be as close to me as I was accustomed to with horses.

Finally, one day, it happened. I had been pressing her away from me for some time, watching for the signals which would tell me she was asking to be relieved of this disciplinary action. She showed me her flanks, locked an ear on to me; she mouthed at me — a silent whisper that she was a herbivore and wanted to try to trust me. Then she dropped her head to ground level and walked along like that, with her mouth inches above the rough terrain.

I backed off, turned at an angle and no longer looked her in the eye. In fact, on this occasion it was a sunny day and we were in a beautiful spot on a promontory overlooking the farm, so I lay on the ground and turned my face to the sun.

The next I knew, Grandma came and lay right beside me. Finally, I'd achieved a near-perfect state of 'join-up' with her. She trusted me. She just lay there, next to me on a hillside in California, with the sun bright in the sky and an eagle floating across the updraughts rising from the valley floor.

I was moved by this long, slow friendship, culminating in this simple, unexciting event on the side of a hill overlooking Flag Is Up.

I learned a lot from Grandma.

I discovered that the flight mechanism of a deer was many times more sensitive than that of a horse. When I made a mistake in one of my movements, I would have to pay for it for a considerable amount of time — sometimes weeks or even months.

It became clear to me that through this super-sensitive flight mechanism one could learn the language 'Equus' more definitively and accurately.

For example, I was encouraging Grandma to come to me on one occasion, so I had my shoulders at a 45-degree angle to her, looking away. However, I wanted to see what she was doing, so I glanced at her out of the corner of my eye. Grandma saw that I'd broken the rules, and she walked off and went 500 yards away. She wouldn't let me close to her for about three days.

I realised I'd been making the same mistake with horses, too; I quite often glanced quickly at them out of the corner of my eye when I wasn't meant to.

I went back to the round pen and started working with a horse, experimenting with the speed with which I moved my eyes as well as trying out different ways of reading the image of the horse out of the corner of my eye without actually looking at them.

I found I could slow down the flight impulse by moving my eyes more slowly. As soon as I understood that, Grandma was much easier to work with.

I also found that spreading my fingers, moving my arms or going from retreat to advance too quickly would set her off, slowing the process of communication.

Again, I experimented with the horses I was starting. I found that when I held out my arms as part of squaring my movements to send the horse away, it would set the horse going quicker and faster if I opened my fingers. I think this has to do with muscle tension; it's part and parcel of the aggressive posturing many animals perform to make themselves look bigger — like a dog's hackles rising on its back.

Without the help of Grandma, I would never have learned this more refined aspect of the language. It was as though this frail old lady was giving me advanced lessons in 'Equus';

she was fine-tuning my responses and taking my qualification to a higher degree. Perhaps it was to repay me for saving her life back in that canyon. Grandma died of natural causes on 2 December, 1995. She is buried here on Flag Is Up Farms.

* * *

By now Johnny Tivio had retired. He was twenty-four years old, and no one had wanted to breed from him for some time. He enjoyed the best of care, with a warm box stall of his own and a field with plenty of green grass in the daytime.

He could watch everything going on from his paddock. This was on the route that the mares took going to and from the breeding barn, and every time a lady went past Johnny Tivio acted the big, bad stallion again, singing out and talking to them and pretending he was only three years old, prancing along by the fence.

On 24 April 1981, I was driving back from the racecourse and instead of going up to the house I turned left and headed straight for the office. When I walked through the door Pat was there, and she immediately stepped forward and embraced me and said, 'Johnny Tivio is dead.'

Apparently, a mare had been taken to the breeding barn and Johnny Tivio had seen her. He'd stepped up on his toes, lifted his tail and was coming over to try to get her phone number, as usual. In the middle of the field, he'd dropped like a stone. Dr Van Snow, our veterinarian,

299

confirmed he'd had a heart attack.

Even though I was struck by a bolt of sadness, my first reaction was, 'Wonderful.' For we were just beginning to have trouble with his feet, and I'd dreaded a long, painful struggle for him when he'd lived such a clean, successful life. It had turned out better than that — he was sound to the last. All our effort had been worth it.

I asked, 'Where is he?'

'We left him where he fell, so you could see.'

I went out to his field. As I walked towards his body lying there, motionless, his death hit me very hard and I found it difficult. His eye was empty; the life had gone.

As I sat there with him, it was like visiting the most wonderful memories.

Early on in our life together, I remembered showing him at Salinas, my home town, on the Competition Grounds where I was raised. It was one of the largest and most important anywhere on the north American continent, and he was so good at everything and so willing that I couldn't decide whether to show him in the cutting division or the reined cow-horse division.

Pat had said, 'Why not show him in both?'

It was unheard of. No one had done it before. It was virtually impossible to do . . .

We entered him for both events. As soon as the entry arrived at the office in Salinas, I got a call back from an old friend, Lester Sterling, who was the chairman of the event, and he asked, 'Monty, have you lost your mind? We can't let

300

you show Johnny Tivio in both cutting and reined cow-horse divisions. It is just ridiculous to think he could perform that way.'

'Is it against the rules?' I asked.

'Well, no . . . but I don't think you ought to embarrass yourself.'

Eventually I persuaded him to agree, however.

As I was preparing Johnny Tivio for these two events, I'd give him one type of bit and bridle when we were training for one event, and a different bit and bridle for the other. He was so intelligent that he read the situation perfectly. He not only entered both divisions, he won both of them as well. It's never been done since.

Now he lay collapsed on his side, with that heavy, final weight that only death brings.

I knew where I wanted to bury him. I'd had it in my mind for some time to make a special graveyard just in front of the office, where I'd give each horse its own headstone. The horses' names and dates and a line or two expressing some of their qualities would be engraved in bronze plates set into the blocks of stone.

It seemed like now was the time to start on this idea.

With some members of our staff, we went over with a low-boy — a type of trailer — to where his body lay. We fitted straps underneath him and lifted him on to the trailer. Towing him back across the field, I remembered 11 years earlier riding him out of the farm, down the drive right there in front of us, when Mr Harcourt had been overshadowing our lives. Johnny Tivio had been confident as ever, and I remembered how his character had seemed like a whole education to me at that time.

When we'd arrived at the Gardner ranch, I remembered, we'd had a visit from that notoriously eccentric woman, Marjorie Merryweather Post Dye. She'd pointed at him in the stable and said, 'Johnny Tivio.'

'What about him?' I'd asked.

'Well, I hear you're in trouble. You need money for a legal defence. Now, I don't give money. No one gets money out of me. But I'll give you anything you want in return for that horse.'

I'd thanked her for the offer, but it was out of the question.

'No!' she'd said, annoyed with my stupidity. 'I don't mean I'd take him away from you. I'd never take him away from you. But I want to buy the papers.'

'The papers?'

'Yes, just for a while. For safe-keeping. Just give me the papers so I can hold them, and point at them, and say I owned Johnny Tivio for a little while.'

We had walked up to the house and I'd given her the papers, shaking my head in wonder at this courageous, strong woman who had so much her own way of doing things. In return, she'd made us promise to call her if we ever needed a loan towards our defence fund.

Now I hoped she'd enjoyed having those papers. They were all that was left of him.

I dug his grave myself, using the little hydraulic digger called a back hoe which we had on the farm. I am not a capable hand at that machine, and I daresay it took me longer than it should have done. It was dark by this time, but the hole was dug and Johnny Tivio's body had to be lowered in.

This was a tough duty. It seemed wrong and ignoble, and I knew I wouldn't see a friend like Johnny Tivio again in my life.

I couldn't back-fill the earth; I'd had enough. Our veterinarian volunteered to carry on while I came back to the bedroom and crawled under the covers. I stayed there until the following morning.

In his time he was undefeated in the stallion sweepstakes — a sort of pentathlon for stallions. He was four times a world champion working cow horse, and was undefeated in Western riding — a form of Western dressage — for 14 separate contests in a row. More than that, though, he was a sterling character: superb intelligence, proud, with an inspiring work ethic. He made it a pleasure to shrug on a coat and walk down through the early-morning mist that often blankets this valley to start on the hours of work that an establishment like this takes to be successful.

The plaque on his gravestone reads: 'Johnny Tivio, April 24 1956 to April 24 1981. Known to all as the greatest all-round working horse ever to enter the arena.'

He died on his twenty-fifth birthday.

★ ★ ★

I was walking up the slope towards the back of the house when I took a bad step; I felt my lower back suddenly clinch, and my legs gave up on me. I was on the ground and helpless, unable to move the lower half of my body at all. There was literally no sensation there. I had a sudden picture of Crawford Hall lying in traction in his hospital bed — now, seven years later, it was my turn.

I pulled myself up the slope with my arms, in excruciating pain. The list of reasons why my back was in bad shape was long enough: stunt-riding, football, team-roping, calf-roping, bullriding, bulldogging. All that extra impact on my spinal column had ruptured the discs, and I was about to find out what would be the cost. I was 46 years old.

The doctor was called and declared me too critical to move to hospital. He wanted to stabilise me first, and try to win back the feeling in my legs.

He arranged for delivery of a rack — that was what it was, like an instrument of torture — and I was strung out on this thing like a rabbit on a spit. I was there for 30 days.

At this point I should put in a word of recommendation for the drug morphine. I was filled with it, and I was doing business and wheeling and dealing like never before. In fact, if I ever get in trouble now with a particular problem, it crosses my mind to hire that rack again and have the doctor come and give me some more morphine, so I can sort myself out.

After 30 days, much of the sensation had

come back to my legs. During that time I'd educated myself in the world of back technology, and I'd settled on a Dr Bob Kerlan as the man who would most likely be able to help me stay out of a wheelchair.

We rented a motor home and wheeled me into that, then I was hauled to Bob Kerlan's outfit in Los Angeles. I was about as much use as a piece of meat.

As soon as possible, I was given a Catscan, after which Bob Kerlan and his team came in to give me their report. They brought in a plastic model of a human spine and were all ready to frighten the life out of me.

'You have very extensive damage to the spine, Monty. Forget riding — boy, don't even think of riding again. You won't be lifting a weight more than 40 pounds again either. You'll probably just about get to walk around the place under your own steam — but be happy with that, because you are on the verge of living the rest of your life in a wheelchair.'

'Believe me, I'll be happy to walk, very happy.'

He pointed to the plastic model. 'OK. You see here, the lower back?'

'Yup.'

'Each of these five discs is ruptured. That's to say, the soft material in the core of the discs has ruptured due to constant heavy impacts on the spine and leaked out, causing stalagtites of invasive material. That's thirty per cent of your problem. The other seventy per cent is fractures and spurs throughout the spinal column. This is what's causing you the pain and the nerve impairment. We can get in there and clean up that stuff, and remove the spurs and you'll be left with five discs which are like doughnuts — the soft middle sections will have been sucked out of them.'

'OK.'

'Normally, we find just one or two gone; but you have all five ruptured in your lower back here. It's going to be a long operation, and we won't find out how successful we've been until it's finished.'

This was definitely not going to be a holiday.

For two or three days I went through preparation. They had to take me off the morphine and the pain was incredible. I wanted to shout 'Fix it!' every second of every minute, at the top of my voice.

Then I went under the knife, with a video-camera positioned to catch the whole procedure . . .

Ten hours later, I woke up. A smiling black lady dressed in a perfect white uniform appeared and she looked like an angel. Had I died and gone to heaven?

Then she said, 'OK, Mr Roberts, shall we visit the bathroom?'

I thought she was joking. 'I can't move.'

'Oh yes, you can. Time to sit up now.'

This definitely wasn't heaven — and it might turn out to be the opposite. Did she know I'd only just come round from the anaesthetic?

She started to pull my feet round and sit me up. The pain shot through me like iron bolts were being driven into my back by Satan himself.

She was holding my shoulders, but every time she let go my body would flop, as if there had been a new hinge inserted somewhere in my middle. 'Wow,' she said, 'they must have done a good job on you.'

She went and fetched some help. Then together they hung me in a wheeled jig in which I could move along. I was in a sorry state.

Later, I saw the video of the operation. It looked for all the world like a gang of carpenters with muscular forearms arriving for work; they had toolboxes filled with hammers and chisels.

After they'd cut through and hooked back the muscles and the soft tissue with giant clamps, they seemed to go at my back like they were mending a house. It was barbaric.

Following my recovery, they sent me home and told me to keep moving, to walk a minute or two more each day. I was in a wheelchair for 10 – 12 days, then on crutches for a further number of months.

I have a scar down the middle of my back from my bottom rib to my tailbone, and my lower right leg is as dead as a doornail — you could stub a cigarette out on it. But I can walk fine, and I can ride. Dr Bob Kerlan did a better job than he thought was possible.

★ ★ ★

In Tissar was a thoroughbred stallion by Roberto out of Strip Poker — in other words, about as classy as you can get. It made him a full brother to the champion Landaluce.

He was purchased as a yearling in the July Keeneland Select Sale in 1979 for $250,000 by Mr Fustock of Buckram Oak Farm, and sent to France to race. He was a good winner early on, but then he was injured and offered for sale at just $220,000.

I thought he'd be a good prospect for syndication, so along with my partners Mr Katz and Mr Semler, we bought him in order to put him to stud. He was a handsome, proud stallion with a superb provenance.

We transported him to California and offered him at $16,000 a share — which is like arranging time-share leases on his capacity as a father.

The 25 shares were sold within two weeks, yielding the partners a gross of $400,000, which meant we were already $180,000 to the good on a cash basis — plus, we had kept back five shares each to be used on our own mares. This was a good piece of business. We were doing well.

I created a syndicate agreement which outlined the duties and responsibilities of Flag Is Up Farms and named myself the syndicate manager.

In Tissar started covering mares in 1983, and for the first half of the season he bred without any problems. Towards the middle of the season, however, I began getting reports that he was being aggressive with his handlers.

I went by the breeding barn and spent some time watching them handle him. The curious thing is that as they brought him out of the stall, if they turned to go to the breeding room he would be fine and would cover his mare with no problem. However, if they turned to go to his paddock he would become aggressive.

It seemed to me that this aggression was a function of his sexuality, so I brought them a metal nose-band stallion halter to use on him, which seemed to solve the problem for a day or two.

Then I was told that the problem had recurred while he was in the breeding room — where he'd previously been willing and co-operative, if a touch over-enthusiastic.

At the same time, rumours reached me that a young man on our night staff had taken it on himself to school In Tissar. I am sure he had good intentions, but it's quite likely he mistreated this stallion, at least in the opinion of the horse.

In Tissar became dangerous and he bit two men quite badly. The situation needed to be controlled.

On a given day, I arrived at the breeding room for a meeting with Dr Van Snow, our resident veterinarian, Darryl Skelton, who was handling the stallions, the breeding-room staff and the veterinary assistant.

It was decided that breeding In Tissar with two 8-foot staves attached to his halter would be effective, to keep his handlers at a distance from him. They bred two or three mares that way, and it appeared to be the answer. The mares were covered and the people involved were safe. In Tissar was happy and didn't object to this careful handling procedure; he even seemed proud of it.

The next time a romantic appointment was booked for him, I came down to watch and see if I might discover if there was any way I could help.

We brought a mare into the breeding room, cleaned her up, bandaged her tail and had her standing in the centre of the room prepared for breeding.

Two men caught In Tissar, put the staves on and led him towards the breeding room. The staves meant that the horse was firmly positioned between the two men, who were approximately eight feet away from him.

The mare was waiting in full heat and well 'let down' in the centre of the room — meaning that she was receptive to the stallion.

The two men entered, leading In Tissar through the large door in the centre of the north wall of this square room, measuring 40 × 40 feet. They brought him about six feet into the room where he planted himself, looking the situation over. There were seven people in the room: two men on the staves, one man with the mare, the veterinarian and his assistant, Darryl Skelton and myself.

I closed the door behind the stallion and Darryl and I walked over to the area where Dr Snow was. In Tissar stood dead still, just looking at the mare and around the room.

Then with no warning whatsoever he struck out with his left front foot, reaching over the top of the stave and slapping it out of the man's hand and onto the floor. The weight of his body snapped it clean in half. The man on that side was left holding one broken portion, while the rest of it was hanging from the stallion's halter, which added to the danger.

A second later, In Tissar reached up with his other foot and slapped the stave out of the other man's hand. The horse was deadly accurate; there was no question in my mind that this was a calculated move, and it wasn't just coincidental that he put his foot right on top of each stave.

This one didn't break; it was just knocked out of the man's hands. This left In Tissar with one full stave about 8 feet long on the off-side, and the half-stave with a jagged end on the near side.

Then he moved fast and attacked the mare in the middle of the room, hitting her at full speed with his mouth wide open. He sank his teeth into her left flank near the last rib, ripping at it like a wolf would do to a rabbit. His shoulder struck her nearside buttocks just to the left side of her tail, and she fell sideways on the floor. He had a hunk of her hide in his mouth. The man holding the mare fled for his life.

In Tissar was now kneeling over the mare, squalling and pawing. The noise in that room was deafening — the excitement and the enormous power of it overwhelmed all of us. My time in the rodeo arena with bulldogging and bronc- and bull-riding gave me the greatest schooling I know to cope with tense and dangerous situations, but it wasn't going to be any use to me now.

I moved over to my right, away from Dr Snow. In Tissar had knocked the mare down near the south wall, and as I moved to the corner he wheeled and took a run at me. I ran back along the wall to gain the protection of the examination chute.

I realised that Dr Snow had moved along with me and he had a shavings rake in his hand. I guess his intention was to protect the mare and the people by holding the stallion off with the rake. In Tissar went for us and ran into the end of the rake, but it had no effect.

Dr Snow turned tail and ran towards the lab which was in the north-west corner of the room. The assistant was standing in the doorway, the doctor ran into him and both of them fell into the lab to escape.

Darryl and I both ended up in the examination chute. I don't know when I've ever felt more vulnerable and less in charge.

The two men who had been holding the staves were outside the north door, which was open about a foot wide, and I'm sure they were prepared to close it if the horse came that way. The man who had been holding the mare was outside the south door, also holding it open about a foot. In Tissar was facing the lab, weaving back and forth as if to say, 'I'm controlling you all. I'm in charge now.'

He had us all at bay.

He turned slowly and walked on the tips of his toes with his tail stuck out and his neck arched high. It was a beautiful, terrifying sight.

He went straight to the mare, who was still lying on the floor, and he stood over her flank as she lay there. He pawed and squealed a couple of times, as a stallion does when courting a mare, and the mare slowly got to her feet. She had a large gash on her left flank and the blood was dripping onto the floor.

In Tissar rooted at that flank with his nose a couple of times, and was fully erect. The mare, incredibly, lifted her tail, displaying that she was receptive to him. He mounted and bred her, still with a stave and a half dangling from his halter.

Each of the people involved stood frozen and watched in fascination: it was a primaeval, powerful experience.

After covering the mare, In Tissar dismounted and walked slowly to the north door where the two men who had held the staves were standing outside. As he stopped and stood there, it was clear that he had no further intention of being aggressive. The men slowly opened the door and took the staves on each side, and they walked him down the alleyway to his stall.

He went quiet as a lamb.

As Dr Snow, Darryl and I walked along behind him, the doctor shook his head and said, 'I'm going to carry my pistol with me from now on, and if he ever does anything like that again he'll have to die. I'm not going to risk losing somebody's life.'

I agreed. Something dramatic had to be done

before someone was killed.

All three of us agreed that the horse wasn't getting enough work to do. Maybe he was over-fed and under-worked? If he was ridden in the hills — and really put to work — perhaps we could change his attitude.

So Darryl offered to ride him each day. Dr Snow and I pointed out that he shouldn't work with In Tissar unless one of us was around, so that we could get help if something went wrong. We were all agreed on what we wanted to do.

On the first day of this new plan of action, we planned to take In Tissar to where we had some very strong corrals and cattle-handling facilities, with a loading chute and a squeeze gate. Then we'd put him in the gate in order to get his tack on and take him for a ride.

Darryl managed to get a shank on In Tissar in the stall and started to lead him over to the corrals. About half-way there, he spotted a mare in a field about a quarter of a mile away and started to play up. Darryl tried to soothe him, but the horse made a move indicating he was going to attack. We were in an area of about half an acre, and he was making some very aggressive gestures.

Moments later, Darryl lost control of the shank and In Tissar was loose. The horse ran all over that area, and no matter where we went, he was after us. We weren't chasing him — it was the other way around.

We managed to avoid being attacked, but if he could spot you from 200 – 300 yards away,

314

he would go for you. We ran around like the Keystone Cops.

He was really angry by now.

Eventually we were able to set some gates so that we could trap him near the heavy-duty cattle apparatus. Darryl was able to get him in the squeeze, and we swung the gate over to him so that he was standing in an area about 12 feet long and 3 feet wide.

When we closed the gate to move him over, he kicked it and then held his near hind leg off the ground for about twenty seconds. We held our breath, thinking he'd broken his leg — the kick was that fierce.

Then he put his leg down and stood on it as normal. There was just a bit of hair off, about mid-shaft on the cannon bone. He wasn't even lame.

Once he was in there, Darryl tacked him up and mounted him. He took him up a hill where he could ride for about 15 miles with no gates to open, and they were gone about three hours. When he returned, he rode him into the stallion round pen, took his saddle off and led him to the wash rack to give him a bath. In Tissar was fine. He looked a picture of health, a fine example of a stallion in the prime of his life. You could have sold him to a schoolgirl — except if her father had noticed that iron-hard, disinterested look in his eye.

We were all pleased, and Darryl started a programme of riding the horse each day. On about the fourth or fifth day, Dr Snow agreed that In Tissar was calm enough now for us to get an X-ray of that hind leg. He had been slightly sore, and we felt we ought to check it out.

We took the X-ray and found that the horse had a significant fracture of the cannon bone. That put us in a dilemma: for how long could Darryl ride him, before it would be cruel?

Darryl cut his work right down. On the second day, when Darryl came back to the round pen and took off his saddle, In Tissar attacked him. Once again, an employee of Flag Is Up had to save his own skin and escape from a dangerous assault.

That was the last straw. At this stage, in the normal course of things, a horse would have to have been destroyed.

I couldn't bear to have him killed, however, and I puzzled over any possible answer. What had gone wrong? It was now too dangerous even to try to help him.

We decided to have one last go at saving his life. In an area next to the stallion round pen, and with the help of four or five construction workers, I invented and built a system by which In Tissar could be stabled, the stable could be cleaned and serviced, he could be groomed, shod, clipped and exercised — all without having anyone in the enclosure with him.

He could also breed a mare, have the necessary washing-up procedures beforehand, could be taken for exercise, have a bath and go back to a clean, prepared stall — without having anyone in the enclosure with him.

He was bred in this fashion for 12 years. During that time we had not one injury, neither to a mare, the stallion himself nor any person working with him.

We now have another remedial stallion, Court Dance (by Northern Dancer) who stands in the same facility.

Court Dance was owned by Robert Sangster and John Magnier when he was sent to my farm. They wanted me to sort out his problems so that they could sell him, but I quickly learned that he was another very dangerous stallion and just not fixable. It was impossible to sell him to anyone because he couldn't be transported or handled.

He has been breeding here under the same system as In Tissar for the past three years, and he is getting along very well.

I would always prefer to come to an understanding with a horse through communication and dialogue, but with these two stallions it wasn't possible.

However, the complicated facility I had built especially to house and care for In Tissar and Court Dance can be regarded as a significant, long-term achievement. Without this system, these two stallions would undoubtedly have had to be put down. Many stallions have been destroyed around the world for temperaments less aggressive than these.

From the accounts I've read about violent stallions like Ribot and Graustark — even In Tissar's sire, Roberto — I'm left in no doubt that there are a significant number of incurably aggressive stallions.

Out of a scale of 1 – 10, In Tissar was a 9.9. He was intelligent and cunning and wanted to harm people. Something in his environment had turned him mean, and he had no intention of listening to anyone.

★ ★ ★

My parents came to stay. This was increasingly unusual, and the fact that they were to be here for as long as a week told us that my mother's cancer was probably worse.

We judged that she was making a last-ditch effort before she died to patch up the relationship between her husband and her son.

There was no doubt about it, she engineered for my father to watch me work in the round pen. She made sure of my schedule before they came, she organised a stool for him to sit on, she made sure he couldn't wriggle out of it. She near as anything told him he had to sit there and take note of what I was doing and acknowledge that it was working.

So my father sat there on his stool, ready to watch me start a raw horse. He was well into his seventies and, as I've mentioned before, his opinion was irrelevant to me on the surface of things. After all, I'd started over 6,500 horses by this time, and above and beyond the working horses I'd trained some wonderful thoroughbreds who'd gone on to win at some of the top racing fixtures in the world. I wasn't a youngster desperate for his approval; I was a man in my forties who wanted his parents to feel comfortable with each other and with their son.

Nevertheless, I also wanted to give it my best shot and finally show him what I'd achieved through many long years of working with horses and — more recently — the deer.

I considered telling him that when I first designed the round pen we were in, around 20 years previously, I'd purposely built it without a viewing gallery, and using tongue-and-groove material so that no one could see inside. It was only recently that I'd added the structure on which he was now sitting, allowing him to look down into the pen where I was about to start this young chestnut filly — a gorgeous creature with a coat on the sandy, fudge-coloured side of chestnut.

I'd never seen her before in my life. I had no idea of her character or her behaviour, although I could see immediately that she was a 'fast' type — i.e. quick to respond, nervous, but intelligent.

I stood in the middle of the ring and coiled my light sash line in my hand. Moving quite slowly because she would obviously go into flight easily, I squared my body to hers, lifting up my arms a touch and opening my fingers, as I'd learned to do with the deer. I locked my eye on to her eye.

The result was dramatic. She fled to the outside perimeter of the round pen, running counter-clockwise.

'OK, Dad,' I called, 'I'm going to tell you everything that will happen — like it's been booked up in advance, like this is a magic show.'

319

I hardly needed to keep this filly going with the sash line at all. She ran comfortably around the outside of the pen and I could control her speed by choosing where to look at her — if I kept my eyes on her eyes, I could increase the speed of her flight from me, whereas if I moved my gaze back to her shoulder, she'd slow up.

At all times, I kept my body square-on to her.

'So the first thing I'm looking for is that inside ear to lock on to me,' I called to my father, who sat still as a post on his stool on the viewing deck. 'It'll happen maybe within a minute.'

The filly's ear settled on me as the words were hardly out of my mouth. My father called, 'Course she's going to listen out for you.'

'It's more than listening out for me. She's keeping the ear on me as a mark of respect. She's allowing me some importance here.'

I pitched the sash line to the front of her, causing her to turn sharply and flee in the opposite direction. Still, the ear nearest me was turned in my direction, constantly.

She settled back to a steady trot.

After another revolution of the round pen, I called out to my father, 'Next you'll see another mark of respect she'll want to offer me. You'll see her licking and chewing. You'll see her tongue come through her teeth, then she'll pull it back and demonstrate a chewing action.'

I was no longer surprised when these things happened; in fact, after many thousands of horses, I would be very surprised if they didn't happen.

Sure enough, she began to lick and chew.

'There it is,' I called to my father, 'she's saying that she's a herbivore, that if she can be allowed to eat safely, if she can be allowed to stop running away, then we can come to an agreement, we can settle our respective positions, live and let live, let's talk.'

We were now about five minutes into the starting procedure, and I explained to my father the final signal I was looking for, before join-up could be accomplished. 'I'm looking for her to drop her head, to run along with her nose a couple of inches from the ground.'

Within a couple of minutes, the chestnut filly was trotting around blowing at the sand in front of her feet, her ear still on me.

'She's telling me it's OK, she understands me, she can trust me, she knows I understand her language.'

Turning my shoulders slightly beyond the filly's action, I allowed my eyes to slide forward also, away from any eye contact.

Immediately, the filly stopped.

I waited, dead still, standing at an angle to her, showing my flanks and avoiding any eye contact — not even glancing at her out of the corner of my eye.

I sensed a reluctance in her; she was finding it difficult to believe that I was talking her language, but she was forced to acknowledge that I'd responded to every signal she'd given me.

This part of the starting process — waiting for the moment I call join-up — is always the most thrilling time for me. Not because there's some doubt over whether it will happen or not, but simply because, when it happens, it proves the possibility of communication between man and horse, and the miracle of this — when a flight animal gives her trust to a fight animal, and man and horse meet across the distance which divides them — I repeat, the miracle of this moment is always fresh for me. I relive it with each and every occasion, and it is a source of satisfaction that has endured throughout my life.

Now this filly took a first tentative step towards me. I wasn't looking at her, but I knew she was weighing it up and deciding there was nothing else for her to do but join-up with me.

Moments later she was standing next to me, her nose at my shoulder. She trusted me. It was a bewildering new experience for her, and I had proved to be her safety zone — someone who understood her language.

I walked slowly in a right-hand circle and she followed me. I took a left turn, and she followed me into that as well. The join-up with this chestnut filly was completely effective.

'That's what I call join-up,' I said to my father.

He asked, 'How many times has that one been ridden?'

'Never, Dad.'

'Paah.'

I didn't take any notice of this exclamation.

The chestnut filly was standing there, waiting for what would happen next on this extraordinary day when everything would change for her. I reminded myself — as I always try to — that although this was an everyday sort of event for me, for her it was possibly the most nerve-racking moment in her whole life.

I called to my father, 'Now I'm going to investigate the vulnerable areas, to confirm that she trusts me completely.'

I walked to the centre of the pen, with the filly following me. I dropped the sash line on the ground and stood at her shoulder. 'The vulnerable areas are where her predators will attack.'

Moving slowly and quietly, I ran my hands over her withers and her neck. 'The big cats will jump up here, clawing into the back of a horse, biting into the top of the neck in an attempt to damage the spinal cord, paralysing the horse or causing it to fall just from their weight.

'If the horse is paralysed, it's easy for the cat to finish him off. If the horse isn't paralysed, then the cat will go to the ground with him and slip his teeth around under the neck, in order to collapse the trachea and shut off his air supply. So it's important she lets me into these vulnerable areas.'

Next I moved my hands slowly across her flanks and under her belly. 'On every continent there's one type of wild dog or another that will prey on horses. One of them grabs the tail, to hinder the animal from running away. Another runs along in front and jumps up and hangs off her nose, which makes it difficult for her to breathe. But the majority of the pack will head for her flanks here; just in front of the hind legs is a favourite spot because it's soft. The dogs will try to rip her open right here, so the intestines drop out through the wound.'

So these were the next areas I investigated with my hands, to confirm the trust between myself and this chestnut filly. She stood reasonably firm, side-stepping only once or twice. I continued until I found an absence of rejection and tension in her.

Then I picked up each of her hooves, sliding my hand down from the knee or the hock over the tendon and then to the rear of the fetlock joint, before asking her to lift her feet one by one, just holding them off the ground for a second or two.

'You see, she's a flight animal and she's just allowed me to pick up her method of propulsion — her feet. She's trusting me, pretty much from top to toe, now.'

We were about 20 minutes into the starting procedure.

Hector Valdez now entered the round pen carrying a saddle, a saddle-pad, a bridle and a long stirrup leather as well as lunge ropes. Hector has been first man up on more horses than I care to remember; having worked for me for so many years, he knew what to do as well as I did. After positioning the equipment in the middle of the round pen, he left again.

The arrival of this new person in the round pen — and more alarmingly, a pile of odd-looking equipment — caused the usual consternation in the young filly. She snorted, blew at the saddle, stared hard, wandered around, and generally came to terms with it.

However, the equipment if anything caused the join-up to work more strongly, because the perceived danger made her need to seek her safety zone — me.

She stood by me as I lifted the saddle on to her back. There was still no lead rope of any description attached to her head. She allowed me to take the girth under her belly and buckle it up the other side.

I called out to my father, 'Now, I want her to get used to the saddle for a while, before Hector gets on her.'

I stepped back from the filly and squared up to her, driving her away again. She went into flight, cantering with an odd, skewed gait as she coped with the strange new feeling of having a saddle on her back.

As she cantered and then trotted around the ring, I waited for the same signals — the licking and chewing, the inside ear settling on me. As always, I wasn't looking to see the head lowering, not with the saddle on. She couldn't trust herself to do that with this weight on her back, all of a sudden; it was too much to ask.

'Now I'm going to try a little experiment,' I said. 'You'll see she has a sweet spot just there in the ring.' I pointed to where I'd recognised she always gave me her full attention. At other points around the circle, she was distracted by something — my father, or the entrance door to the round pen, or the light fixed to the overhead beam. I knew from long experience that most babies have a sweet spot — and it's best to wait until they're in it before trying the more subtle signals of 'Equus'.

'I'm going to hold my hand across the front of my body like this, and when she reaches her sweet spot I'm going to do nothing more than simply open my fingers. You'll notice her pick up speed considerably.'

I did exactly as I'd told him I would. I simply held my hand across in front of my chest, and when I opened my fingers she broke into a canter.

'See? That's how much she's reading me. She knows she can let a cat walk right past her, but if that cat has its claws open she has to flee, and pretty quickly.'

I set her going in the opposite direction, allowing her to become familiar with the saddle; and after three or four revolutions, she was asking to come back in to me.

I tightened her girth a notch, to make sure it stayed in place.

'Now for the bridle,' I called to my father. 'You know,' I added, 'once the join-up is achieved, it's pretty much of a formality. The join-up tells me she trusts me. And with horses, that's not too big a step away from her offering to work as hard as she can for me.'

She was now wearing her first bridle, unconcernedly standing there, chewing at the bit which sat across the bar of her mouth for the first time.

'Now that the bridle's on, we can long-line her.'

We were now about 25 minutes into the procedure, and it was going fine.

I long-lined this filly in both directions; this was the first time she'd ever walked into the reins and I wanted to get her used to them before Hector was on her back, just to give him a bit of a steering wheel.

After the long-lining, I backed her up a step. As soon as that backward step was taken, I released the pressure on the long-lines, rewarding her immediately. Then I pulled her girth tighter by a further notch, ready for Hector to ride her.

Hector came into the ring and made himself known to her. He too rubbed her vulnerable areas, until she was happy with his presence. He brushed her new saddle lightly with his hands.

Then I lifted him on to her back and he lay across her for several moments, while I turned her head this way and that to make sure she caught sight of him draped over her middle like that.

Carefully, slowly, Hector lifted a leg over her back — and she was being ridden for the first time.

Hector walked her around the ring, not bothering with her mouth or whether or not she jigged sideways or broke into a trot or anything else she might want to try in order to take stock of what was happening on her back.

I checked my watch. 'Half an hour,' I called to my father as he sat on his stool. 'Which is about average.'

My father didn't say much at that stage, but

got off his stool and went off to quiz the hired help. He wandered around the establishment, questioning them about what they were doing.

Then he returned to the viewing deck at the round pen and sat on his stool again. Because my mother had carefully chosen the right day in my schedule for their visit, I'd started some ten young horses by the time darkness fell.

Each time he'd seen the same process, with the same key markers, the same language spoken between the horse and me. Each animal was different, of course, but we were all using the language 'Equus', and we achieved the same result — Hector Valdez in the saddle and riding them comfortably around the ring within approximately half an hour, with no restraints used, no harsh words, not a whip in sight.

By the end of the day, my father had seen me start more horses than he would have believed possible to 'break' in six weeks. He came down from the viewing deck and we stood outside, hardly able to see each other's faces in the gloom.

I asked him, 'What d'you think of that?'

But he couldn't let go of his way of life. Even faced with such proof as I'd shown him again and again, it was too much to ask of him to admit the old ways weren't the best ways. He replied, 'Keep doing it that way, and they'll get you.'

Up at the house that night, my mother was especially anxious to know what he'd thought. In her mind, a lot hung on this. It was a question of justice for her son, I think, and an agreement that might be reached between two men she loved probably equally but in different ways — one as a son, the other as a husband.

She kept away from the topic for some while, as though it hadn't been her idea in the first place. Then she could hold out no longer and asked, 'So, Marvin, how'd you enjoy what you saw today?'

'Fine.'

This wasn't nearly enough for her and she pressed on. 'What d'you think of it all?'

My father replied, 'It's suicide.'

She would just have to go on living with the same divided loyalty that she'd had to put up with for so long.

As it turned out, my mother's intestinal cancer took her away from us not long afterwards, and we found ourselves making the journey up to Salinas for her funeral.

We arrived at their house, where my father had some years ago built a block of stables and a few paddocks. Until recently he'd given riding lessons, and had still been involved with horses. Now, however, with the death of his wife, he was in a sorry state. He couldn't believe it had happened.

He greeted us on our arrival with the words, 'Come on in, your mother'll be back in a while.'

Pat and I looked at each other to check we'd heard right, and then walked inside with him. I reminded him, 'Dad, she won't be back, she died.'

He waited for a long while and then admitted,

'Yeah, I suppose she did.'

Half an hour later, we were ready to go to the funeral service. As we were leaving the house my father stopped in his tracks and said, 'Hold on, we have to wait for Marguerite. She's not back yet.'

Again we reminded him, 'Dad, she's waiting for us at the funeral home. This is her funeral.'

'Yeah, OK.'

By a strange coincidence, the funeral home was located four doors down from our old house in Salinas, 347 Church Street. It seemed to me now such a small neighbourhood compared with what I remembered. The houses had shrunk in size, and the road was just a strip of pavement.

The funeral home was called Struve and LaPorte. We had the whole LaPorte family as riding students, back in the 1940s at the Competition Grounds. Now this man with grey hair was coming out to greet us, and he'd been one of my students all those years ago. Jim LaPorte was in charge of the family business — who would have thought it? I could only remember him as a small boy bouncing around on the back of a horse.

As we headed inside, my father played his trick again. 'Wait, we have to get your mother.'

Jim LaPorte told us that this was a common phenomenon among elderly people separated after many years together.

We attended my mother's funeral service at the local Catholic church. There were only a few people there as mass was said and she was taken out and buried. Her life had been spent entirely in the service of her husband and her children.

My brother Larry and I were naturally concerned about how fast my father was heading downhill following our mother's death, and we wondered how he would cope. I called his doctor and suggested we should find him some accommodation on Flag Is Up Farms, where we could keep an eye on him.

His doctor reported that he was as healthy as a mule, and that the last thing he'd want was to move anywhere else. He had someone to come in and see he was all right, and he had enough to eat, and all we should do was telephone him as often as we could and visit frequently.

Larry and I arranged a programme for calling and visiting him. I'd ask how he was on the phone, and he'd say, 'Fine. Got that filly going nicely now, you know, and the palomino colt is a good horse.'

'Dad, you're not doing anything with those horses.'

'God, I am!'

'Well, OK.'

Silence. I knew he wasn't doing a stroke, he was hardly going outside the house.

'Dad, would you like for us to move you down here and you can stay with us for a while, until you find your feet?'

'No way, I'm not moving. What are you talking about?'

On Larry's next visit, he called us to say that my father was sinking fast. He wasn't eating and had stopped caring about his own person. He was visibly failing.

I agreed to come later the following day, but the next morning, in fact, Larry found my father dead. It was just 42 days since our mother had died.

Late that evening, I felt compelled to visit the Struve and LaPorte funeral home where my father was lying at rest. I rang my old student, Jim LaPorte, and asked if I might be admitted. He agreed.

I arrived at the appointed time and Jim let me in. He ushered me into a small room, which was very clean and bare except for a stand of flowers and a trestle at one end holding the coffin. There was no light in the room save a soft glow aimed directly onto my father.

Jim left me alone and I walked forward to look into the coffin. My brother Larry's words came back to me: 'He's shrinking to nothing in front of my eyes.' He seemed only 5ft tall, and the flesh had almost disappeared from his bones.

I'd always had this exact picture of my father; ever since I was a small boy, I knew there'd come a time when he was in a wooden box and I'd be looking down on him. Throughout his punishments and beatings, I clung to that fact. It was an image which had tracked me for my whole life, and I had to come and see it for real. Cowering under his blows when I was a child, I promised myself that my father would fit in the same-size box as any other man, and when that day came he wouldn't be able to hurt me any more.

It was a cathartic moment, but I didn't shed a tear. The truth is, I didn't care that he was dead. I don't believe my reaction meant I was an unforgiving person, it's just that I felt anger for the penalties that he'd imposed on me as though they'd happened yesterday and not 40 years ago.

Well, he couldn't hurt anyone now. He was relieved of the burden of whatever it was in him that made him like that. And whatever it was — violence, anger — I wanted gone from this earth altogether. From my small corner of the world, it was a big moment.

After leaving the funeral home, I was moved to drive down to Chinatown and find the Golden Dragon Saloon where all those years ago I'd watched my father's cruel arrest of the black man.

It was still the downtrodden area of town and now there were drug addicts lying around as well, which wasn't the case in 1943.

I noticed it was a one-way street, so I could do just as my father did that night and pull right across the street and park on what was (back then) the wrong side of the road.

I looked around, but there was no Golden Dragon. As I was searching for where it might be, a police car swung by and I saw the driver had noticed me. My Lincoln Town car was an unusually smart vehicle for this area. He parked right behind me.

The officer approached the passenger-side

window carefully, and I buzzed it down so he could speak.

'You're lost, right?'

'No, I'm not lost. I'm back here to visit — it's more than 40 years since I last sat in this spot.'

Because I hadn't immediately asked for his help getting out of this dangerous neck of the woods, he was suspicious that maybe I'd come to buy drugs and his manner became more guarded.

'Oh yeah?'

I went on, 'There used to be a saloon here called the Golden Dragon — you know what happened to it?'

'The Golden Dragon was torn down a year ago maybe.'

'Right. Well, on this occasion, more than 40 years ago, it was a bad night. My father made an arrest in there. I came by just to remember it.'

The officer brightened up. 'Your father was a policeman?'

'Yes, he was. For 12 years, as it turned out. He retired from the force quite a few years ago now, though.'

'What was his name?'

'Marvin Roberts.'

'Oh yeah. There's a big funeral for him tomorrow. There's a lot of officers going to that.'

And he was right — at my father's funeral service on the following day, there was an enormous contingent of Salinas policemen filling the church.

It was packed . . . whereas at my mother's funeral only six weeks earlier, the church had been virtually empty.

★ ★ ★

All the time that I was working with the elderly doe I called Grandma, I thought how nice it would be to start with a young deer, one with a malleable mind who had not yet been traumatised by life. I wanted to see if he or she would respond faster than Grandma, who was carrying all of her life's baggage with her.

There weren't a lot of deer around when I came to Flag Is Up in 1966. The day I met Grandma, I'd lived on the farm for 11 years, and throughout that time I can remember only ever seeing a maximum of 3 – 4 deer in a group. However, during the first 4 – 5 years I worked with Grandma, I saw a marked increase in the number of deer making their home on the farm.

So I picked out a young male and began to work with him. Later on I'd call him Yoplait, from the brand of yoghurt he particularly liked eating. I'm sure he was a better student than Grandma, but I'm also sure I understood more about the language by the time I took him on.

Within six months, his behaviour had altered significantly. I could draw him from the other deer, give him a rub around the neck and head and stroke him. He always seemed a rather indifferent character, and I assumed that that was the personality of deer in general. I would

335

later come to understand that they all have different personalities, and indifference is not the general rule.

Yoplait would ignore me for long periods of time, staring in the other direction and not paying any attention. I assumed I was making mistakes, and that was probably true to a certain degree.

However, after working with others subsequent to Yoplait, I've learned that his indifference was unique to him. I wouldn't now call it a joyful relationship I had with him, but it went on for 12 years before he died in an accident on the highway in October 1994.

During his life, Yoplait came to believe very strongly that Flag Is Up was his property. He would often go to the highest point to the north overlooking the farm and lie there as if surveying it. He would become aggressive with people and other animals whom he thought were intruders.

When strangers came to the property he would position himself between them and me, brushing them away from me. He had become jealous of my attention to other people. This is a tendency deer have, which I now know to be pervasive in the species.

Also, my employees told me that when I left the farm he became very uneasy; he would look for me, and at night he'd come and lie just outside my bedroom. He seemed to be attempting to find me or get close to me.

Later, I tried an experiment. On the day of my departure, I took an undershirt that I'd worn and put it near a tree. As I left, I briefed some of my employees to watch for his reactions. They later reported that he would lie near the undershirt for inordinate periods of time until I returned.

Later still, I took undershirts, put them in plastic bags and tied them in knots to hold the smells, leaving them with my employees so that they could change them every 3 – 4 days. I was conditioning Yoplait to think that I was still there.

This seemed to work. Without the undershirts he would get restless, often leaving the farm. He was seen walking into the village of Solvang when I was away for extended periods of time.

It's still a part of my routine today, to organise some dirty underwear for the deer. On extended trips I even have to mail used undershirts back to the ranch, to keep everyone happy.

During Yoplait's formative years, my wife Pat had a dog by the name of Jay. Yoplait took a dislike to both Pat and her dog. He regarded them as competition, and made it abundantly clear that the dog should stay in the house and that Pat should stay away from me, at least while he was around. He had the dog — a Queensland Heeler — completely intimidated. He'd lower his head and drive him back into the house at the slightest provocation.

Once, when I was away for quite a while, Pat decided to plant some flowers in the back garden. By now the deer had increased to 60 – 70 in the family group; several of them spent most of their lives close to the house, and there were only a few plants they wouldn't eat.

However, Pat had discovered that deer wouldn't eat blue flowers. On this occasion she had worked her way round outside the kitchen and laundry room, planting these blue flowers that deer wouldn't touch, when she discovered that Yoplait was coming along behind her, pulling the plants out of the ground and dropping them without attempting to eat them.

She picked up a broom which was outside the door and waved it at him, driving him off the hill and down towards the farm.

Discouraged with the wasted effort, she went to the garage and warmed up her Jaguar, opening the garage door so that the exhaust fumes could escape. Then she went into the house to get some things she needed to take down to the office.

When Pat returned to the garage, she found that Yoplait had made his way back up to the house and was now standing on top of the car. She hadn't had it for very long and was proud of it, but Yoplait had damaged the paint on every panel with his antlers and feet. He had danced on the trunk, on the hood, and he'd used his antlers to rake the sides. The whole car had to be repainted.

I'm going to be taken away in a straitjacket for mentioning this, but he'd also knocked a photograph of Pat and Jay off the wall in the garage. There are about 50 photographs hanging there, but he'd dislodged that one and now Pat saw it broken on the ground, with deer faeces on it. I'm very happy to count that as a coincidence — just so no one comes to take me away to an asylum — but it's an odd one.

Pat telephoned me that evening and suggested she might be having venison for dinner!

★ ★ ★

The voice on the other end of the telephone said, 'It's Lyman Fowler here.'

'Lyman Fowler!'

'That's right. I wonder if you remember, but I used to teach you at high school?'

'Of course I do.'

'You might also remember, I had you do a paper?'

'I remember it distinctly.'

'Well, now, I'm retired as you can imagine.'

'Yes, it was a long time ago.'

'But I have a favour to ask of you.'

'Go ahead.'

'I'm the social director of my church group and every year we try to go somewhere pretty . . . you know, somewhere civilised. No muggings or any of that, because we're quite a geriatric group as you might expect.'

'OK. What can I do for you?'

'I thought it might be possible to bring them out to have a look at your place. We wouldn't be any trouble; we'd only take up an hour or two of your time, but we've read about you in the papers of course and it occurred to me that it might be possible.'

'That'd be fine, sure. I'll give you a tour of the place.'

When we'd fixed a schedule, I put the phone down and shook my head in disbelief. I remembered Mr Fowler and that paper all right, with its big red 'F' written across it. He'd rejected my proposal as being too extravagant — and now he was coming to visit the establishment which bore quite a resemblance to those plans I'd submitted to him!

It was a beautiful summer's day when the coach arrived at Flag Is Up Farms, and Mr Fowler was the first to step out. He was a very tall man — around 6ft 5ins — and he didn't stoop at all. He was smartly dressed and had the same olive complexion and prominent eyes. His hair had turned completely white, and his face was lined; otherwise, it was the same man.

He offered me a long, graceful hand and spoke in his precise way. 'Monty, hello.' Then he kept coming and gave me a heartfelt embrace — which was unlike him.

People were filing off the coach and now stood in a semi-circle. There were about 50 elderly people looking at me expectantly.

Lyman Fowler made his introductory speech. 'Ladies and gentlemen, this is Monty Roberts, whom I've told you about, and he's kindly offered to show us his establishment, Flag Is Up Farms.'

After walking around the immediate area, much of the tour of the farm had to be conducted from the coach because they were all quite elderly people and not able to walk far. It had a public address system, and I used this to explain what they were seeing as we drove around.

They had all lived in an agricultural community, so they were interested in the planning of the farm. In addition I'd arranged for some horses to be cantering on the practice track, and we could park right alongside and watch the animals breeze past from the coach.

After doing a full circle of the property, we drove up the slope to the house, where everyone came inside to look around. Then we went on to the terrace, from which the whole farm could be seen spread out below. We provided some refreshments, and they also asked questions about the deer who were grazing on the lawn.

Mr Fowler made a speech in his precise, articulate voice that I will always remember. We stood together as he said, 'As you all know, I taught Monty when he was a young man. However, he taught me something — and it's possibly the most valuable lesson I ever learned.'

He paused, and then announced, 'A teacher does not have the right to put a cap on the aspirations of his students — no matter how unreal those aspirations might be.' He waved a long, elegant arm at the buildings and paddocks below us. 'There was a time when I told Monty that this was unattainable. Now we've all had a good look around, and seen how he proved me wrong.'

I felt a great warmth towards Mr Fowler, that he enjoyed telling this fable so much.

IV

An Invitation That Changed My Life

I N April 1989 I was invited to go to England to give a demonstration of my work in front of Her Majesty Queen Elizabeth II, Prince Philip and the Queen Mother. I have described the early part of that experience in the opening pages of this book.

The impact of this visit on me can be imagined. It was as though I was finally allowed out into the daylight, blinking a bit in the fierce glare of publicity — but with my work recognised as valid and genuine. It wasn't long, it must be remembered, since I'd built the viewing deck above the round pen at Flag Is Up; before that, I didn't show what I could do to anyone, because I thought it had been proved to me that people wouldn't accept it. Now, one of the most important figures in the horse world — and I mean world — was actively taking part in promoting demonstrations of my work to members of the public. It was the seal of approval which people needed to allow them to believe that what they were seeing was not a trick, but a genuine example of mankind communicating with horses using the language 'Equus'.

The point I'm making — that it took someone with the authority of the Queen to believe in me, before anyone else was able to — was to be brought home to me conclusively during the course of that day at the royal mews.

The first demonstration — on the Queen Mother's filly — had gone like a dream, and I'd revelled in the close attention paid to my work by all the members of the royal party.

Afterwards, we went with Sir John Miller and about 12 people, most of whom were journalists, to the Savile Gardens Restaurant in Windsor Park. Happy and excited at the warm reaction we'd received, we were looking forward to the afternoon session in front of a different audience.

During lunch, Sir John changed positions several times in order to have conversations on his radio-phone. I didn't hear what had been said, but as we were preparing to leave to go back to the castle and continue with our demonstrations, he mentioned to me that the stable staff were picking up two new horses.

This wasn't part of the schedule.

Much later, however, I would learn that the Queen had spoken with her staff and they'd suggested to her that I had done something underhand with the horses when I was supposedly taking them through the ring to acclimatise them — in short, they suspected some form of trickery.

The Queen hadn't agreed with their judgement but, nonetheless, she'd asked what they would need to see in order to be convinced that my work wasn't fraudulent.

They'd suggested that a truck be sent over to Hampton Court to pick up two very large, three-year-old piebald stallions, who were very raw and had barely been handled; they'd certainly never seen me or the round pen. They proposed to take them one at a time off the truck and see if I could start them — predicting I would fail.

Sir John told me he wanted me to start these horses without acclimatising them to the ring. Because my working methods were new to him, I suppose it didn't seem like much of a request. However, it's unfair to expect horses to go through an experience that must rank as the most traumatic of their lives and be introduced to a frightening new environment at the same time.

This new plan concerned me, as there was enough pressure on the event already. I was in a fish-bowl. It was important that everything went well, and naturally I wanted the right measures taken to give me the best chance.

When we arrived back at the Windsor mews just outside the riding hall, there was a small van parked there with the two piebald stallions shoe-horned into it. They were sweating and banging around. When the first was taken off, the other screamed fiercely and the first one was hollering back. They had always been kept together in a field at Hampton Court, and were obviously in love.

There were 100 guests invited to see the demonstration that afternoon, as well as the stable staff who were now lining up against the wall — and I knew they were expecting me to fail and so my work would be judged as false.

Sir John took the microphone and stepped into the round pen to introduce me. The huge piebald colt came charging towards him and slapped his big front feet on the ground, exhibiting anger over the whole situation.

So, Sir John stepped quickly back outside the gate and made the introduction from the other side of the fence — and you couldn't blame him.

I was not happy about these new circumstances, which I felt were unfair as well as dangerous. This big colt was aggressive and, in addition, continually distracted by his friend's calling from just outside the building.

Suddenly, everyone stood up — the Queen had walked in. She wasn't scheduled to be here, but she had turned up to see the outcome of this. She went to an area behind where the seats were located and gestured to everyone that they might sit down.

Sir John continued with his introductory speech and explained what they were about to see.

I couldn't do much else but step through the gate into the round pen, pick up my line and give it a go.

The big piebald colt circled me, acting with an all-male arrogance. I pressed him a touch harder to go away — and he did just that. As he left me and went to work, cantering a good circle against the fence, he forgot about his partner outside and became tuned in to my presence and what I was doing. He was working hard for me.

After about 3 – 4 circles of the round pen, I was receiving a good response from him and was confident that the demonstration was going well. My voice rose a few decibels in volume.

'I'm looking to have the same conversation with him. And I can assure you, he will talk to me. Watch out for the inside ear. The licking and chewing. The head down, skating a couple of inches above the ground. Great! There he goes . . . '

I wanted to drive it home to the stable crew that this was a legitimate process, that this horse was communicating with me, and I felt a good deal more comfortable conversing with him than I did explaining my work to them. After all, this colt believed me within a few minutes and trusted me after seven minutes.

As we progressed, the large piebald stallion got better and better. Sean rode him without any problem at all, well before the 30-minute mark. It was a perfect demonstration, and the Queen's reaction was one of pleasure and satisfaction — her confidence in my work had been well-founded.

As the big colt was taken out and I waited for them to bring in his companion, the stable-hands started to filter out of the room and back to their work areas. I followed them and politely asked them to come back and watch me start both of the horses from Hampton Court, not just the one.

They returned and lined up against the wall again, but perhaps with slightly more open minds by now. I then started the second horse and the demonstration went equally smoothly.

I continued with demonstrations for different

audiences for the rest of the week, and I did not sense the scepticism that I had felt directed at me on the Monday. It may have been there, but in that case it was suppressed.

The Queen and others — most of them involved with royal horses of some description — continued to ask guests to come and see what I could do. We had a count of about 200 people each day, Monday to Friday.

On the Tuesday morning, the Queen again arrived unexpectedly and spent the morning watching the horses work. She returned on Tuesday afternoon, Wednesday morning, Wednesday afternoon, Thursday all day and Friday morning. It was an exhilarating feeling to have won her commitment to the extent that she changed her diary. We share a real fascination with horses and it's a great pleasure to talk with her about them. Her continued support prompted in me a genuine warmth for her.

At one point, John Bowles arrived from California. As I described earlier, he is a friend of Sir John Miller and also my neighbour in California; it was he who brought Sir John to my farm in January of 1989. He's a real Southern big-boy with a strong accent.

When John Bowles arrived at the stable area, I was talking with the Queen. He walked up behind her, off to one side, unaware who she was, and stuck his hand out with a big smile, ready to say hello to me.

When he suddenly realised that I was in the middle of a conversation with the Queen, a look of consternation fell across his face.

I had been spending all my time with Sir John so-and-so and Lady this-and-that for three days by that time, so when plain old John Bowles came up, I shook his hand and very confidently said, 'Your Majesty, this is Sir John Bowles.' He'd received an instant knighthood from his old friend as a reward for his good services.

During that week we started 16 of the Queen's horses, four ponies for Prince Philip, the Queen Mother's filly and one show-jumping prospect that was owned by a friend of the Queen's — a total of 22 completed during the five days.

In addition, we'd decided to ride the Queen Mother's thoroughbred filly each day and bring her on a bit, so that before we left the Queen Mother could watch her ridden in the open parkland surrounding Windsor Castle. There was the risk of embarrassment because a baby going outside for the first time can do silly things, no matter which way they've been started; however, I was willing to take the chance.

That Friday in mid-April 1989 must be written in the record books as one of the most glorious, sunny days that England has ever experienced. There were blue skies with the occasional billowy white cloud sailing through, and Windsor looked as beautiful and civilised and old as only England can.

The Queen Mother was chauffeured in and I stepped to an area near the car to greet her. However, before the car actually stopped rolling, she opened the rear door with a big smile on her face and greeted me as though she had known me all her life.

She walked over, gave her filly a rub on her nose and spoke with Sean. Then she greeted Roger Oliver and said hello to Sir John and to my wife.

Sean rode out on the filly, accompanied by the head groom, Roger Oliver, who was riding an experienced older horse in front. Together they went into the gardens, and it was one of the most beautiful sights that man and horse could ever create, which might have been taken straight from a fairy tale. Sean put the filly through her paces beautifully.

The Queen herself had an important engagement that day, but she'd asked to be informed when the filly was being ridden in case she could slip away to see her.

As we walked back up the hill, approaching the castle, we saw the Queen coming out of her apartments. Dressed for her engagement, she greeted us with a warm smile and was generous in her praise regarding how the filly looked being ridden around.

The Queen and I had a 10 – 15-minute discussion; she thanked me for spending the week at Windsor Castle and outlined the plans she had for the countrywide tour on which I was due to embark. Then she departed for her meeting and we all strolled down to the riding hall.

As I was enjoying this day and thinking about everything that had happened, I realised that it had been one of the most rewarding times of my life. The pressure had gone — and our visit had been a success. It had been a storybook week for myself, my family and Sean.

That afternoon, we went back to Shotover House to stay the night. Sean was particularly looking forward to seeing Sir John's butler again — a man who went by the name of Horseman. Horseman's wife also worked at Shotover House and Sir John called her 'Horsewoman'.

When I'd first arrived at Shotover House, I'd been greeted by Horseman. As he hurried from the portico over the front entrance of this gracious, square-built manor house, he matched exactly what you'd expect of an English-butler type.

He was probably no more than 60, but he looked about 85 years old. Stooped and grey, he had a sad droopy face with big watery eyes. He was dressed very properly, but his collars and his cuffs had seen a lot of wear. Although he attempted to move quickly, he wobbled on his feet like his joints were giving him trouble. With each step he mumbled something or other, and occasionally this mumbling would become louder and take on a strangled quality, so that you thought he might literally be about to die . . . then he'd go back down to his regular mumbling as if nothing had happened. He never gave an explanation for these outbursts and certainly didn't look for any reaction to them on my part.

When I first turned up at the house, he'd trotted as fast as he could across the gravel and attempted to lift up my case, muttering away,

'Oh-oh-oh-oh, I'll get that.' It didn't seem fair to ask him to carry anything, but he wouldn't hear of my taking the case.

Sir John introduced him. 'Ah, this is my butler Horseman, he'll show you to your room.' Horseman's arms were being pulled out of their sockets as Sir John went on, 'The Canopy Room, Horseman.'

The shallow stone steps into the house were trouble enough, but now we faced a couple of flights of stairs as well. Horseman soldiered on; he wouldn't accept any help. Several times he had to stop and rest, breathing and clutching his chest and muttering to himself.

He settled me into my room and showed me the bathroom and so on. It seemed he had to make four or five trips to fetch towels, and he also came back again with a pitcher of water and a glass. Each trip he took, I thought it might be his last.

During dinner we saw his wife — this was 'Horsewoman' — who looked somewhat similar, but less dishevelled. She was in charge of the kitchen, I think — certainly she was helping him bring the food out and lay it on the sideboard.

When Sean arrived later in the week he came straight to me and, with disbelief written all over his face, he asked, 'D'you see that butler guy?' He was entranced by this unique figure. Sean's room was a flight further up than ours, so God knows how long it must have taken for him to be shown to his room.

One evening Sir John was expecting important company for dinner and he asked Horseman,

'Can we have the sitting room in tip-top condition, please, for tonight? Give the room a thorough going-over.'

By the end of the day Horseman hadn't managed to reach this item on his list of duties, so he was in a hurry — and we happened to see his version of 'a thorough going-over'. He skipped into the sitting room, muttering away under his breath and carrying a feather duster, just batting at anything that got in his way. Then he took the 15-foot-high curtains and banged them against the walls, pushed a pile of newspapers to one side, and that was it — the room was ready.

Before dinner, we were all in this sitting room and Sir John was involved in a long telephone conversation. Horseman took orders for drinks from the assembled company and disappeared.

Sir John remained on the phone and the minutes ticked away. No one was sure where Horseman had got to. After more than 15 minutes had passed, everyone was a little concerned, and since Sir John was still on the phone Sean volunteered to go and find out what had happened to him. I'm sure it crossed all our minds that it might be bad news.

Sean followed Horseman's tracks and found him leaning up against a sideboard in the hall. As Sean watched, Horseman lifted a heavy glass decanter to his lips and took a long pull from it. Then he picked up a different decanter and tried that one as well.

By this time Sean was right by him, and Horseman started mumbling away nineteen to the dozen and shifting the decanters around as if they were pieces on a chessboard. Sean could pick out enough words to understand that it had been necessary that the butler drink from all these different decanters, so as to find out which was which.

By the end of that evening, Horseman was flying. His manner became imperious; he was playing the part of an English butler to the hilt, and he announced the names of new arrivals as though he was having to shout over hundreds of people. He was magnificent.

Sean fell in love with Horseman and followed him around like a puppy, a smile always on his face. He came to me to report once that he'd seen Horseman cleaning out his — Sean's — bath. Horseman had stood over the tub holding the corner of a wet cloth which just hung there. Then, with an effortful movement, he had spun the cloth in a circle a few times and the job was done.

Sean and I split our sides over that man — and we were genuinely fond of him. He was priceless. He and his wife are both dead now, but they gave us a lot of pleasure and I know Sir John must miss them.

Now, however, it was time for Sean, Pat and me to say goodbye to Shotover House and take off on a nationwide tour. The Queen had lent us a Ford Scorpio which was a steady, rock-solid, bulletproof car, so we felt pretty safe.

As the Oxfordshire hedgerows slid past the windows of our vehicle, I could hardly believe it — we were going to show what I could do to people all over Britain. In 1966, when I'd built the round pen at Flag Is Up Farms, I'd designed it without a viewing balcony so no one could see in. Since the time I'd shown Ray Hackworth what I could do with starting the mustangs in the mid-1940s, I'd shown my work to no one — not until the mid-1980s. Now I was going to drive hundreds of miles every day in a foreign country to show as many people as possible. I was actively seeking their support and approval.

The response I received was incredible.

In Newmarket we found five of the wildest two- and three-year-olds you could ever imagine. They were just a tick quieter than mustangs would be, extremely raw and green, but they were very healthy and well-fed.

The weather was hostile — driving wind and rain on the second day — and I couldn't imagine that people would stand there and watch me start these 'wild horses', but they did; there must have been 200 – 300 people there. They braved that weather unbelievably and the horses went well. One of them was filmed by Channel 4, which televised it all over the British Isles. Sheik Mohammed and a contingent of people from the Arab Emirates came, and I'm told they liked what they saw.

We stayed at Sandringham, on the Queen's property, with Michael Osborne and his wife. They had a wonderful dinner party arranged, and I had many questions to answer.

Later we stopped at the Yorkshire Riding Centre for the Bartel family, who were the hosts of the event.

357

Then we travelled to the impressive Gleneagles hotel and leisure facility in Scotland. Between 400 – 500 people attended and asked questions in their extraordinary Scottish accents. I really needed an interpreter.

It was in Scotland that Sean said something which made me laugh. He'd just ridden a four-year-old stallion — an aggressive animal, as I remember, 16.2 hands high and over 1,200 pounds in weight, full of grain. When he caved in and forgot about being a stallion, this horse went like a charm. Up on his back for the first time, Sean could relax, and he called to me in a loud voice, 'Fifty-first fluke in a row!'

I had to explain my laughter to the audience. 'You know,' I said, 'every place we go, there's always someone who says that what they're watching must be a fluke. It's become a standing joke, that there's always a person who says it was a fluke. New audience, new fluke! Well, as Sean mentioned just then, this is our fifty-first fluke in a row in this country — and I'm not even counting the many thousands of horses I've started before I landed at Heathrow!'

We then flew to the Isle of Man, where we had perhaps our oddest experience.

We were picked up at the little aerodrome by a woman in her late sixties dressed in the English country style with gaberdine trousers and so on, who went by the curious name of Dizzy Wriggle. She'd seen a lot of the wind and sun, and she had a warm, smiling outlook. From the outset she was gracious and hospitable, and did everything she could to make us comfortable.

On the way, she told us she'd had a round pen built for us, but she was worried about it. When she took us to see it, it was quite clear that any young wild horse would be able to escape easily enough. She'd had some stakes driven into the ground in a circle, and nailed some wooden straps to them. But there was no sand in the bottom, so they'd be sliding around in the mud.

She set her people to buying some more lumber and making the pen into a more solid structure, but it meant the audience would be unable to see in so easily.

Then she took us into the cobbled stable area, telling us that she and her husband lived in the stable block now, as the old house was too big for them. 'It's just too much work, you know, what with Billy's condition.' Her husband was in a wheelchair, and went by the name of Billy Wriggle.

As I walked past the tack-room, I saw a lunch table laid out in there with cold cuts, egg and salad and all sorts. None of it was covered up, so it looked like she was about to have a party.

She said to us, 'But you're staying in the big house.'

Pat, Sean and I followed her up there and were shown into the most ancient house I've ever seen; it was close on a thousand years old and hadn't been lived in for a long time, let alone kept up. I remember going in one room where there was a foul smell — I guessed something must have died in there. As I approached the fireplace, the smell was getting worse all the time.

Then I saw what it was — a horse's foot was standing there on the mantel! Dizzy Wriggle had had someone saw the foot off a favourite horse, and she'd just stood it there without boiling it or curing it in any way.

There were huge old toilets with spiders in them, and cracked wooden seats left over from the dark ages. When you turned on a tap, leaves and twigs came out.

Dizzy Wriggle walked ahead of us, showing us the way to our bedrooms. We thought we'd probably need to lay a piece of string to find our way out again.

She went into the first bedroom and started shouting at the top of her voice. We didn't know what was happening and quickened our pace so that we could maybe save her from a gang of intruders — only to see when we got there that she was throwing a whole tribe of dogs off our bed. Now they thundered past us — whippets and spaniels and setters. Dizzy Wriggle was re-arranging the bed and straightening the pillows. 'It's perfectly all right, everything's clean.'

We wondered, did the dogs live in the house by themselves?

That night, we had dinner in the main house. A group of people had been invited, and they were the most stimulating company. They were so far afield from our experience of life, yet they received us with such hospitality and genuine interest.

A very pretty girl was coping with the Aga and was managing to produce some excellent food — but all the time I was wondering what was happening to the spread laid out in the tack-room. I hoped someone had eaten it.

These were upper-crust English people and although the plates were chipped and the glasses leaked, everything was done properly. Vast quantities of wine were consumed.

Billy Wriggle, his white hair greased back over his head, sat at the end of the table in his wheelchair, stoic in his demeanour, talking in a voice as loud as a bugle. He'd spilled generous quantities of food down his canary-yellow jersey.

The lady sitting next to me engaged me in an extremely odd conversation.

She said, 'D'you know about pot-pourri?'

'Yes — it's that stuff in a basket that smells good.'

'No, but do you really know about its origins?'

'No, ma'am, I don't.'

'Well, washing yourself is unhealthy. All this soap — destructive to your skin.'

'I see.'

'Bathing is unintelligent. And, you know, our ancestors knew this. In former times, they didn't do all this silly washing. When they went to the toilet, they merely dipped their hands in a bowl of pot-pourri and emerged fragrant and refreshed.'

I just didn't know how to answer that.

Then there came the most extraordinary thing — the ladies were asked to leave the room.

Dizzy Wriggle stood up and announced in an imperious voice, 'Ladies, this way.'

When they'd gone, Billy Wriggle produced a box of Havanas which looked like they had been around since the house was built, and everyone proceeded to try to set these things alight. Port was served, and the whole scene looked like a painting you might see in a Bond Street art gallery.

There were more questions, disagreements, discussions and quite a lot more to drink. Then they toasted the Queen. One by one the men pushed back their chairs, stood up straight and delivered what sounded like old military speeches of some kind. Sean and I were bowled over; we'd never seen anything like this in California.

After each of the military-type pronouncements, there'd come the toast: 'God Save the Queen.'

When it came to Billy Wriggle's turn to speak, he became very animated and gave his speech in a deliberate, emotional manner. From time to time he would bang the table, then the glass in his other hand would jump and the port would splash onto the yellow sweater. Then pretty soon he'd bash the table again.

After a while the ladies returned and the party began to break up. Dizzy Wriggle wheeled Billy Wriggle from the room and out to the front entrance. I helped her load him into the car so that they could drive the short distance to the stable block where they lived. I must admit I was worried if they would ever make it, and my fears turned out to be well-founded.

362

Pat, Sean and I excused ourselves at that stage of the evening as well — although I'm sure other members of the party were set to continue until dawn.

We went up to our room where Pat went to bed fully dressed; she was sure that she'd have to jump up and run away from something in the middle of the night — spiders or ghosts or whatever.

The next morning the three of us walked down to the stable block to catch up with what was going on. As we approached, we saw the same pack of dogs all gathered in a circle, noses to a point on the ground and tails wagging in a fan.

We wondered what they'd found, and thought it was probably a rabbit or a rat. But when they separated in front of us, we saw that they were lapping at quite a large pool of blood.

We greeted Dizzy Wriggle some minutes later, and she told us she'd had the most awful night. She'd driven the short distance from the big house to the stable-yard without incident, but then — when she was transferring Billy from the car to his wheelchair — she'd dropped him, and he'd suffered a very bad cut on his leg which had bled profusely onto the cobbles.

Dizzy had had to leave him there lying on the ground while she went to call for an ambulance. He was still at the hospital now, recovering.

Boy, was this a glimpse into old-fashioned, upper-class English life!

When we caught the flight back to the mainland, we saw the good-looking girl who'd managed to kick-start that old kitchen and make us our dinner. It turned out she was the Wriggles' grand-daughter.

I hardly dared ask what her name was, as I imagined it was going to be 'Twiggy Wriggle' or 'Piggy Wriggle' or something like that.

No, she had a different surname, lucky for her.

After the Isle of Man we went to Chichester, a country town in the south of England, and did some New Forest ponies and wild horses mostly for Pony Club and horse-show people.

Various other dates took the head-count up to 98 horses and ponies. We averaged 27 minutes per horse to accept saddle, bridle and rider.

Returning to Shotover House, we spent a day with Sir John giving him an account of our tour. I also wrote a report for the Queen and left it with him to deliver personally.

When we flew home to California at the end of this trip, I somehow had the feeling that life wouldn't be the same. As the plane lifted away from that beautiful, crowded island, I imagined all the horses down there whose lives we'd touched briefly and I wanted to continue — I wasn't tired out yet. I thought I would probably return to Britain many times in the future.

I was right. *Horse and Hound* magazine, through a man by the name of Michael Clayton, became interested in sponsoring a trip in the fall of 1989. It was to include two venues, Stoneleigh and Towerlands; there were to be full-day teach-ins at each location.

Also, it looked as if my association with the

royal family's horses would continue. The Queen had asked if she could send people to California to study my techniques, so that they might return to England and start her young horses using the methods she'd seen.

Victor Blackman from Dick Hearn's yard, and later from Lord Huntington's yard, was to do just that, and returned to take charge of starting the Queen's yearlings.

Corporal Major Terry Pendry, who was in charge of starting the horses for the Household Cavalry, and Richard Maxwell, also the Household Cavalry, were to study extensively with me.

New opportunities were being offered, and I was glad to accept them.

* * *

My tour of the UK prompted another invitation — I was asked to make two tours of Ireland in 1990.

My Irish contact was Hugh McCusker, who is famous for his hunter show-horses. It put a different spin on my visit there and opened up a different world for me. His nickname on the English show-horse scene is 'The flamboyant Irishman', and I'd go along with that description.

I found the Irish people down-to-earth and interested in testing me to the maximum. They brought me tough horses and demanded honesty and openness in my dealing with them. A couple of events, particularly, are worth relating here.

Hugh McCusker had scheduled a demonstration in the town of Kill, near Dublin. The property we were to use had just been bought by the president of the Irish Draught Horse Association, and he was keen to have us come there and introduce his facility to the public via the demonstration. He asked me to do a pair of fillies, and said there would possibly be a third horse.

As was routine by now, we arrived beforehand just to introduce the horses to the round pen. We found a very nice building with the pen all set up for us.

We also found this flashy three-year-old Irish draught colt, called Stanley. He had feet the size of dinner plates and a neck you'd have trouble fitting both your arms around. This was the mysterious 'third horse'.

I put Stanley through the normal procedures to acclimatise him to the pen and to the building. While doing it, he seemed to be quite alert — an 'all-boy' sort of animal. He was aggressive and unco-operative.

I asked Hugh McCusker about the history of this colt, but he wasn't sure what had been done with him before, only that he'd never been saddled, bridled or ridden.

After he was acclimatised to the pen and the building, I said that Stanley could go back to the stall, and I recall seeing two boys come in. They worked as a team to take him from the round pen to the stable. This didn't seem out of line at the time, but looking back, I realise there was a reason for two boys doing the job instead of just one.

After the colt was taken back, I put the two fillies through the same procedures; they were both nice and looked the type that could give us a good demonstration. I felt it would be best if we just did the two fillies, since we allow about an hour per horse including introductions and questions and answers. A two-hour demonstration would be plenty long enough.

When we arrived in the evening to do the demonstration, it was clearly going to be well attended. There was seating for 500 people, and it was just about full.

After a 20-minute introduction to my methods of working, I did the first filly and she made a good example of herself.

Following about 15 minutes of questions and answers, the next filly was brought in. My opening remarks were quite short, since they'd heard the explanation before. She was a nice filly, and it proved to be a very good demonstration of 'join-up'.

After another 15 minutes of questions and answers, Mr McCusker came to me and said that the owner would like to call an interval for some refreshments but that he wanted me to do the big colt, Stanley, after the break.

Fair enough, I agreed.

Somebody announced over the public address system that Stanley would be done after the refreshment time — and it seemed to me that everyone was familiar with the name of this

367

animal. A ripple of interest ran through the crowd. My experience in match racing and rodeos in small towns in America told me there was definitely something in the wind.

As the crowd filtered back into the building after the 20-minute break, I saw there were more people here after the intermission than there were before — which is pretty unusual for ten o'clock at night. The seats were filled, and a lot of people were standing up.

I asked Mr McCusker how this could have happened. He said that when everyone heard that Stanley was going to be started without a lead rope attached to his head, they'd all gone and telephoned their friends to tell them to come and see this cowboy get eaten alive!

When Stanley was brought into the building, he was being led by the two lads, each with a lead rope, one on either side. They were keeping their distance from him, and a lady was walking behind to shoo him from the rear.

The two boys went through the gate well in front of him, being very careful about how they handled the whole procedure. When he was inside, they gently released the two lead ropes.

With the adrenalin surging in his body from being under the lights and having probably 600 people watching him, Stanley marched around the pen and appeared very much in charge of the situation. I didn't need to be told that this was a colt with some reputation.

I switched on my lapel microphone and announced to the crowd that I was ready to go ahead. As I walked towards the gate leading into the round pen, you could have heard a pin drop. Suddenly there wasn't a single person rustling a crisp packet, nor a single cough.

I opened the gate and stepped into the pen. At that time Stanley was on the far side, about 50 feet from me. As I closed the gate behind me and stepped away from the fence, he arched his neck and marched about three steps towards me. Then he pinned his ears back, bared his teeth and came at me, full-speed. The audience gasped.

I tripped the latch on the gate and stepped outside. The colt slammed to a halt inches from the fence and turned away to show off his supremacy.

I said to the audience, 'Wow! What are you trying to do to me here?' I shook my head and put my hands on my hips, looking around at the banks of people sitting and staring. 'Surely the nice people of Ireland wouldn't set me up for something like this, would they, by any chance?'

Not a word was spoken, and not a sound could be heard.

I stood there for a while, then I sat down on a chair near my gate and gave the impression that I was very worried about going into the pen and dealing with this horse.

Then I addressed the audience again. I said, 'On this trip I've met a lot of sceptical Irish horsemen who feel that some of my work is less than believable. Now, I know that Ireland is filled with good horsemen — in fact, I'm sure there are a lot of them in the building right now. And since I'm a 56-year-old man who's completely out of shape and has had half his backbone surgically removed, I'd very much like to ask for a volunteer to come and deal with this horse. It would be interesting to see what an Irish horseman could do with a horse as aggressive as this.'

I sat there for a few seconds and listened to this deep silence. To tell the truth, I wanted to see a few red faces. And then I said in a surprised voice, 'No volunteers? Come on, think about it. Let's get some young kid down here who's in good shape, and he can go ahead and do this horse. I'll make some suggestions from outside the ring.'

Again there was not a motion, nor a sound. It was absolutely dead silent in that room, except for the sound of the colt's breath and his giant foot pawing at the floor of the round pen.

Then I said, 'Well, I guess I'm going to have to go ahead and do him.' I went to my equipment bag and got out my nylon lariat rope, leaving my light sash line outside the pen.

I went through the gate and immediately started to swing a loop in my rope.

Well, this young Irish draught horse had never seen a cowboy before, so he stood off and moved around the perimeter of the pen and looked me over. He was confused enough by this loop whirling around my head; he wasn't going to try to charge through it.

We circled one another for a few seconds and I started to close in on him. He went into a high-stepping trot near the fence. I continued to close on him and he picked up speed.

When the time was right, I threw the loop which caught him around the neck. This was real Western stuff and I'd been doing it all my life.

The colt went crazy. He bucked and he balled and he did everything he could do to try and shed this rope. Now he had a new concern — I wasn't his problem, it was the rope. I would just give him a little tug now and then, and he would go into orbit again, expressing himself with all the rage that he had locked up in him. This went on for 30 – 40 seconds, then he settled down and came to a stop.

At that point I slipped in near him, and I wound the rope around his head in a fashion I have used for about 40 years, called a come-along, which I mentioned earlier. It's a way of connecting the pressure points in the rope against certain nerve ganglia.

And then I started to school him on the come-along. His aggressive tendencies were clearly obvious for the first minute or two, maybe up to five minutes. Then he began to settle and respond to me; he started giving me the early signs of 'join-up'; he opened up an ear to me, according me that much respect anyway. Then I observed his tongue come out from between his teeth, and he was licking and chewing. He was prepared to engage in a conversation with me — and I understood his language. I was communicating with him pretty well within 5 – 8 minutes.

Rather than go through the loose horse or free

horse 'join-up', I continued to work with the come-along on him, because he'd have been a very dangerous horse to work with had I released him in the pen.

When he was comfortable, I put the saddle on his back and he had a few complaints at that, but not too many. His heart started to calm down a bit, and he was beginning to have confidence in me. The bridle went on, and then I put the long-lines on and I long-lined him pretty hard for about 10 – 12 minutes. I brought my rider in and put him on — and I must say, he was a game lad to climb on such a monster animal which would have the power of two normal horses.

Now, however, this colt was acting very well and I was giving him lots of encouragement.

Once the rider was up and he was working in a controlled circle, we went ahead and gave him about 10 – 15 minutes of trotting and cantering. The colt performed well.

It should go down as one of the best demonstrations I have done. The people were amazed and full of questions, I could have stayed there for hours talking with them about what they'd seen, but I was ushered away to a party at the owner's house.

When I arrived there, the owner told me the story behind this colt. It turned out that he had been the champion in-hand Irish draught at the Dublin Horse Show the year before as a two-year-old, but he'd become very aggressive and he'd been kept in a dark stall ever since.

As I heard this, I was more than anything

pleased to have got him out of that darkness. Now he could shrug off his reputation and put the trauma behind him, if he was handled properly from now on.

I returned to the same place — Kill, near Dublin — in 1996. I saw they had some show-jumping fences set up in one corner of the arena, but I thought nothing of it. But after the demonstration, the organisers had a surprise for me. 'Monty, this is Stanley, and he's now Ireland's finest show-jumping Irish draught horse'. They brought him in and a young rider put Stanley through his paces. He went over those poles beautifully — all his power and grace was now controlled and fluent. It was a great experience.

★ ★ ★

The Irish National Stallion Show was being held at Balinsloe, and to understand my consternation at this story you have to remember that I was born and raised in California.

This stallion festival was a very large event held in the bowl of a valley which seemed to me to be pretty rapidly filling with water. It was a quagmire. Sheets of rain were falling. We only have drops of rain in California — sometimes pretty big drops, I grant you, in a storm — but I'd never seen these curtains of water drifting across the entire countryside. I couldn't understand why they weren't cancelling the event, but Hugh McCusker pointed out that if they started cancelling events because of rain, there wouldn't be any left to go to!

Sure enough, these brave Irish people were turning up and staying to watch the different events. By the time we'd engaged 4-wheel drive and made our way into the ground, there must have been around 3,000 people there. The place looked like Woodstock, except everyone was in oilskins — and probably wearing waders, for all I knew.

The two stallions which had been arranged for us were in their box on a nearby promontory, so we slogged our way up there. They were squeezed into a tiny trailer which was bursting at the seams, completely closed up. Steam was rolling from the air vents set into the top, and there was a lot of banging and kicking going on. The whole outfit looked like it would take off down the hill at any minute.

A young Irish guy of maybe 22 was there, soaked to the skin, holding on to some equipment which was also drenched.

We agreed not to unload the horses to show them the round pen; we weren't sure we'd be able to swim back up again. This was a once-only effort.

When the time came, the round pen was a sea of mud and I was standing in the middle of it. I asked for the lapel microphone and they said, 'Ah yes, the remote microphone.'

'No,' I reminded them, 'the lapel microphone.'

The short answer was, they only had a remote microphone, which was the size of a cucumber and had no way of attaching to me.

I pointed out, 'I need both my hands.'

They had a good answer for that too. They took my coat off, my shirt off, and taped this cucumber microphone to my chest. Then they squeezed the water out of my clothes and allowed me to put them back on.

Our first stallion was sliding down the hill now, towing the young lad behind him like one of those dinghies you have at the back of a boat. His neighbour in the box was screaming, and he was screaming back.

When the stallion stepped into the round pen, his feet were sucked into mud a foot deep. He probably couldn't have run away from me if he'd wanted to.

I started my usual introduction. 'Ladies and gentlemen . . . ' But with a fizz and a crackle, the microphone had given out.

By this time, I didn't care. I was just going to go on, try to rescue some sort of demonstration and get out of there.

Then I saw Hugh McCusker running to the announcer's stand. Seconds later I heard his voice come over the public address system, loud and clear: 'Monty Roberts' microphone has been drowned out, so I'm going to take over, and I know he would have said something along the following lines: 'Good afternoon, ladies and gentlemen, my name is Monty Roberts and we're here today to . . . '

Hugh McCusker was my voice for that whole demonstration, and he did just fine.

Probably the horses wanted to get out of the rain as much as we did, and they were begging to join-up with me. In the event, I'm not sure what happened — who joined up with whom, or what we said to each other — or how we kept our shoes on, even. All they wanted was to finish with this circle of mud they found themselves in.

Afterwards, Hugh McCusker and I headed straight for the nearest supply of best Irish malt whisky.

* * *

When I returned to California from Ireland, I swear I still had steam rising from my back and mud under my fingernails.

Arriving home, I noticed that Flag Is Up seemed curiously empty. I asked, 'Where is Yoplait?'

Nobody knew.

As it turned out, my male deer, Yoplait, had crossed the highway in front of the farm and had been hit by a car. He broke his right hip, and his right hind leg was swinging like a flag in the breeze.

I found him — on the front lawn of the house as though begging for help.

I had some Flag Is Up staff help me to lift him in the back of my pick-up. Then I took him to one of the stables and put him in a box stall.

I thought that if I could put the leg in a cast, then maybe I could save his life. Together with the vet, we made an attempt to do this; but Yoplait wasn't going to stand for having someone else work with me to get a cast on him. Because of his resistance, it would have done him more damage than good.

So, I continued to try to help him by myself — and he settled enough to lie on a very deep bed with enough straw to prop his broken leg in place. I put grain, hay and water within reach. He lay there for two weeks without standing on his feet. It was about 14 – 15 days before I saw him stand, and I noticed that the leg had started to mend and was fairly rigid.

He didn't put any weight on it for another 2 – 3 weeks — and it healed.

Ultimately Yoplait walked without even a noticeable limp. The healing properties of deer are incredible; many times Yoplait and others have overcome injuries that would have been fatal to any horse. Later he would break his jaw in many places and knock several of his teeth out in another altercation with a car on the highway. That time I had to feed him hot gruel to keep him alive. His jaw healed and while he had a funny smile on his face thereafter, he was able to live comfortably and it didn't affect his ability to eat.

By now I had begun to work on another male deer, Bambo. He was a dramatic success and joined-up strongly. He's so tame now that I can run at him, slapping my thighs, and all he does is ignore me and come closer. At 12 years old, he has gone through all the jealousy traits that I saw in Yoplait and the other deer I've worked with, but to a lesser degree.

Although Bambo is naturally of a sweeter disposition and takes less offence to strangers, he is still possessive and watches over our relationship intently. He spends a great deal of his time near our house, and is diligent about greeting me in the morning and coming around at dinner-time when he knows I'll be home.

I work with him continually to strengthen the join-up phenomenon. It's reached the point now where should I want to walk, say, 5 miles back into the hills, I could literally take Bambo with me and bring him back to the house again, controlling his movements by using these communication skills.

It was only in 1990 that I started to work with a young female we call Patricia. She is similar to Yoplait in that she is distant and cold and will ignore you for long periods of time, but she is virtually expressionless in her communication.

The difference between Patricia's character and Yoplait's is that she is in no way surly. She has no ill-intent towards anyone, even a stranger, but is simply aloof and distant, ignoring strangers and moving away from them. She is by far the greatest challenge I've had in terms of getting one to warm up and to reach a position where I could predict her responses. Patricia isn't great fun, and she tests my ability to communicate each time I work with her.

Some years later, I took on another female called Feline (pronounced Fe*leen*). There are distinct differences in the personalities of these two females, Feline and Patricia. Feline is one of the sweetest, kindest, most attentive deer that I've come across. She doesn't ignore me and her responses are dramatic. When I ask her

378

to go away, she expresses herself with great displeasure, as she considers it a horrible form of discipline. She shakes her head and will actually balk, round her back and jump up in front, which is the same reaction the horse has when it roots its nose out in a circle: 'I don't want to go away. I didn't mean that. I'm sorry for what I did.'

When you invite her back, you can almost see her smile. She returns fast, full of reaction, totally unlike Patricia. Yet, I've worked with the two of them simultaneously.

One morning Feline showed up at the house and I spent some time working with her, only to find that she had been bitten by a spider or some other insect. Her muzzle and the bridge of her nose were swollen to almost double their normal size. It was bothering her to eat because her gums were swollen.

Almost all the deer I've chosen as subjects have come to the house quickly when injured and presented themselves on the lawn, as if to say, 'I need your help and attention.'

Feline was all right, and the swelling subsided in a few days. She has been a joy to work with — her responses are keen and more advanced than any horse I've dealt with.

Once there was a doe on the farm that gave birth to twins, one male and one female (twinning is common). She then proceeded to walk away from them and not return. I saw them a couple of times on the side of the hill about 300 yards from the house. The first time they were still wet, new-born and unable to stand.

About 4 – 5 hours later, I came by and the doe was still nowhere to be found. While they were up and walking around a bit, the twins were still quite weak and hungry.

Around sunset of the same day, there was still no mother to be seen. The twins had moved down the hill 50 feet or so, and were starting to bump into one another looking for a way to nurse. I decided to let them go through the night and see how it was the next morning, hoping that the doe would come back and suckle them during the night.

The following morning they had progressed down the hill another 50 feet or so, and there was still no mother in sight. By this time they were looking pretty sad. I decided to let it go until midday and see if the mother would return.

But she didn't come back.

About 28 hours after I first saw them, I gave them each three ounces of goat's milk, which I had frozen from a goat which had just given birth so that I got the first milk — colostrum.

Then I left them where they were.

By sundown the next day the mother still hadn't returned, so we took the two babies to the breeding barn and started to feed them with the goat's milk at four-hourly intervals for about three days.

To have a thoroughbred breeding farm makes this easy; there's a night foaling attendant who is trained at this kind of work. Then I brought in a female goat who was fresh with milk and fostered them onto her, and they began nursing.

Cyrus and Reba, as we called them, were successfully established into the wild at about three months of age. They spend most of their time a few hundred yards from the house, and are so responsive to the communication process that they virtually talk to you in English. They are a joy to have about. Both of them have wonderful personalities and are extremely friendly with the people around us as well as with strangers. I can take them with me or leave them at home at will. They will eat out of my hand and they will, if you're not careful, follow you through the door into the house.

I have to say that in one sense these deer that I've chosen to work with have received no great favours from me. Living in the wild is a challenge for them once they've lost their full desire to flee from danger. I've assumed responsibility for their protection. I've learned to keep things as natural as I can, except for the communication work.

When I speak with horse groups around the world and mention working with deer in the wild, their perception is that this is impossible — the deer will run away, there is no way to communicate with them.

Yes, the deer will go away — but if you follow, and then read a curve they make, they will often circle around to stay within a given area. They do not continue simply to go away. You can confine their movements to a reasonable area, 2 – 3 miles in diameter, where you can work with them.

It's a time-consuming activity which very few

people have the inclination to pursue. If I have been silly enough to accumulate this knowledge, others can learn from me and avoid having to walk about on a hillside for weeks at a time.

I can promise that it has worked for me virtually without fail; that if I create in my mind's eye a round pen a couple of miles in diameter, and if I think about the deer as horses in a round pen, I will in fact communicate with them effectively.

I have to be twice as tenacious and twice as delicate in my responses, but it *does* work.

The extra level of refinements that I've added to my technique — courtesy of the deer — I've put to good use with my own horse, called Dually.

Dually is a registered quarter-horse gelding, dark bay in colour with a black mane and tail and black points. He has a white pastern on his near hind leg and a white, irregular star between the eyes with a strip that runs down to his muzzle. He's 14 hands 3 inches high and weighs 1,200 pounds — so quite a solid guy, is Dually. In fact, this affectionate name I have for him refers to a type of pick-up we have here in the USA — called a dually — which has a beefed-up rear end with twin tyres at the back, so that they can tow a trailer. They look massively broad and strong, if you stand behind them — and that's how Dually looks. His rear quarters are like a couple of small hills jammed together, and the power they give him is incredible. He's a turbo-charged, twin-engined type of rocket-horse; and he also has the balance and coordination that's bred into the modern-day examples of the breed.

There's no way he can replace Brownie and Johnny Tivio, but Dually is a natural successor to them — both in terms of my affection for him and in his achievements. He too is a world-class, championship-winning animal in his own right.

From my first day with Dually, I felt I had the opportunity to create a near-perfect working animal.

After join-up, Dually bonded with me very strongly and, like Johnny Tivio, he will follow me around the farm without any headgear on. I can wander up to the promontory which overlooks the farm and he'll walk alongside as if there were an invisible thread connecting us. He's been schooled from start to finish only using the methods which I have described in this book. I haven't trained him, I've created an environment in which he's wanted to learn. I've never struck him or pulled at his mouth, ever — in fact I could have used a piece of cotton thread instead of leather reins. Yet, on totally loose rein, he'll slide to a blinding halt from a full gallop just hearing a single word, 'Whoa', and at the same time feeling my weight settle back in the saddle. Again on a loose rein, he'll spin like a top, just feeling the gossamer weight of the rein against his neck and a slight pressure applied to the inside.

He has an immense heart, does Dually, which is just as well because to train him using these experimental methods takes patience and hard work from both of us. However, learning from my experiences with Brownie and Fancy Heels, among hundreds of others, I've paid careful attention to ensuring that his appetite to work isn't dulled by repetition and overwork; it's been essential to our progress together that he should remain fresh and keen as ever.

He's six years old now, and in the prime of life. The understanding between us is mature and well-founded, and we can enjoy ourselves as much in the show-ring as we can when walking around this beautiful property, Flag Is Up — he, without a care in the world of course, while I puzzle out how to deal with this or that horse, or how to stop the deer from metamorphosing into human beings.

★ ★ ★

There are events for all of us which serve to change the pattern of our lives. The first of which was in 1943 when my father killed the black man. I remember the second of these as being my conversation with Brownie in 1948. The third was on 16 June 1956, when I married Pat. Her support and her tolerance for my shortcomings, failings and maniacal approach to my work is absolutely essential, I know now. Somehow I was lucky enough to find that person at the first attempt. Then, as I said earlier, the birth of our children — Debbie on 10 April 1957, Lori on 12 January 1959 and Marty on 1 February 1961 — these were events that changed the character of my life.

In dealing with horses, there was my life before

Johnny Tivio and my life after him. I've never dealt with a horse with the kind of brain that Johnny Tivio had. He was the one who trained me — not vice versa.

Then perhaps there is the Monty Roberts before April of 1989, when I spent my first week with the Queen and her family, and there's a different Monty Roberts afterwards.

A horse called Lomitas has provided me with my most recent landmark event. He was born in England in 1988. His sire is Nininski and his dam is La Colorada, by Surumu, owned by Walther J. Jacobs of Bremen, Germany.

Placed in training in Bremen with a young trainer by the name of Andreas Wohler, Lomitas was a good-looking chestnut colt who would race in the colours of Gestut Fahrhof, the Jacobs stud farm.

By early 1990 he began to show potential by doing a few speed works in February and March. By early that summer, he appeared to be a very good prospect.

He won both of his starts in 1990, and was the high-rated two-year-old in Germany that year. Gestut Fahrhof was no stranger to top horses, but it is always an honour to have a champion two-year-old. You can look forward to the Derby, and other three-year-old classics present themselves as exciting targets. This was the kind of horse Lomitas was.

In April of 1991 came the first sign of trouble. Lomitas was prepped and ready for his debut as a three-year-old, and on the day he was to be shipped he proved to be quite a problem when they attempted to load him on the truck to go to the race meet.

After he arrived at the meet, there was a bigger problem: getting him into the starting stalls. They led him up — and each time he balked at going inside. He threw his head up, side-stepped, pulled back; he refused every which way. All the other horses and their jockeys were in their stalls, having to wait for Lomitas. No one likes this situation, least of all the other jockeys, for whom it's always a nerve-racking time.

After 15 – 20 minutes it was decided that he would be scratched from the race, and he'd have to be taken home and schooled to return another day.

You can imagine the apprehension in the Gestut Fahrhof camp when the champion two-year-old refused to run in his first race as a three-year-old.

After about two weeks of re-schooling and going through tests for the stewards, another race was targeted in Cologne. It was difficult to load him into the van — but what happened on the racecourse that day is incredible.

He was the last horse to be put into the starting stalls — but he wouldn't go in. The rest of the horses stood and waited for about 20 minutes while they wrestled with Lomitas. Eventually they put a blindfold on him, and they had his tail up over his back and over the shoulder of the jockey. They had a dozen men attempting to get him to accept the stalls. At that point he became vicious, attacked the men and caused injuries.

He ended up lying on the ground, exhausted from the fight. The race started with Lomitas immobile, flat on his side, behind the stalls on the turf course.

Immediately after the race, word came down from the stewards that Lomitas was banned from racing for life. He was to go home and never return to the race-track.

The owners, Mr and Mrs Jacobs, left the racecourse in despair. Their young champion horse was not only a non-performer, but he was a convicted criminal sentenced to a lifelong ban from racing.

By this time, I had an established reputation for the successful treatment of remedial thorough-bred racehorses; I was someone who was known to be able to deal with difficult cases, around the world. I received a call from Andreas Wohler, Lomitas' trainer, asking if I would fly in and straighten him out.

So I put my life aside on 12 June 1991, and left California for Germany.

At the airport, I saw a man in riding breeches who looked too young to be a trainer. Nevertheless he *was* in breeches, so perhaps this was someone Andreas had sent to meet me. I walked up to him and asked, 'Do you know Andreas Wohler?'

He smiled and said, 'I'm Andreas Wohler.' I didn't know how young he was, but he looked too young, given his list of achievements.

We drove immediately to the Bremen Racecourse (where several trainers like Andreas leased facilities for training and stabling their strings of horses) and I met this superstar, Lomitas, for the first time.

I went into his box stall and there he was, turning his head to look at me. A registered thoroughbred stallion, foal of 1988, 16 hands high, 1,150 pounds, chestnut in colour with a white pastern off-hind, a star between his eyes with elongated strip that widens and ends between his nostrils. I said out loud, in awe, 'Gorgeous!' I could see every point of his skeletal frame hitting its mark — he had a perfect thoroughbred racehorse conformation. 'Correct of limb, in every way,' I said.

I walked over to where he was munching hay, standing against the back of his stall, and greeted him with a stroke on his neck. 'Hello, Lomitas, you're a fine man, eh?' I proceeded to move my hands back along his body and I felt that he wanted to move into my hands, away from the wall. I held out against the pressure, and he immediately kicked out behind.

I logged this as being a possible response to any number of things, and continued making his acquaintance. He really was a breathtaking animal, and with a look in his eye that spoke of very high intelligence. I'd travelled a long way to be standing here, and suddenly I was very pleased to have made it.

So there we were — and my task was very specific: I had to cure this beautiful, intelligent animal of his fear of the starting stall.

As we had discussed between us before my arrival, Andreas had constructed a solid-wall, permanent training stall for our mission, which was much safer than the conventional racing stall. I could work with Lomitas on good footing in the centre of a riding hall on the Bremen Racecourse.

They checked me into the Silinger Hotel, a few miles from the stable, and picked me up about 7 a.m. the following morning. When I asked Andreas to give me someone who could speak English, but most importantly who had had some horsemanship experience, he introduced me to a young man by the name of Simon Stokes.

As this story progresses you will see that, as is often the case in successful remedial stories, the people are as important to the success of the project as the horses. Simon Stokes was about 5′ 6″ and weighed 130 pounds. He was a jump jockey from Chichester in England, whose nose had been broken many times from pushing fences over head-first.

In addition to steeplechasing, he also rode on the flat and was an assistant to Andreas in training the horses. He had been living in Germany for 11 years and spoke fluent German. This was a dream for me, to be assigned an assistant who could speak the language of the country fluently, who understood horses and could speak English.

To make that dream even better, Simon Stokes — as I was to find out later — is a man who is talented, courteous and respectful. When he smiles at you and you get to know him, he is one of the most wonderful human beings.

I walked into this dreamland on 13 June 1991 and found Lomitas, an equine superstar, Andreas Wohler, an outstanding horseman, and Simon Stokes — this was a rare combination.

But there is still one personality missing in this scenario: the owner. While I didn't spend much time with Mr or Mrs Jacobs during the early days with Lomitas, I have subsequently come to know them quite well. Walther Jacobs is probably the greatest owner this industry has ever known. In 1991, he was 84 years of age. His courage and determination will become evident as the story of Lomitas unfolds.

8 a.m., 13 June 1991. A set of horses left the yard of Andreas Wohler to go the short distance to the racecourse for training. I had explained to Andreas that while he was out with this set, I would just take Lomitas into the covered ride and spend some time with him, to get to know him.

This covered ride was like a small oval race-track, about 16 feet wide, covered with a roof. One lap around the oval would amount to about 200 yards.

I walked Lomitas into this covered ride and simply stood with him. Then I moved to the end of the rope and asked him to step towards me. He seemed reluctant to step into my space.

I raised one arm sharply above my head, and then the other arm. He didn't seem unduly alarmed, which told me that he hadn't been abused with the type of punishments that come from a raised hand.

Then I stood next to him and lifted my knee

and leg under his keel. Again, there was no discernible tightening of the abdominal muscles, no sudden grunt or lifting of the thorax. Plainly, he hadn't been abused in that area either.

Then I took a short length of rope and swung it near his head. He paused and looked at me, then moved sideways and paused again. He was struggling with a desire to understand me in a most intelligent fashion, but his lack of panic told me he hadn't been whipped.

Finally, I led him closer to the wall and placed my hands along his side, as if to hold him closer against it. Immediately, he kicked out and plunged forward, showing classic signs of claustrophobia.

So, although his relationship with the human species was clearly a good one, he was prepared to blame us for placing him inside these enclosed structures such as starting stalls and vans — and he was perfectly happy to express that discomfort with his handlers by using this aggressive behaviour.

I stopped, to allow the pair of us a breather. Looking at his fine build and marking the extraordinary intelligence in his eye, I thought, 'I am in the presence of greatness. I had better be patient; I must do my job with diligence and competence, because I am in the presence of something special.'

So he was not an abused horse, but he believed he had been mistreated by being imprisoned in these claustrophobic structures. His perception was that people were treating him in an unfair manner.

In testing whether or not Lomitas had been abused, it wasn't that I distrusted my new acquaintances, Andreas and Simon, but I always give my horses the respect of asking them to speak for themselves because while I have been lied to by human beings, a horse can't lie — it's not within his scope.

Lomitas was telling me, 'I think I've been treated unfairly. I fear it's going to become worse.'

When Andreas and Simon returned to the stable, I was back near Lomitas' stall, leading him around. I asked, 'Can we use a round pen or lunging ring somewhere nearby, so I can work him?'

'Hmmm . . . that might be difficult.'

'The thing is, I need to turn him loose, to let him go on his own and win his trust.'

I felt that if I could join-up with him and gain Lomitas' trust, maybe he would also trust the confined positions we asked him to walk into.

Andreas thought about it and replied, 'Well, there's a show-jumping ring about ten miles away, but we'd need to get him into a transport truck to take him there, which counts that out.'

'No,' I replied, 'hang on, we can do the van, I'm sure we can. We can order a van for this afternoon and have it parked here, and I assure you we can overcome his difficulties with loading right away.'

Andreas and Simon were both nervous about this, but clearly it had to be done. So they ordered a van and it was there just after lunch.

Having Simon translate Andreas into English, it was like a double-act always, when they spoke to me. I suppose it was quite comic. '*Gehen wir hinein?*' asked Andreas, and Simon would repeat, 'Shall we go inside? Andreas is suggesting, let's back the van into the barn here, so the ramp is in the centre aisle, and it'll give Lomitas less room to run around the side.'

I replied, 'He's going to have to learn to enter the van like a gentleman one day, and we might as well start as we mean to go on. Let's have it out in the middle of the yard and do it properly from the outset.'

With the van parked there, the ramp down and waiting, I attached long-lines to Lomitas and schooled him for about half an hour. I didn't see any problem with the schooling process; he was obedient, hard-working and well-mannered. There was nothing but to load him into the van, because until he showed me a problem I was going to treat him like a normal horse.

He walked up the ramp and he followed me right into the van, without any problem. The minute he was inside, the helpers standing by ran to lift the ramp, but immediately I said, 'No, leave the ramp down. I'm going to walk him off and on several times.'

A couple of the lads there who spoke English said, 'No, don't. If you bring him off, you'll never get him back on again.'

I asked them to have some faith in me and what I wanted to do. So they left the ramp down, and I walked Lomitas off and on the van without any problems probably 15 – 20 times before we closed it up and made our trip to the show-jumping yard.

When we arrived at the yard, I found a building with good footing, but it was about 150-feet long and 100 feet wide. For my purposes, I needed a 50-foot round pen.

They had a lot of jump poles and stands there, so in one corner of the building I made a makeshift round pen. I actually built it right around Lomitas while he stood there watching me. Then I went to work.

Free of any rope on his head, he went into flight immediately when I pressed him away from me. He cantered steadily around the perimeter of this makeshift arena, with one ear already locked on to me. Within a minute or two, he understood what I was doing and I began to observe some licking and chewing.

He was a most intelligent horse, and it was only 10 – 15 minutes before he was in full conversation with me. It was clear that there would be no problems at all; I had a good 'join-up' very quickly. He trusted me.

Now I wanted to take this trust a bit further. I dismantled the jump poles, so that we were now occupying the main arena. It took a few minutes. He ran away from me for a while and thought he was going to take charge, but as soon as I told him to go away, further away, he was pressing to come back and join-up with me. I was able to go anywhere in the building and he was right there with me, his nose to my shoulder.

When that happened, I felt confident I was dealing with a horse with supreme intelligence, and that we could work through the problems with the starting stalls.

When we loaded him on the van to go home, he walked right up like an old horse who'd never had a problem with vans in his whole life.

By the time we got back to the stables in Bremen, we were ready to call it a day, and we put him away, fed him and left him to have a good night's rest.

On 15 June 1991, I started to work Lomitas in the permanent training stall. I was banking on his trust, and also on taking it a step at a time and creating within him a desire to go into the stall. Within a short period, he was going in and out with no problems.

Later that morning Simon put some tack on him and sat on his back while I led him in and out. We were able to close the gate behind him and start the process of letting him walk out in a very relaxed manner.

This took us through the morning.

In the afternoon, Andreas had invited the head starter from the Bremen Racecourse — Herr Dunca — to watch Lomitas walking in and out of the training stall.

Herr Dunca spent about an hour with me that day, and was impressed with what he saw. He told us that he would go back and recommend to the stewards that they reassess the situation and give Lomitas another chance, as long as he could pass all the necessary tests.

It was arranged with the Bremen Racecourse that the following morning, 16 June, we would have the proper racing stalls to school in. Herr

Dunca returned to watch.

Lomitas was troubled and he was a bit difficult at times, but he was trying hard for me and before the morning was over he was going in and out of the proper stalls easily.

Herr Dunca told us that he had had a meeting with the stewards and they had arranged a stalls test for Lomitas on 18 June. They'd want to see him achieve the same steady behaviour with other horses around him in the starting stalls.

At the prescribed time, the stewards were there to watch as he passed that test with flying colours. They had a different impression of Lomitas — what he did that morning looked very impressive. For me it was an accomplishment to be sure, but it still wasn't the way I wanted it. He was a little tentative going in and a little nervous while he was in there.

Andreas told me there was a race here at Bremen on 23 June, and he wanted to run Lomitas. The stewards said they would require another test — and would want him to be nearly perfect. They'd consider reinstating him only after they saw him in that second test.

They came back on the morning of the 20th and we were at the centre of the home straight in front of the grandstand. We had three horses for company.

Lomitas was as near perfect as you could want a horse to be. The stewards said they would give him a reinstatement and tentative approval for one race, and reassess it at that time. They added a proviso that I had to come with him, and that nobody from the racecourse would handle him. It was also suggested that Lomitas should be the last horse to enter the starting stalls, so he wouldn't have to stand in there for a long period. These arrangements were agreed among all the parties.

The race was just three days later, and I'd only been working with Lomitas for seven days. When the morning of the 23rd came around, it was a tense time for me. I was in one of the grandest fish-bowls you have ever seen.

At race time, it seemed as though 20,000 people were there when I went to the starting stalls which were on the home straight (the race was a mile and a quarter). It also seemed that every one of those 20,000 people had made their way down to the stalls to see their national hero, Lomitas, who had become something of a legend — the horse who had fought with his trainers and refused to race. He had that sort of following amongst the public.

When I arrived at the back of the stalls and started to walk Lomitas around, I had parents holding little children over the fence saying, 'Oh, Lomi, Lomi, Lomi.'

It seemed that we walked around behind those stalls for an interminable length of time. Finally I realised that something was wrong. All the other horses in the race were huddled over to one side of the track and the jockeys were in deep conversation. Andreas was speaking with the head starter and with a group of officials. They were all talking in German, and I knew nothing of what was going on.

After some time, Andreas came to me and

said that the jockeys were boycotting the race unless I was the first one to go in. They'd said they were tired of being put in the gates and waiting for Lomitas to have it out with the starting-stalls crew; they refused to ride if he wasn't put in first.

I said I didn't mind; it didn't make any difference to me, I would go first. Andreas told the head starter, who called to the jockeys, 'Come on, everybody, let's load the stalls.'

They pointed to my stall and I walked Lomitas right in — he was good as gold.

As I stood there with him, thanking him for giving us a good result on this important occasion, I realised that there was a starting-stall attendant opening the gate in front of us. After he opened it — and left me standing directly in Lomitas' path — he went round behind and closed the back gate.

Normally this is never done, because it is extremely dangerous. I could have been severely trampled.

Then I realised what was going on, that the starting-stalls crew did not want this to work, and they did everything they could to cause Lomitas to misbehave. With their straps and ropes and blindfolds, they would accidentally brush him and hit him as they went behind him, trying to make him jump forward.

However, Lomitas stood there calmly while they loaded the other horses — and with superb irony, they had considerable difficulties with some of the others. This seemed like poetic justice to me.

After all the horses were in, the attendant came round and closed the gate in front of Lomitas. I vacated my precarious position.

They started the race and Lomitas sprang from those stalls, the keenest of all of them. Seeing the great leap he made — which catapulted him clear to the front of the field — my heart made a leap in sympathy as it were. It was an undiluted pleasure to see this complex, intelligent horse cover the ground substantially quicker than anyone else from start to finish — and take his rightful place in the winner's enclosure.

This triumph was the first of a series of victories for him which propelled him to champion three-year-old of that year and Horse of the Year. His earnings reached about 1,600,000 deutschmarks.

Going through something like this with a horse of this quality brings a bonding and close association between man and beast which is not easy to describe. In just a short time, I felt the same degree of love for Lomitas as I had for Johnny Tivio, Brownie and Ginger.

Lomitas finished his year with three Group I victories in succession. He was the highest-rated German racehorse in the history of the country.

Andreas Wohler gave Lomitas an easy time through the winter of 1991 in order to prepare for the 1992 racing season. With high hopes for another outstanding year for him, we weren't to know how events would unfold to prevent that.

Early in 1992, before the racing season began,

Mr Jacobs received a blackmail letter demanding 400,000 deutschmarks, otherwise Lomitas would be harmed or killed. He told me they were taking special precautions with security, and naturally he was concerned about the situation.

I recall having a conversation with Pat shortly after that and saying that of all things you have to go through in the horse business, and of all the problems you have to meet and overcome, no sooner are we on top of things than we have to deal with some crackpot who wants to extort money from an owner and threatens a horse's life.

By this time, Mr Jacobs was 85. It occurred to me that he might simply want to retire Lomitas from racing and back away from the whole situation. However, in subsequent conversations with him he seemed stronger than ever and determined to meet this situation head on.

I went to Hamburg in June of 1992 and watched Simon handle the horse at the starting stalls. Lomitas had no problems and he won that race, too. Everything seemed to be fine.

However, Mr Jacobs told me that the blackmail letters were still arriving on a regular basis. The extortionist was adamant that he be paid or else he would harm the horse. In order to send a signal of his intent, he burned down a hay barn on the Gestut Fahrhof stud.

Extra guards with dogs were hired around the clock, and additional security was arranged for the Bremen Racecourse.

Lomitas was due to race in Dusseldorf in late July 1992. He made the trip, went in the stalls

OK and ran in the race; but he finished fifth, giving a very lack-lustre performance.

After the race, it was clear that Lomitas was not himself, so he was transported to Gestut Fahrhof for tests to see if the extortionist had sabotaged him in some way. Around the time he arrived there, a letter came saying, 'We only gave him enough to make him sick.' It hadn't been their intention to kill Lomitas, but to show that it could be done if the money was not paid.

With this sombre turn of events, things really swung into action. It was arranged that Lomitas would go into hiding, when he was well enough to travel to England. From there, he'd be quarantined and taken to the United States, where he was to be sent to California to race.

I was amazed at the strength and tenacity of Mr Jacobs through all of this. Here was a man with the Horse of the Year, and he could easily have backed off and hidden from this blackmailer, but he stepped right up and said, 'The man will not stop me from racing my horse if I want to race him.' So he set in motion the plan to ship him to California.

We had to wait for about 15 days before moving him, because Lomitas became very ill. The letter had told us he'd been given a heavy metals poison, and it had affected his liver and other vital organs. It was a cruel sight, to see him. This beautiful horse hung his head, and his eye was dull and uninterested; he was turned in on himself, concentrating on the illness and the pain. We all felt great anger, and incomprehension that anyone could be capable of doing this.

Lomitas fought off the results of that poison within 8 – 10 days. His head came up, he began to eat a little. A measure of interest returned to his expression.

As quickly as possible, he was shipped to Newmarket, England, where we hid him in Susan Piggot's yard. We gave him a false name: 'Pirelli'.

Simon stayed with him during the four-week quarantine period. Gradually he was able to put him back to work, and after Lomitas had spent his month in England he was in pretty good health again and training well under the circumstances. Simon then flew with him to California, where he arrived in mid-September and was placed in training with Ron McAnally at Santa Anita.

Lomitas trained along quite well through October and November, and was in fairly heavy work during early December in preparation for starting the race meet at Santa Anita right after Christmas.

In mid-December I was told by the barn foreman that Lomitas had come back to the stall with a quarter crack on the off-fore foot. This was a blow to me, for Lomitas had never had a foot problem like that, not during the whole of his training and racing in Germany. A patch was applied to the crack and training continued. But it wasn't long before there was a crack on a rear foot, and then a crack on the near-fore foot. All this was within a three-week period. The cracks were near the rear of the foot, and they started at the hair line and proceeded downward a half to three-quarters of an inch.

Lomitas' trainer, Mr McAnally, told me he knew of a very good quarter crack specialist in New York by the name of Ian McKinley. We had him flown out from New York and I met with him at the track, together with the veterinarians and other farriers. We had a round-table discussion about this situation.

Then McKinley asked me, 'What happened to this horse about five months ago?'

It clicked, and I replied, 'He was poisoned.'

McKinley showed me where there was a band of disconnected foot wall about half an inch wide right around all four feet. Why I had never thought to tell the farriers to be alert for potential foot problems because of this poisoning episode, I don't know. I just didn't make the connection until Ian McKinley asked me that question.

You could literally see this band of tissue that had darkened around the entire foot. As the foot had grown down, this separated area had become more critical to the strength of the rear portion of the foot, and so these cracks had started to occur.

Mr McKinley used a substance called 'Equilox' to put patches on each of the quarters of Lomitas' feet, whether they had cracks or not. He was strengthening the wall artificially by laying this space-age polymer over the top. We were then able to train without further cracks, but it meant it was February before he could race.

In his first start he was named the winner because he was interfered with by the horse that crossed the line before him.

His next start was in April at Hollywood Park — and he started out from the stalls 9 lengths behind, because he'd been distracted in his stall just as the gates opened. Even as the field turned for home, he was probably 12 – 15 lengths behind.

Then he made a blinding run at them. He ran the fastest last quarter ever at Hollywood Park, as far as we can tell. He was just two ticks away from setting a world record.

However, Lomitas' feet continued to plague us and it was decided to retire him to stud. He left the United States in 1994 to stand at Gestut Fahrhof near Bremen, Germany for the breeding season of 1995.

While his American initiative fell short of my hoped-for goals, Lomitas earned approximately $100,000 and served notice that he was a formidable competitor on the American race scene.

The German breeders have responded strongly to Lomitas as a breeding prospect, and he was booked to 50 mares in 1995. Like a true champion, he does this job well, too. He has a conception rate in the 90 percentiles.

It will be interesting to see if Lomitas can pass along his talents to the next generation. It is my hope that his story is just beginning.

Concerning the extortion attempt, an arrest was made; the letters have ceased.

An English country house in the dead of night is a ghostly place.

As I tied the cord of my dressing-gown, I looked at my watch and saw it was 3 o'clock in the morning. I went out of my room and began to pace up and down the upstairs landing. What could I do with this horse, Prince of Darkness? What was the answer? Where was the gap in my understanding of this big, highly-charged animal?

Now I heard something — almost indiscernible, but yes, footsteps. I stood as quiet as a cat and listened.

A door opened and Sir Mark Prescott appeared, also in his dressing-gown. The two of us blinked at each other.

'Ah, Monty.'

'Sir Mark! I'm sorry if I disturbed you, but I couldn't sleep.'

'Not at all; I couldn't sleep either.'

'I've lain in a hot tub and all sorts, but I can't seem to get my brain to stop working.'

'I know exactly what you mean.'

Sir Mark took up position at the window, his face cast in moonlight. Suddenly, his expression sharpened. 'Well, I'll be darned,' he muttered softly.

'What?'

'Come and see.'

I went and stood next to him.

He pointed. 'Look . . . '

From the window, we could see over the

sloping roof of the house to the stable-yard. In the moonlight we could clearly make out Prince of Darkness, his head appearing first at the window of his stall and then at the door as he walked around. He was as awake as we were.

Sir Mark sighed and said, 'That's three of us trying to work out what's wrong, then.'

Prince of Darkness was trained by Sir Mark Prescott in Newmarket, and owned by Pinoak Stables of Kentucky with English partners including Graham Rock, Graham Moore, Neil Greig and Wally Sturt.

He was a large-framed horse standing about 16.3 hands high, very muscular and long in the body. The normal starting stalls were really not large enough for him — his nose would be touching the front, and still the rear gate would bump into his hindquarters. He was so broad that the rails touched him on each side.

As with 80 per cent of the cases involving problems with the starting stalls, the first few times in his life he'd gone into them without any trouble. Then one day they were loading him into the stalls in a training session on the heath in Newmarket, and he didn't step fully in. An attendant had just slapped him on the outer thigh with his hand and the horse kicked out, hitting the side of the starting stall.

After this incident he developed a negative attitude towards the stalls, whether he was walking towards them, getting in them or standing once he was inside.

I'd come over to sort him out once already

and thought the job had been done, but I hadn't been back in California for three days before I got a call from Sir Mark. He told me they'd gone to the stalls on the heath and Prince of Darkness had been upset from the time he'd arrived there. They'd got him in, but then he'd tried to kick the stalls to pieces. After that, they couldn't get him anywhere near them.

I'd been disappointed. I stand behind the work I do. Sir Mark agreed to fly me back to England on a no-fee basis, to deal with the problem.

So here I was, back again, with a real puzzle that was keeping us all awake in the middle of the night.

As soon as that long body of his was inside a starting stall, Prince of Darkness panicked and burst out through the front — very angry about the whole thing.

I couldn't understand what had changed him so much since I'd had him going in and out like a dream.

That night, having dinner with Sir Mark, I asked him what Prince of Darkness was like to transport in a van. He said the horse was no problem, whether the stalls were narrow or wide. This was hard to believe, given what I had been through all day in the starting stalls, so Sir Mark suggested that we book a van with adjustable stalls so that I could see for myself.

The following morning a van arrived early and I briefed the driver while we familiarised ourselves with the interior of the van.

'OK. This is what we're going to do. You'll be driving, while I'll be standing here at Prince

407

of Darkness' head, so I can talk to you and at the same time observe him.'

'Right y'are.'

'First we'll load him in and give him a pretty wide stall.' I pointed at the fixings on the floor of the van. 'So, we'll fix the partition here. Then we'll drive slowly around the place — it doesn't matter where — and I'll observe.'

'OK.'

'Then we'll bring the partition in tighter, and increase the speed with which you drive. The aim is to try and identify what's causing him to feel claustrophobic.'

We loaded Prince of Darkness into the van and started a tour of Newmarket — first of all driving slowly and making careful turns. Prince of Darkness was completely at ease in his stall, so we stopped and narrowed the partition so the walls of the van were now closer to his flanks.

Still, he seemed comfortable.

I asked the driver to increase his speed and make more aggressive turns. He began to haul on the steering wheel a bit and the engine note rose an octave.

In front of me, Prince of Darkness was unconcerned. He braced himself against the corners and seemed unaffected by any part of the van touching his body.

I called, 'Can we go a bit faster still?'

The van leapt forward as the driver put his foot down.

Now we were sailing around the town. Anyone following us must have thought a couple of crooks had stolen the van as we squealed around corners and took roundabouts at hair-raising speed. Myself and Prince of Darkness were rolling around like it was a ship on the high seas, while the driver hauled on his wheel as if he was driving an ambulance on an emergency call.

Prince of Darkness was in the narrowest possible stall and the driver was risking his licence to give us all the ride of a lifetime. There was no kicking, no leaning, not the slightest bit of resistance or anger from Prince of Darkness — unlike what I'd observed the previous day in the starting stalls.

So — what was the difference between the stall in the van, in which he was happy, and the starting stall, which he'd kick to bits?

Once we'd arrived safely back at the yard, I stared hard at both of them. I puzzled about the psychology of it — where was the fear coming from? If I could find the source of his fear, I'd be home and dry. It wasn't claustrophobia, because he'd been happy in the van. There was something about the starting stall which spooked him, but I couldn't find out what it was.

That night I really wanted to tell Sir Mark that I was going to have to quit and refund him the money, but I just couldn't get the words out. The thought of losing was killing me. We had been three days and I didn't feel any closer to success. I decided to give it one more try.

The following day was the toughest of all. It turned out to be another 8 – 9 demanding and dangerous hours. Geraldine Rees, a friend of Sir

Mark's, came along and patiently watched the proceedings.

I stood in front of Prince of Darkness as he was led into the starting stall, in the same way as I'd stood in front of him in the van. I wanted to observe every small nuance of behaviour as he went in, to try and find a clue as to his behaviour.

He walked into the stall, creating a high old fuss. He was no sooner in than he lunged forward, scattering from that stall like there were wild Indians arranged all along the sides poking him with lances. He had no concern for me being in his way at all and charged right through me, knocking me to the ground.

I stood up and dusted myself down. The trouble was, I needed to get even closer.

The next time he blasted from the stall in a flurry of legs and tail and tossing head, he knocked me down again, and still I had no clue as to what was causing it. This wasn't a game for a man of my age and with part of his spinal column missing, but I was determined to go in closer.

Once again he jumped forward and bowled me over, stepping on my leg, side and ear. Then he ran to the end of my come-along rope and turned around and stood there looking at me from about 20 feet away.

I was hurting badly — physically speaking — but then, in a flash, it came to me. Although my brain was pretty muddled by this time, I had noticed that just before he jumped up and ran over the top of me, Prince of Darkness had rolled his eye back to look at his off flank and his attention seemed to be focused on the off-side rail.

I stood there, bruised, battered, with a trickle of blood running into my collar, but I'd found it: the source of his fear was the rail itself — of course! A trailer has smooth sides to the stall, whereas the starting stalls have rails running along each side. That must be the difference. I could have kicked myself for not realising sooner, but I felt a sudden excitement that I'd found out what he was afraid of. It was that specific. Something in the character of those footrails running along the inside caused him great fear.

After a few tests, I knew I was right. I was lucky to still have both my ears attached to my head and no broken bones, but I had the answer: if it wasn't for those rails along the side of the stalls, he could be raced tomorrow.

That evening Sir Mark and I discussed the situation, and with mounting excitement he phoned the various racing officials to investigate the possibility of removing the rails from inside a given starting stall.

It wasn't long before we realised that when you remove the rail from one horse's stall, you also remove it from the next because of the way they're constructed. Obviously this would not be acceptable to the stewards.

Early the next morning — it was the day before Good Friday, I remember — I outlined an idea that was going through my mind. If we could manufacture something like the picador's

411

horse wears in the bullfighting ring — a drape made of heavy leather to go over his rear quarters, heavy enough to protect his flanks — then we could maybe convince him he had enough protection from those evil rails.

It was just a wild thought, and I didn't really think it would be practical. Many years before, I had used a leather cape that fitted over the horses' haunches and attached to a Western saddle so that when asking a horse to make a sliding stop from extreme speed, it encouraged him to drop his hips in order to hold his rear feet in the ground and support the weight of the cape.

I felt that if I could use something like this to protect Prince of Darkness' sides from those rails, he might accept the stalls.

Geraldine Rees said, 'What if we used carpet?'

All kinds of flashing lights went off in my head. Using carpet instead of heavy leather might be a practical solution. So we jumped into her car, went into Newmarket and bought a roll of remnant carpet. Then we went to Gibson's Saddlery and I started to design the kind of thing I thought might work.

The prototype was just carpet sewn on a stable blanket so that it hung down on the sides with double thickness. The carpet was sewn both inside and outside the blanket, and then sewn together. We got it done in just a few hours and went back to the stables to try it out.

When I put him in the starting stalls with his special blanket on, I immediately knew we were on the right track. I gave Geraldine Rees a big pat on the back. 'Look, he's still frightened and not very confident, but he's staying in there, isn't he?'

It felt pretty good, to be able to stand in front of that huge animal and — at last — stay on my feet.

The more he rubbed against the sides of the stall, stepping backwards and forwards, the more Prince of Darkness realised that he had protection from the rails. He relaxed and calmed down. We were making progress.

We raced back to Gibson's Saddlery, because this was the Easter holiday period and we risked not having access to his shop, but Gibson's was good enough to work that evening and the next morning to develop the prototype a bit further and make up a blanket that was cut in half around the horse so that it would just fit the hindquarters, behind the saddle. There were straps woven into the forward edge of the blanket, which lay under the girth of the jockey saddle, in order to hold it in place. Lastly, we sewed a ring on the blanket just above the root of the tail so that you could fasten a rope onto it and hold it — the idea being that the horse would actually break from the stall and run out from under the blanket.

On Easter Sunday morning I was back in Henry Cecil's yard, and we worked for about four hours in the permanent stall and the regulation stalls.

Sir Mark had to go to France and left

413

instructions that we should race the horse at Warwick on the Tuesday, so that Sunday afternoon we arranged to take him with company to the starting stalls. I did my routine of letting him break very slowly, using the blanket for protection. He responded very well.

On Monday morning we schooled him again, and that evening I spoke to Sir Mark on the telephone and told him I thought the horse would make a good start from the stalls at Warwick on the following day.

I rode to the races at Warwick with George Duffield, the jockey for Prince of Darkness. George was game to try this new-fangled carpet technology, but a little embarrassed.

'Carpet? He's wearing a carpet?'

'That's what it's made of, sure.'

'Is it patterned carpet or plain?'

'It has a slight pattern, I suppose you'd say.'

'Oh no,' he groaned.

'Don't you like patterned carpet?'

He held his hands in the air in mock surrender. 'No — it's fine, I don't mind looking like an idiot. Maybe I ought to wear the same pattern. The same colour. Let's go for it. Trade in the silks. Can we stop at the carpet store on the way and measure me up for a tufted Wilton?'

I promised him, it was his only chance of getting a start at all — Prince of Darkness had to have his fitted carpet!

When the race was due to begin I met Prince of Darkness at the starting stalls. The

414

head starter was rather apprehensive about the blanket, but he had given Sir Mark permission to use this unconventional apparatus so he couldn't back down now.

I put the contraption up behind George Duffield and it certainly drew a lot of comments from the other jockeys — and it was a touch ignoble to have someone holding on to the rear of your horse with a piece of rope when you were hoping to run a race in a few seconds' time. As we loaded him into his stall, I was hoping the invention would work the first time. Inventions seldom do.

Now they were under starter's orders. I dug my heel in and wrapped the rope around my shoulder, ready to take the strain as Prince of Darkness left the stall.

And they're off! There was a terrific kick on the rope and then it went dead as Prince of Darkness broke from underneath his blanket with perfect timing. The carpet lay there in the bottom of the stall. Success!

There were 18 horses in the race, and at Warwick they run about 7 furlongs and make a hard left. When they made the turn, Prince of Darkness was the clear leader. He didn't win, but he made the best start that day. He went on to be a winner.

I didn't know it then, but this experience would lead me to invent 'The Monty Roberts blanket' for horses with similar fears. It has now been used on more than 1000 horses.

★ ★ ★

I've just recently seen a wonderful sight. In order to share it, I first have to introduce a gentleman by the name of Greg Ward.

Greg Ward was born in 1935 in Bakersfield, California, the son of a realtor. His mother was a primary school teacher. Living in the suburbs of Bakersfield, Greg became intrigued with horses. At the age of eight or nine, he began to express that interest to his parents and his older brother, none of whom had any interest in horses.

Greg was a star athlete in high school, excelling in track, football, basketball and baseball. Many of the people involved with his high school athletics thought he could have been an outstanding professional athlete in one of these sports if he'd chosen that course.

On 19 October 1952, he was driving a tractor on a nearby farm to earn extra money to buy and support a horse so that he could learn to ride. While clearing brush on the side of a hill, Greg got his tractor in a bad position and it rolled over, throwing him off and rolling over him, driving a piece of metal into his head and leaving him unconscious and blind.

He spent many weeks in the hospital and, after numerous operations including the fixing of a plate in his head, his muscles returned to normal and his sight came back — except, that is, for a major part of his peripheral vision.

Without peripheral vision, however, he had no future on the athletic field.

As soon as he was healthy enough, his parents helped him to buy his first horse, who had the glamorous name of Blackie. Blackie was approximately eight years old when Greg bought him for $350, including a good saddle as part of the bargain.

In September of 1953, almost a year after his accident, he went to Cal-Poly University in San Luis Obispo, taking Blackie and his saddle with him. Greg had been at Cal-Poly for two years when I arrived there. He had been asking a lot of questions, getting tips and watching the riders in competition so as to learn as much as he could in an attempt to get on the rodeo team at the school.

I recall watching Greg ride Blackie and laughing about the little fat horse with no class at all and thinking, 'Why is he wasting his time? What will that horse ever be?' I was young, and I had championships under my belt, and I didn't have much time for an ordinary horse like Blackie.

When I look back on it now, I realise how wrong I was to laugh at that horse. He was the most important horse on the face of the earth to Greg. In fact, he was one of the most important horses for the entire working-horse industry because he was teaching Greg Ward, who was later to become one of the greatest horsemen who ever lived. I should have known better, because I'd had a horse called Brownie who'd been very important to me.

I liked Greg; he was a good friend while we were in school and I shared whatever bits of information I could with him — even my best secrets.

Little did I know that he would learn very

quickly and so well. Greg ultimately made the rodeo team and while he was still learning, he contributed to points earned in the two national championships we won in 1958 and 1959.

Greg was able to put together 43 acres near Tulare, and he built the training establishment which he still owns. He has improved the facility to a great degree with two covered training arenas, several outdoor training areas and a half-mile track.

Greg was married to Laura Odle in 1957 while still at Cal-Poly. In 1959 their son, John, was born, followed by daughters Wendy in 1961 and Amy in 1963. All three children have ridden and shown in his operation. The daughters are now married and away from the ranch, but John is continuing in his father's footsteps and is practically running the entire operation at this time.

Horses trained at the Ward ranch, either by Greg or by his son John, have for the past 30-plus years amassed one of the most incredible records ever. The Ward ranch horses have won twelve world championships in cutting and reined cow-horse events. They have won literally millions of dollars in prize money.

In addition, young horses bred on the Ward ranch have sold for millions and won several million in the show ring. The most popular stallion in their industry at this moment is Dual Pep, who was bred and raised by the Wards and whose value is currently around $2 million. Dual Pep won over $300,000 in prize money and has a breeding income of a half-million dollars per year.

I could write 50 pages on the accomplishments of the Wards and their horses, but suffice it to say that their operation is arguably the best that north America has ever known where cow horses are concerned.

As Greg's son, John, is carrying a major portion of the workload on the ranch now, this gives Greg a chance to experiment with training techniques which he might not otherwise have time to do.

This brings me to the reason why I want to describe a particular sight that can be encountered at the Ward ranch, when Greg's starting his group of youngsters.

These are not cheap young horses. The latest crop of 32 is probably valued at $2.5 – 3 million. One colt in the group is said to be worth around $1 million alone. Economics dictate the need for Greg's horses to perform extremely well in competition to earn back their value.

I suppose what I'm trying to say is that Greg's training methods aren't the result of some wishy-washy notion he has of being kind to animals — although he would never be anything but incredibly kind and respectful of them. They are the best methods, as proved in the very toughest competition, and also the kindest.

I saw something that thrilled me when I arrived at Greg's ranch in Tulare. 'Monty,' he said, 'come and have a look at my new babies.'

I watched as five people led the young horses in from the field without even so much as pulling on their lead ropes. They allowed them to go wherever they wanted and simply walked around, following these young, excitable animals until they were able to take advantage of the horses' wanting to go into the yard themselves.

They were saddled up and the riders carefully mounted.

'During the first twenty days of riding,' said Greg, 'we allow them to do whatever they want. There's no tension on the reins whatsoever.'

I watched as the riders were led out of the yard and down a lane, on to the practice race-track. The gates were closed, so the horses couldn't leave, but other than that they were free to wander where they wanted on this half-mile oval track.

A sixth person was riding an experienced saddle horse and carrying a long wand with a plastic flag on the end, so that he could keep the horses from endangering one another should the situation arise.

Greg pointed and said, 'It doesn't matter which direction they take. They can do what the hell they like.'

I watched these five horses with their riders, wandering around. If they wanted to stop and graze on the grass along the fence line for a while, they stopped. If they wanted to cross the track and go to the other side, they crossed it. If they wanted to canter along for a bit, they did so — and ran until they wanted to stop. If they just stood there — then that's all they did. If they wanted to lie down and roll, that was fine too; the rider dismounted and watched his mount roll, completely unconcerned.

In short, whatever the young, freshly started horse wanted to do, he did.

'How long does this go on for?' I asked.

'Twenty days.'

I marvelled at this sight and the correct thinking behind it. These horses were learning to carry the riders' weight, and of course they hadn't the slightest suspicion that they might be punished for anything. They were gradually getting used to the idea of having riders on their backs. There wasn't a chance that they would cultivate resentment or foster aggressive tendencies towards their human partners.

Because of the success of methods such as these and others that I have outlined during the course of this book, I firmly believe that — taking all this evidence together — it constitutes a new beginning in the relationship between man and horse, and it has been my privilege to make a contribution to this spirit of understanding.

It's a most fitting picture, and one that precisely demonstrates a wholesale commitment to the theories in which I believe.

★ ★ ★

Passing through England recently, on my way back to California, I received an invitation to meet the Queen, to bring her up to date on my work and give her my views on the world of horses in general.

Corporal Major Terry Pendry drove me through the now-familiar grounds of Windsor

421

Castle. 'You'll be meeting Her Majesty outside . . . ' he said, as part of briefing me for the upcoming meeting.

Outside? I wondered what he could mean. Were we going to stroll around the grounds together, or meet in the mews and look over some of her horses?

Terry Pendry pulled up to one side of the lawn which sweeps graciously down in front of the castle and got out of the vehicle; so I did likewise.

He pointed: 'There she is.'

In the middle of this expanse of perfectly manicured green lawn was a small table with a figure seated at it. Trailing back from the table, a white cable snaked all the way back to the castle and disappeared inside.

I began the long trek over the lawn, and as I drew near I recognised Her Majesty sitting there. The corners of the snowy-white tablecloth flapped idly in the slight breeze, and various pieces of bone china and silverware stood ready for our tea.

Her Majesty greeted me in a very informal way and I sat down at the table. She pressed a button fixed to the end of the cable and the signal travelled all the way back to the castle. As we began to talk, a member of her staff brought tea and refreshments.

It was a perfect occasion in the most beautiful surroundings. We talked about horses, and once again she proved to be an interesting and informed owner. She wanted to know my views on everything, and I felt thoroughly privileged to

422

have met this woman whom history has placed in such a unique position.

It was difficult to believe that here I was, completely alone, taking tea with the Queen of England in the middle of the lawn in front of Windsor Castle, conversing like old friends.

For my part, I was happy to bring her up to date on the course which is being run now at West Oxfordshire College under the directorship of Kelly Marks, dedicated to furthering the training methods which I've described in this book — the first time ever that a course of this nature has been specifically designed and built into the curriculum.

I related my recent experiences with the racing officials about starting stalls problems.

I told Her Majesty that I looked forward to the future, when students of my methodology would have advanced our understanding so much further that they'd describe my practices as archaic. Even as I write this, certain veterinarians are developing the capability of 'listening' to horses in order to determine which part of the animal's gut is hurting, identifying where the trouble is in the duodenum loop, in the small or the large intestine.

Finally, long after the tea party was scheduled to end, we rose to our feet. Our parting was genuinely warm and informal, and she returned to the castle while I strolled back across the lawn to where Terry Pendry was waiting for me.

I had a sudden vision of what this scene would look like from the ramparts of the castle itself: the white square of the table set in the middle of the green lawn, the remains of our tea, the chairs set askew, the Queen of England strolling in one direction and this cowboy from California walking the other way, shaking his head in disbelief at the curious circumstances in which he found himself.

Nearly 800 years ago, a very different ruler, a conqueror named Temujin, had a very different attitude to horses. His mongol empire grew to encompass the shores of the Pacific and the northern stretches of the Black Sea. Standing astride a quarter of the world's surface, he changed his name to Genghis Khan, meaning 'master of all' — and deservedly, now, that name conjures the idea of unimaginable cruelty, an iron will and an inflexible resolve.

His chief ally in this remarkable expansion of power and influence was the horse.

Using ropes, whips and every cruel tactic he could think of, Genghis Khan harnessed the horse's strength, stamina and speed.

The horses had no answer to his cruelty, had no voice. But . . . they did have a language. No one saw it, no one tried to see it, but it was there then and it's still the same one now. It's a language that's been around for 45 million years and has remained virtually unchanged. Just to put this into perspective, mankind has been on this planet for only a few hundred thousand years, and already his language has fragmented into thousands of different tongues.

The absence of communication between man and horse has led to a disastrous history of cruelty and abuse. Also, it has been to our detriment. We haven't captured the willing co-operation of the horse nearly as much as we might have done, and that is our considerable loss — both in emotional terms and with respect to the performance and work we might selfishly gain from them.

It's a balance which I've been happy to try and redress during a lifetime's work with horses. I've been doing it for 61 years so far, and I'm still going strong.

V

Join-Up — A Step by Step Guide to the Monty Roberts Method

YOU can achieve the Monty Roberts method of JOIN-UP as long as you believe in your own mind that you can do it and as long as you are not frightened of horses.

To begin, I would like you to discard all preconceived notions you hold about starting the young horse. I want you, however, to hold on to the experiences that have taught you not to fear him and also your ability to move around him safely and effectively. Hold in your mind the idea that the horse can do no wrong; that whatever action he takes was most likely influenced by you, especially the young unstarted horse. We as horsemen can do very little to teach the horse. What we can do is create an environment in which he can learn. I believe it is much the same with people. The human student who has knowledge pushed into his brain learns little, but he can absorb a great deal when he chooses to learn.

ACTIONS SPEAK LOUDER THAN WORDS

This is a saying we humans use quite often. Generally, however, we do not live by it too successfully. The horse has a very predictable, discernible and effective language.

429

The incredible thing about this language is that these animals need no interpreters. Around the world they are understood by all of 'EQUUS'. It is amazing that we, as humans possessing the most phenomenal brains on earth, often need help to communicate with one another.

Just like any other form of communication 'EQUUS' requires some effort to master. If we refuse to believe that the horse can communicate fluently, it is possible through the use of pain to train him somewhat effectively. But if we believe in his skill of communication, then we must give him credit for possessing the ability to form an adversarial relationship with us if we train with pain. Consider for a moment what you would feel if on your first day of school, your teacher put a chain through your mouth or over your nose, gave it a jerk, and then took a whip to you when you tried to get away. What do you believe the balance of your relationship would have been, and how do you think you would view school from that point on?

I suggest to you that while the horse's brain is not as complex as the human's, there would be, to some extent, the same reaction. The point of my method is to create a relationship based on trust and confidence, a relationship by which the horse wants to

JOIN-UP,

be part of the team, to wear the same colour jersey. It is my opinion that most 'conventionally started' horses form an adversarial relationship with the people they work for and, while they may agree to perform, it is with a reluctant attitude.

The first rule of this method when starting a fresh horse is

NO PAIN.

We will not hit, kick, jerk, pull or tie or restrain. If we are forced to use some restraint, we want it to be of the mildest nature and without the feeling 'You Must' communicated to the horse. We want to eliminate that feeling from the environment we create.

We can suggest that we would rather 'he did' but not that 'he must'. If any restraint is used it should be done so as to encourage him to stay with you but not to demand that he stay with you.

The horse is the quintessential flight animal. When any pressure is applied to the relationship, he will almost always choose to leave rather than fight. It is with this in mind that I have developed the knowledge of a phenomenon already in place in most animals of the earth. 'Advance and Retreat' is obvious in relationships animal to animal, both inter and intra species, and human to human. We all use it every day when we push a situation and then back away to see what effect we've had. This is evident in personal and business relationships. An example is the fourteen-year-old boy just starting high school. He is attracted to a girl in his class and follows her incessantly. She states that she

431

can't stand him and moves away. He will persist, generally about sixty days, and then will give up. Soon we will note that she starts to appear where he is and shows interest in him. What we will study and develop is a knowledge of this very phenomenon.

Let's move to the practical act of starting the young horse (I never use the term 'breaking'). Our intention is to cause this animal to accept the saddle, bridle and rider with no trauma. I do demonstrations where I take a young horse who has not been saddled, bridled or ridden and attempt to have him accept all this in approximately thirty minutes. If I demonstrated with a horse that had been mouthed before the demonstration, the viewer might be sceptical, and believe that more than mouthing had been done. Demonstration aside, it is best to take a few days to accustom the baby to the bit and to a small measure of communication through long lines and the mouth of the horse, than to move directly to the starting procedure.

THE FOLLOWING IS A LIST OF GOALS TARGETED IN THE STARTING PROCESS:

1. JOIN UP
2. FOLLOW UP
3. VULNERABLE AREAS
4. PICK UP FEET
5. SADDLE PAD
6. SADDLE
7. BRIDLE

8. LONG LINES
9. RIDER
10. FULL CIRCLE RIGHT
11. ONE STEP BACK
12. FULL CIRCLE LEFT
13. ONE STEP BACK

EQUIPMENT LIST

2 LONG LINES (30-FEET EACH)
1 SNAFFLE BIT, FULLY EQUIPPED
1 SADDLE (YOUR PREFERENCE)
1 SADDLE PAD
1 STIRRUP LEATHER
HEADCOLLAR ON HORSE

I use a round pen in my operation, and while that isn't absolutely necessary, it certainly makes the job easier. My pen is fifty feet in diameter (16 metres) with a solid wall eight feet high (2.4 metres) and roofed over. My pen has a sand surface with about a two-inch cushion. I have, however, started horses in the wild with no fences, and rode a horse to aid in travel. A square pen can be used, but it is much better if you can panel the corners out. Fifty feet in diameter is optimum in my opinion for mid-range sized horses. Good footing is important for the safety of horses and people.

Bring the horse into the pen with the headcollar on and have with you one long line, preferably a light sash thirty feet long (9 metres). Stand near the centre of the pen and introduce yourself by rubbing with the flat of your hand (no patting) the horse's forehead, even if you are already acquainted. Now move away and toward the rear of the horse, staying out of the kick zone. When you are behind the animal or he flees, whichever comes first, pitch the line toward the rear quarters. The line can fall on him, but you **DO NOT HIT**. At this point, almost all babies will take flight and proceed around the pen. The horse is retreating so you must advance. Keep the pressure on. Pitch the line about two times per revolution or whatever it takes to keep your subject retreating. You must maintain an aggressive mode: your eyes drilled on his eyes and your shoulder axis square with his head. Maintain forward movement as much as possible, but do not enter the kick zone. You should try to get your subject to canter five or six revolutions, one way and then reverse and repeat, except that during the second direction you are readying the horse for a message that he would like to stop all this work. Watch the inside ear particularly. It will slow up its movement or stop altogether, while the outside ear will continue to move to observe his surroundings. The head will begin to tip, ears to inside, nose to outside, and the neck will bend slightly to bring the head closer to the centre of the circle. He will probably lick and chew, running his tongue right out. Finally, he should crane his head down near the surface. The ear gives you respect. Coming closer means just that. Licking and chewing is to say 'I am a flight animal and I'm eating so I can't fear you'. Craning the head down means 'If we could have a meeting to renegotiate, I would let you be the chairman'. Experience will sharpen your senses to this communication, but when you observe the horse in this mode, he is asking you to take the pressure off, he wants to stop.

Coil the line at this point and assume a submissive mode . . . your eyes down. Don't look at his eyes. Bring your shoulder axis to a forty-five degree position. This is his invitation to come to you, or at least look your way and stop retreating. If he will come to you, that's great! If he stands and faces you but does not move forward, then you start to move closer to him, but do it on arcs or semi-circles, not straight at him. If he leaves you, put him back to work for a few more laps. Then repeat the process.

As you move closer do it with your shoulder axis on forty-five degree angles to his body axis showing, for the most part your back to him. He should voluntarily move toward you and reach out with his nose to your shoulders. That's JOIN-UP.

When you can approach his head, give him a good rub between the eyes and then walk away moving in circles. I like to start by circling on the right hand about 10 feet in diameter. After the right is accomplished, circle left and repeat several times. He should follow you or at least move to maintain his head in your direction. If he doesn't, then you will find yourself toward his rear and you put him back to work. Stay out of the kick zone. Working this way you should accomplish JOIN-UP and FOLLOW UP.

Once FOLLOW UP is evident, you should

435

be able to have him follow you to the centre of the pen and stand comfortably for the next step which is to enter his vulnerable areas. Starting on the near side, use both hands to massage neck, withers, back, hips, fore flanks and rear flanks. Do the same on the off side and you are ready to pick up the feet. Pick up each of the feet using safe, horsemanlike procedures.

Having completed the preceding steps, you are ready to bring the balance of your equipment into the pen and place it on the floor near the centre. Allow the horse time to look the equipment over, moving between the equipment and the horse several times in both directions until your subject prefers to follow you instead of examining the tack. Once you have his attention, clip one line to the headcollar, placing it over your left arm about three feet from the clip. Pick up the saddle pad and gently place it on his back, first up ahead of the withers and then slide it back in place. If he should leave, don't punish him just ease him around, cause him to JOIN-UP and repeat the process (very few will do it). Once the pad is in place, pick up the saddle, irons up and girth over seat. Slide your body along the near side of the neck to the point of the shoulder. The saddle is on your right hip. Gently place the saddle on his back and move past his head giving him a rub to the off side. Take the girth down slowly and smoothly without hesitation, adjust the girth to reach approximately mid-fetlock joint, move smoothly back to the near side giving the head a rub on the way by. Stand near the fore leg and bring the girth up and place the front buckle on the front billot, draw it snug, reading your horse, so as not to make it too tight but tight enough not to turn should he buck. Next, place the back buckle on the back billot and snug it up a bit tighter than the front one. Go back to the front one and level the two up. Unclip the line and step back cautiously, line in hand, moving backwards away from your horse. Favour the rear portion, staying out of the kick zone, send him away with the line and be careful not to encourage joining up and bucking at the same time.

STAY CALM

Your horse must believe that he is the only one bothered by this saddle, or he will be more inclined to buck. Watch for the signs that he once again wants to JOIN-UP but only when he is travelling comfortably with the saddle do you allow it.

As soon as he is back with you, put the bridle on and place the reins under the rear of the saddle or some other safe attachment. Leave plenty of slack in the reins. Now, take your extra stirrup leather and drop it through the off-stirrup iron so that it hangs half way through. Then move to the near side and carefully pick up both ends of the leather and buckle it through the near iron. The stirrups are buckled together under the horse. Take both lines at the clip end and place one over the seat of the saddle allowing the clip to just reach the ground on the off side. Then place the second clip through the near iron (back to front) and clip it on the near side bit ring. Move to the off side and repeat. Move back to the near side. Pick up the two lines at the side of the horse and move backwards and laterally outside the kick zone towards the rear of the horse. You are now justified in moving him forward and swinging the right rein over his hips to the long lines. If you are not experienced with long lines, keep things slow. You want to accomplish a little communication through the mouth, but do it cautiously. It would be advisable to practise this process with older, more experienced horses for a significant period of time before you try it with a first-timer. You could hurt your horse or yourself. If you are experienced with lines, ask your horse to circle at the canter and the trot both ways. Ask him to negotiate turns and stops. Finally, stop him, facing away from the centre and ask him to rein back one step.

At this point most of the horses I do are ready to be ridden. You may elect to ride him yourself or have another person do so, either is fine. Make sure the saddle is adjusted properly and the girth is tight enough to prevent the saddle from turning. If you are using a rider then at this point bring your rider in with all proper safety equipment. Clip a line on the near side bit ring. Give your rider a minute or two to get acquainted with the horse, rubbing both sides and treating him as you have. I then leg my riders up. First I ask them to just 'belly over' (belt buckle on pommel). Then I move the horse carefully, first in two or three left circles and then to the right two or three times. If the horse is happy and accepting the rider lying over him, you will guide the rider's foot into the near iron as he mounts. Repeat the circles. If your horse is relaxed and accepting the seated rider make larger circles leading your horse nearer the perimeter, carefully unclip the line and assist the rider to accomplish a circle of the pen in each direction. No cantering, walk and trot will suffice. After each revolution I like my rider to rein back one step.

Do not be a hero, if your horse is not ready to be mounted, do it another day. Remember that when I do my demonstrations they must be done in one session or the viewers cannot see the entire procedure. This does not mean that you have to do the same. This system will save so much time that you will be well ahead. It is the quality of your work that is important not how fast you accomplish it. We all want the well-behaved happy and willing horse at the conclusion. It is on this that you will be judged.

At this point you will have accomplished the goal of your horse accepting saddle, bridle and rider. The horse should NOT be traumatised and should elect to stay with you rather than go away.

Remember, let your animal be free, DON'T RESTRICT. Make it nice for him to be near you and put him to work if he wants to be away from you.

NO PAIN

If you can accomplish this process then you have helped me in my quest to

Make The World A Better Place
For The Horse.

Debts of Gratitude

I must thank my wife, Pat, all my children and close friends for allowing me the space necessary to do this book and Pat's special efforts typing, reading and critiquing for months on end.

I also owe a debt of gratitude to others who gave great effort to create this book: Sue Freestone, my editor, who enthusiastically supported me throughout my first adventure into the literary world; Sam North, who travelled half-way around the world to spend several weeks with us working diligently to edit my words brilliantly; Jane Turnbull, my enthusiastic and totally supportive literary agent who believed in me from the start; Kelly Marks, who organised superbly for me in England; and my clients who stood by me during this project such as Sir Mark Prescott, Henry Cecil, Walther J. Jacobs and Dr Andreas Jacobs.

A special thanks must go out to Her Majesty, Queen Elizabeth II, who brought light to my work, to Sir John Miller, who was instrumental in making the Royal connection and Terry Pendry, my friend and ardent supporter.

My nine students who have risen to the level of 'Advanced Professional' must be acknowledged: Crawford Hall, Sean McCarthy, Kelly Marks, Richard Maxwell, Terry Pendry, Tim Piper, Satish Seemar, Simon Stokes and Hector Valadez.

441

Other titles in the Charnwood Library Series:

PAY ANY PRICE
Ted Allbeury

After the Kennedy killings the heat was on — on the Mafia, the KGB, the Cubans, and the FBI . . .

MY SWEET AUDRINA
Virginia Andrews

She wanted to be loved as much as the first Audrina, the sister who was perfect and beautiful — and dead.

PRIDE AND PREJUDICE
Jane Austen

Mr. Bennet's five eligible daughters will never inherit their father's money. The family fortunes are destined to pass to a cousin. Should one of the daughters marry him?

THE GLASS BLOWERS
Daphne Du Maurier

A novel about the author's forebears, the Bussons, which gives an unusual glimpse of the events that led up to the French Revolution, and of the Revolution itself.

CHINESE ALICE
Pat Barr

The story of Alice Greenwood gives a complete picture of late 19th century China.

UNCUT JADE
Pat Barr

In this sequel to CHINESE ALICE, Alice Greenwood finds herself widowed and alone in a turbulent China.

THE GRAND BABYLON HOTEL
Arnold Bennett

A romantic thriller set in an exclusive London Hotel at the turn of the century.

SINGING SPEARS
E. V. Thompson

Daniel Retallick, son of Josh and Miriam (from CHASE THE WIND) was growing up to manhood. This novel portrays his prime in Central Africa.

A HERITAGE OF SHADOWS
Madeleine Brent

This romantic novel, set in the 1890's, follows the fortunes of eighteen-year-old Hannah McLeod.

BARRINGTON'S WOMEN
Steven Cade

In order to prevent Norway's gold reserves falling into German hands in 1940, Charles Barrington was forced to hide them in Borgas, a remote mountain village.

THE PLAGUE
Albert Camus

The plague in question afflicted Oran in the 1940's.

THE RESTLESS SEA
E. V. Thompson

A tale of love and adventure set against a panorama of Cornwall in the early 1800's.

THE RIDDLE OF THE SANDS
Erskine Childers

First published in 1903 this thriller, deals with the discovery of a threatened invasion of England by a Continental power.

WHERE ARE THE CHILDREN?
Mary Higgins Clark

A novel of suspense set in peaceful Cape Cod.

KING RAT
James Clavell

Set in Changi, the most notorious Japanese POW camp in Asia.

THE BLACK VELVET GOWN
Catherine Cookson

There would be times when Riah Millican would regret that her late miner husband had learned to read and then shared his knowledge with his family.

THE WHIP
Catherine Cookson

Emma Molinero's dying father, a circus performer, sends her to live with an unknown English grandmother on a farm in Victorian Durham and to a life of misery.

SHANNON'S WAY
A. J. Cronin

Robert Shannon, a devoted scientist had no time for anything outside his laboratory. But Jean Law had other plans for him.

THE JADE ALLIANCE
Elizabeth Darrell

The story opens in 1905 in St. Petersburg with the Brusilov family swept up in the chaos of revolution.

THE DREAM TRADERS
E. V. Thompson

This saga, is set against the background of intrigue, greed and misery surrounding the Chinese opium trade in the late 1830s.

BERLIN GAME
Len Deighton

Bernard Samson had been behind a desk in Whitehall for five years when his bosses decided that he was the right man to slip into East Berlin.

HARD TIMES
Charles Dickens

Conveys with realism the repulsive aspect of a Lancashire manufacturing town during the 1850s.

THE RICE DRAGON
Emma Drummond

The story of Rupert Torrington and his bride Harriet, against a background of Hong Kong and Canton during the 1850s.

FIREFOX DOWN
Craig Thomas

The stolen Firefox — Russia's most advanced and deadly aircraft is crippled, but Gant is determined not to abandon it.

THE DOGS OF WAR
Frederic Forsyth

The discovery of the existence of a mountain of platinum in a remote African republic causes Sir James Manson to hire an army of trained mercenaries to topple the government of Zangaro.

THE DAYS OF WINTER
Cynthia Freeman

The story of a family caught between two world wars — a saga of pride and regret, of tears and joy.

REGENESIS
Alexander Fullerton

It's 1990. The crew of the US submarine ARKANSAS appear to be the only survivors of a nuclear holocaust.

SEA LEOPARD
Craig Thomas

HMS 'Proteus', the latest British nuclear submarine, is lured to a sinister rendezvous in the Barents Sea.

THE TORCH BEARERS
Alexander Fullerton

1942: Captain Nicholas Everard has to escort a big, slow convoy . . . a sacrificial convoy.

DAUGHTER OF THE HOUSE
Catherine Gaskin

An account of the destroying impact of love which is set among the tidal creeks and scattered cottages of the Essex Marshes.

FAMILY AFFAIRS
Catherine Gaskin

Born in Ireland in the Great Depression, the illegitimate daughter of a servant, Kelly Anderson's birthright was poverty and shame.

THE EXPLORERS
Vivian Stuart

The fourth novel in 'The Australians' series which continues the story of Australia from 1809 to 1813.

THE SUMMER OF THE SPANISH WOMAN
Catherine Gaskin

Clonmara — the wild, beautiful Irish estate in County Wicklow is a fitting home for the handsome, reckless Blodmore family.

THE TILSIT INHERITANCE
Catherine Gaskin

Ginny Tilsit had been raised on an island paradise in the Caribbean. She knew nothing of her family's bitter inheritance half the world away.

THE FINAL DIAGNOSIS
Arthur Hailey

Set in a busy American hospital, the story of a young pathologist and his efforts to restore the standards of a hospital controlled by an ageing, once brilliant doctor.

THE COLONISTS
Vivian Stuart

Sixth in 'The Australians' series, this novel opens in 1812 and covers the administration of General Sir Thomas Brisbane and General Ralph Darling.

IN HIGH PLACES
Arthur Hailey

The theme of this novel is a projected Act of Union between Canada and the United States in order that both should survive the effect of a possible nuclear war.

RED DRAGON
Thomas Harris

A ritual murderer is on the loose. Only one man can get inside that twisted mind — forensic expert, Will Graham.

CATCH-22
Joseph Heller

Anti-war novels are legion; this is a war novel that is anti-death, a comic savage tribute to those who aren't interested in dying.

THE ADVENTURERS
Vivian Stuart

The fifth in 'The Australians' series, opens in 1815 when two of its principal characters take part in the Battle of Waterloo.

THE SURVIVOR
James Herbert

David is the only survivor from an accident whose aftermath leaves a lingering sense of evil and menace in the quiet countryside.

LOST HORIZON
James Hilton

A small plane carrying four passengers crash-lands in the unexplored Tibetan wilderness.

THE TIME OF THE HUNTER'S MOON
Victoria Holt

When Cordelia Grant accepts an appointment to a girls' school in Devon, she does not anticipate anyone from her past re-emerging in her new life.

THURSTON HOUSE
Danielle Steel

At forty four, Jeremiah, a mining baron was marrying for the first time. Camille was a captivating eighteen-year-old girl. But can money buy happiness, a family . . . or love?

THE FOUNDER OF THE HOUSE
Naomi Jacob

The first volume of a family saga which begins in Vienna, and introduces Emmanuel Gollantz.

"THAT WILD LIE . . . "
Naomi Jacob

The second volume in the Gollantz saga begun with THE FOUNDER OF THE HOUSE.

IN A FAR COUNTRY
Adam Kennedy

Christine Wheatley knows she is going to marry Fred Deets, that is until she meets Roy Lavidge.

ONCE IN A LIFETIME
Danielle Steel

To the doctors the woman in the ambulance was just another casualty — more beautiful than most . . .

AUTUMN ALLEY
Lena Kennedy

Against the background of London's East End from the turn of the century to the 1830's a saga of three generations of ordinary, yet extraordinary people.

LADY PENELOPE
Lena Kennedy

Lady Penelope Devereux, forced to make a marriage of convenience, pours all the affection of her generous nature into her children . . . and her lovers.

LIZZIE
Lena Kennedy

Tiny, warm-hearted but cruelly scarred for life, Lizzie seems to live only for, and through, her burly, wayward husband Bobby.

GOING HOME
Danielle Steel

Gillian and Chris pledged their love for always, their happiness seemed complete. Until a moment's infidelity broke the bond they shared . . .

ACT OF DARKNESS
Francis King

What happens inside a family when an act of brutal violence suddenly erupts without warning or explanation?

THE LITTLE DRUMMER GIRL
John Le Carre

The secret pursuit by Israeli intelligence agents of a lethally dangerous and elusive Palestinian terrorist leader.

ACCEPTABLE LOSSES
Irwin Shaw

A strange voice in the dead of night full of menace and loathing shatters the confidence of Roger Damon, a respected literary agent.

CROSSINGS
Danielle Steel

Armand de Villiers, the French Ambassador, was crossing the Atlantic, with his American wife, Liane, when they meet Nick and Hilary Burnham. The spark between Nick and Liane is instantaneous . . .

THE SHAPIRO DIAMOND
Michael Legat

Set in the late 19th century, the story of a man struggling against fate to prove himself worthy of his family's name.

THE SILVER FOUNTAIN
Michael Legat

Jean-Paul Fontaine came to London in 1870 with a burning ambition to be the proprietor of an exclusive restaurant.

THE CRUEL SEA
Nicholas Monsarrat

A classic record of the heroic struggle to keep the Atlantic sea lanes open against the German U-boat menace.

RED FOX
Gerald Seymour

Two unconnected events make headlines. A British businessman is kidnapped and Italy's most wanted woman terrorist is captured.